Anonymus

The philosophical dictionary for the pocket

Anonymus

The philosophical dictionary for the pocket

ISBN/EAN: 9783741182860

Manufactured in Europe, USA, Canada, Australia, Japa

Cover: Foto ©Andreas Hilbeck / pixelio.de

Manufactured and distributed by brebook publishing software (www.brebook.com)

Anonymus

The philosophical dictionary for the pocket

THE PHILOSOPHICAL DICTIONARY FOR THE POCKET.

Written in FRENCH by
A SOCIETY OF MEN OF LETTERS,

And Translated into ENGLISH from

The last GENEVA Edition, corrected by the AUTHORS.

WITH NOTES,

CONTAINING

A REFUTATION of such Passages as are any way exceptionable in regard to RELIGION.

LONDON:
Printed for THOMAS BROWN,
M.DCC.LXV.

ADVERTISEMENT.

THE great noise which the following work has made in foreign parts, on account of the author's freedom in regard to matters of religion, may probably occasion some people to be offended with the publication of it in English. But an exception of this kind must surely be the effect of prejudice, and is impossible to be defended upon the principles of reason and philosophy. True religion is not afraid of bearing the strictest examination; the attacks of infidels, instead of weakening her authority, rather contribute to her triumphs. She is ever ready to hear what her adversaries have to oppose; and calmly endeavours to refute their errors. This is a maxim agreeable to sound sense, and the contrary doctrine is calculated only for the meridian of the inquisition.

It must be acknowledged, however, that in writings of this sort, some regard ought to be shewn to the illiterate and the vulgar; neither is it fit that their minds should be unhinged in their assent to the true religion. This indulgence to the public is shewn in the following translation, which has been undertaken chiefly to prevent the work from being rendered into English by some other hand, who would perhaps have been glad of the opportunity of spreading its errors. Care has therefore been taken to make proper strictures on such

ADVERTISEMENT.

such passages as are most exceptionable, and even to refute at large some articles which may be suspected to have a dangerous tendency.

These are blemishes, which, as a judicious critic observes*, are capable of disfiguring, but not of intirely destroying the merit of this work. Tho' our author is no divine, he is a poet, an historian, a philosopher, and in many respects a most agreeable writer. In such a multiplicity of articles he has an opportunity of displaying not only his wit and humour, but likewise a great fund of erudition. Where he does not intermeddle with religion, he is very entertaining, and oftentimes instructive. Even when writing on religious matters, he is not always deserving of censure; for instance, his article of toleration contains excellent doctrine, and shews him to be endowed with good-nature and humanity. This appears even in the singularity of many of his notions, which were owing to the favourable opinion he entertains of mankind. He thinks that we are not naturally prone to vice; that virtue consists only in doing good to our neighbour; that neither the Greeks nor Romans were idolaters; opinions, which, however erroneous, are an indication of his benevolent disposition.

---

* See Critical Review, December 1764.

A PHILOSOPHICAL DICTIONARY.

ABRAHAM.

ABRAHAM is a name famous in Asia Minor and Arabia, like Thaut among the Egyptians, the first Zoroaster in Persia, Hercules in Greece, Orpheus in Thracia, Odin among the Northern Nations, and many others, known rather by their celebrity than by any authentic history. — Here I speak only of prophane history; for as to that of the Jews, our teachers and our enemies, whom we believe and detest at the same time, the history of this people having manifestly been written by the Holy Ghost, we have for it all the sentiments we ought. We here address ourselves only to the Arabs, who boast of being descended from Abraham by Ishmael, and believe that this patriarch built Mecca, and that he died in this city. The truth is, that Ishmael's progeny has been favoured by God infinitely more than that of Jacob. Both races, indeed, have produced robbers, but the Arabian robbers have prodigiously surpassed the Jewish. Jacob's descendants

ants conquered only a very small country, and that they afterwards lost; whereas the descendants of Ishmael have extended their conquests over a part of Europe, Asia, and Africa, have founded an empire greater than the Romans, and have driven the Jews from those holes of theirs, which they called the Land of Promise.

To judge of things only by the instances of modern histories, it is not likely that Abraham should have been the father of two nations so very different: we are told that he was born in Chaldea, the son of a poor potter; who subsisted by making little earthen idols. Now how should this potter's son go and found Mecca, at the distance of three hundred leagues, and over impracticable desarts? If he was a conqueror, he certainly would have bent his arms against the fine country of Assyria; and if only a poor man, as represented to us, he could hardly found kingdoms in foreign parts, his only monarchy must have been his home.

Genesis makes him seventy-five years of age when he left the country of Haran, after the death of his father Terah the potter. But the same book says, that Terah having begotten Abraham in his seventieth year, he lived to the age of two hundred and five years (A), and that Abraham

did

(A) M. Voltaire is ready to start objections, but never offers to give any solution. The scripture says, Gen. xi. that "Terah, after having lived seventy years, begot Abraham, "Nachor, and Haran." Now though Abraham be named first, it is not certain that he was the eldest of the three: on the contrary, it seems probable, that he was not born in the seventieth year of Terah; because it is expresly said, in the following chapter, that Abraham going from Haran immediately after the death of his father, who departed this life at

the

did not leave Haran till after his father's deceafe: thus from Genefis itfelf it is clear, that Abraham, when he left Mefopotamia, was an hundred and thirty five years of age; and he only went from one idolatrous country to another, called Sichem in Paleftine. And wherefore did he go thither? why leave Euphrates' fertile banks for fo rocky, fo barren (B) a country, as that of Sichem, and withal fo remote? The Chaldean tongue muft have been very different from that of Sichem, neither was it a trading place. Sichem is above an hundred leagues from Chaldea, and with many defarts to pafs through: but God ordered him on this journey, intending to fhew him the country

---

the age of 205 years, was then only feventy-five years old. The confequence is, that Abraham was born in the 130th year of the life of Terah, and not in the feventieth: fo that Terah having begun to have children in the feventieth year of his life, Haran and Nachor muft neceffarily have been born before Abraham: therefore Abraham departed from Haran in Mefopotamia, not in the 135th, but in the 75th year of his age.

— (B) The author, upon all occafions, reprefents the country of Paleftine as a barren difagreeable fpot, and not at all anfwering the defcription in Holy Writ, where it is called a Land flowing with Milk and Honey. But we may obferve, with the learned Dr. Shaw, that, were the Holy Land fo well peopled and cultivated at prefent as in former times, it would ftill be more fruitful than the very beft part of Syria and Phœnice. The barrennefs or fcarcity, which fome authors, either ignorantly or malicioufly, complain of, does not proceed from the incapacity or natural unfruitfulnefs of the country, but from the want of inhabitants, and the great averfion there is to labour and induftry in thofe few who poffefs it: otherwife the land is ftill capable of affording its neighbours the like fupplies of corn and oil, which it is known to have done in the time of Solomon. Thus there is no forming an idea of its antient flourifhing ftate from its prefent barren condition, which is entirely owing to the want of culture.

which

which his issue were to possess many centuries after him. The reasons of such a journey are what the human mind can never conceive (C).

No sooner has he reached the little rocky country of Sichem, than a famine obliges him as hastily to decamp, and he goes away to Egypt, in quest of a subsistence. Memphis lies two hundred leagues from Sichem; now is it natural to go for corn so very far, and where one knows nothing of the tongue? These are odd peregrinations for a man near an hundred and forty years old.

With him he brings to Memphis his wife Sarah, who, in age, was little more than a child to him, being only in her sixty-fifth year. As she had a great share of beauty, he was for turning it to account: make as if you were only my sister, said he to her, that I may have kindness shewn to me for your sake. He rather should have said to her, Make as if you were my daughter.—The king became smitten with young Sarah, and gave her sham brother abundance of sheep, oxen, he asses, she asses, camels, and man servants, and maid servants; a proof that Egypt, even then, was a very powerful and well policed, and consequently a very antient kingdom; and that brothers coming to make a tendre of their sister to the kings of Memphis were magnificently rewarded.

Young Sarah had, according to scripture, reached her ninetieth year, when God promised her that Abraham, then full an hundred and sixty, should get her with child within the twelvemonth.

— (C) One would imagine our author had never heard of such a memorable æra as " The Call of Abraham," when this holy man was made choice of to be the stock and father of all believers.

Abraham,

Abraham, being fond of travelling, went into the frightful wilderness of Kadesh, with his pregnant wife, who, it seems, was still so young and pretty, as to kindle in a king of this wilderness the like passion which the Egyptian monarch had felt for her. The Father of the Faithful here enjoined her the same lie as in Egypt: and thus his wife, passing for his sister, got more cattle and servants; so that Sarah turned out no inconsiderable fortune to him. Commentators having written a prodigious number of volumes to justify Abraham's conduct (D), and reconcile chronology, to those commentaries we must refer the reader. They are all the works of men of great parts and sagacity, consummate metaphysicians, void of all prepossession, and the farthest in the world from any thing of pedantry.

ANGEL.

ANGEL, in Greek a MESSENGER; it matters little to be informed that the Persians had their Peries, the Hebrews their Malacs, and the Greeks their Demonoï.

But what may, perhaps, be more interesting to know is, that the supposition of intermediate beings between the Deity and us, prevailed among the first men; these are the demons and genii feigned by antiquity; man has always made the

---

— (D) There is no necessity for justifying Abraham's conduct: though Sarah might have been Abraham's sister by the father's side, and consequently the expression be true; yet it was ambiguous, and calculated for deception, and therefore cannot be justified. Abraham, though father of the faithful, was subject to human infirmities, and here, in particular, he betrayed his distrust of God's providence.

gods in his own likeness. As princes were seen to signify their orders by messengers, the Deity of course also dispatches couriers. Mercury and Iris were celestial couriers and messengers.

The Hebrews, that chosen people, under the immediate guidance of the Deity itself, at first gave no names to the angels whom God, after some time, was pleased to send to them; but, during their captivity in Babylon, they borrowed the names used by the Chaldeans. The first word we hear of Michael and Gabriel is in Daniel, then a slave among those people. Tobias, a Jew, who lived at Nineveh, knew the Angel Raphael, who took a journey with his son, to help him in getting a sum of money due to him by Gabel, likewise a Jew.

In the Jewish laws, i. e. in Leviticus and Deuteronomy, not the least mention is made of the existence of angels, much less of worshipping them; accordingly the Sadducees believed no such thing.

But in the histories of the Jews they frequently occur; these angels were corporeal, and with wings at their back, as the Mercury of the Pagans had at his heels. Sometimes they concealed their wings under their apparel. Bodies they surely had, for they ate and drank; and the inhabitants of Sodom were for abusing the angels who had come on a visit to Lot.

The antient Jewish tradition, according to Ben Maimon, makes ten degrees or orders of angels. 1. The Chaios Acodesh, pure, holy. 2. The Ofamins, rapid. 3. The Oralim, the strong. 4. The Chasmalim, the flames. 5. The Seraphim, sparks. 6. The Malachim, angels, messengers, deputies. 7. The Eloim, the gods, or judges. 8. The Ben Eloim, children of the gods. 9. Cherubim, images. 10. Ychim, the animated.

The

The history of the fall of the angels is not to be met with in the books of Moses; the first word of it is in the prophet Isaiah, who, in a divine rapture, calls out to the king of Babylon, " What is become of the exacter of tributes? the fir-trees and cedars rejoice at thy overthrow: how art thou fallen from heaven, O HELEL, thou morning star?" This HELEL has been rendered by the Latin word Lucifer; the appellation of Lucifer has afterwards been allegorically transferred to the prince of the angels who dared to make war in heaven. And lastly, this name, originally signifying Phosphorus, and the dawn of day, is come to denote the devil.

The Christian religion is founded on the fall of the angels: the rebels were tumbled down from the spheres of bliss into hell, in the center of the earth, and became devils. A devil tempted Eve under the figure of a serpent, and brought damnation upon mankind, till Jesus came to deliver them, triumphing over the devil, who, however, still tempts us. Yet is this fundamental tradition to be found only in the apocryphal book of Noah (E), and there quite differently from the received traditions.

St. Austin, in his hundred and ninth letter, expressly attributes ethereal or very thin bodies both

―― (E) If our author means by fundamental tradition the " Fall of the angels," as he seems to do, he is certainly mistaken when he says it is to be found only in the apocryphal book of Noah: for in the 2d of St. Peter, c. ii. ver. 4. it is expressly said, " For if God spared not the angels that sinned, but " cast them down to hell, and delivered them into chains of " darkness." The like we find in the epistle of St. Jude, ver. 6. " And the angels, which kept not their first estate, but left " their own habitation, he hath reserved in everlasting chains " under darkness."

to good and bad angels. Pope Gregory II. has reduced the ten degrees of Jewish angels to nine choirs, to nine hierarchies or orders. These are the Seraphim, the Cherubim, Thrones, Dominions, Virtues, Powers, Archangels, and lastly, the Angels, from whom the other eight hierarchies receive their appellation.

The Jews had in the temple two cherubim, each with two heads, one of an ox, the other of an eagle, with six wings: but for some time past they have been painted as a flying head, with two little wings under the ears, as angels and archangels are under the figure of young persons, with two wings at their back. As to the thrones and dominions, the pencil has not yet presumed to meddle with them.

St. Thomas, question 118, article 2, says, That the thrones are as near to God as the cherubim and seraphim, because it is on them that God sits. Scotus has computed the angels to amount to a thousand millions. The antient mythology of good and bad genii having spread itself into Greece, and so on to Rome, it has there been sanctified, and to every man has been assigned a good and evil angel; one assisting him, and the other annoying him, from his cradle to his coffin: but, whether these good and evil angels continually shift stations from one to another, or whether they are relieved by others of their order, is not yet known. Hereupon St. Thomas's Summary of Divinity may be consulted.

Neither is it exactly known, where the angels keep themselves, whether in the air, the void, or the planets; this God has thought fit to conceal from us.

DICTIONARY.

ANTHROPOPHAGI,

Or Man-eaters.

THAT there have been Anthropophagi, or man-eaters, is but too true; such were found in America, and there may be some still; and in antient time it was not the Cyclops alone who sometimes fed upon human flesh. Juvenal relates, that among the Egyptians, that people so famous for its laws, so wise, and so very devout as to worship crocodiles and onions, the Tintirites ate one of their enemies who had fallen into their hands. And this is not a tale on hear-say: this inhuman act was committed almost under his eyes, he being then in Egypt, and but a little way from Tintira. He farther quotes the Gascons and the Sagontines, who used to eat their countrymen.

In 1725, four Mississippi savages were brought to Fontainbleau, where I had the honour of conversing with them. One being a lady of the country, I took the liberty to ask her, whether she had ever eaten men, to which, with an unconcerned frankness, she answered in the affirmative. On my appearing something shocked, she excused herself, saying, that it was better, after killing an enemy, to eat him, than to leave him to be devoured by beasts, and that conquerors deserved the preference. We in pitched battles or encounters kill our neighbours, and, for a most scanty hire, prepare a most plentiful meal for ravens and worms. Herein it is that lies the horror, here is the guilt: what signifies it to a dead man being eaten by a soldier, or a crow, or a dog?

We shew a greater respect to the dead than the living; but both claim our regard. The policed nations,

nations, as they are called, were in the right not to spit their enemies, as from eating neighbours they would soon come to eat countrymen, by which the social virtues would be reduced to a low ebb. But the policed nations, far from having been always so, were, for a long time, wild and savage, and amidst the multitude of revolutions in this globe, the human race has been sometimes very numerous, sometimes very thin. The present case of the elephants, lions, and tygers, whose species are very much decreased, has been that of man. In times, when a country was bare of inhabitants, they lived chiefly by hunting; scarce any other arts or trades were known among them; and the custom of feeding on what they had killed, almost naturally led them to treat their enemies like their deer and boars. The sacrifice of human victims was the effect of superstition, the eating them was owing to necessity.

Which is the greater crime, to hold a solemn assembly, in order to plunge a knife, by way of honouring the Deity, into the heart of a beautiful girl, adorned with fillets and ribbons; or to pick the bones of an ugly fellow, whom we have killed in our own defence?

Yet we have more instances of sacrificing girls and boys, than of eating them; there is scarce a known nation where such sacrifices have not obtained. Among the Jews it was called the Anathema; this was a real sacrifice, and the 27th chapter of Leviticus enjoins not to spare the souls which have been devoted: but in no place are they ordered to eat them; they are only threatened with it; and Moses, as we have seen, says to the Jews, that if they fail in observing his ceremonies, they shall not only be plagued with the itch, but that

mothers

mothers shall eat their children (F). In Ezekiel's time, indeed, the eating of human flesh must have been common among the Jews, as he foretels them in chap. xxxix. That God will give them not only to eat the horses of their enemies, but even the riders, and the other great warriors. This is clear and positive (G); and indeed why might not the Jews have been man-eaters, since this only was wanting to render the chosen people of God the most abominable upon earth.

I have read, in the anecdotes of the history of England, in Cromwell's time, of a woman who kept a tallow-chandler's shop at Dublin, whose candles were remarkably good, and made of the fat of Englishmen. Some time after one of her customers complaining that her candles were not so good as usual, why, said she, for this month past I have had few or no Englishmen. I would fain know who was most guilty, they who murdered the English, or this woman who made such good candles of their tallow?

— (F) This is donounced as a curse, that the mothers shall eat their children through extreme hunger.

— (G) This is a strange perversion of Ezekiel: the chapter above-mentioned contains God's judgment upon Gog, Israel's victory, and the feast of the fowls. The prophet foretels a complete victory over Gog, his princes, and his army. The field where they are slain is compared to a table of entertainment, and the feathered fowls and beasts of the field are invited to partake of it. "Come and gather yourselves to my sacrifice, ye shall eat the flesh of the mighty, and drink the blood of the princes of the earth; ye shall be filled at my table with horses and chariots," that is, with horsemen and those who ride in chariots. Is this a proof, that the eating of human flesh was common among the Jews, because, after the slaughter of an enemy, their dead bodies were exposed to the feathered fowls and beasts of the field?

APIS.

APIS.

WAS it as a god, as a symbol, or as an ox, that Apis was worshipped at Memphis? I am inclined to think that it was as a god by the fanatics, and only as a mere symbol by the wife, whilst the stupid people worshipped the ox. Was it well in Cambyses, when he had conquered Egypt, to kill this ox with his own hands? why not? He gave the weak to see, that their god might be roasted, and nature not stir a finger to revenge such a sacrilege. The Egyptians have been greatly cried up; but I, for my part, scarce know a more contemptible people. There must ever have been both in their temper and government, some radical vice, by which they have been kept in a perpetual servitude. I allow that in those times of which we have scarce any knowledge, they over-ran the earth, but since the historical ages, they have been, subdued by all who thought it worth their while; by the Assyrians, the Persians, the Greeks, the Romans, the Arabians, the Mamelucs, the Turks; in short, by every body except our CROISES, these being more imprudent than the Egyptians were cowardly. It was the corps of Mamelucs which defeated the French. Perhaps there are but two tolerable things in this nation; the first, a freedom of conscience; they who worshipped an ox never compelling those who worshipped a monkey to change their religion; the second, the hatching of chickens in ovens.

We have many pompous accounts of their pyramids; but these very pyramids are monuments of their slavery, for the whole nation must have been made to work on them, otherwise such unwieldy

unwieldy masses could never have been finished. And what is the use of them? Why, forsooth, in a little room within them is kept the mummy of some prince or governor, which his soul is, at the term of a thousand years, to reanimate. But if they expected this resurrection of the bodies, why take out the brain before embalming them? Were the Egyptians to rise again without brains?

The APOCALYPSE.

JUSTIN MARTYR, who wrote in the year 170 of our æra, is the first that mentions the Apocalypse, attributing it, in his Dialogue with Tryphon, to the apostle John the Evangelist. This Jew asks him, whether he does not believe that Jerusalem is one day to be restored in all its former splendor? Justin answers him that it is the belief of all Christians who have a right way of thinking. "There was," says he, "among us a "respectable person named John, one of Jesus's "twelve apostles; he has foretold that the faith- "ful shall dwell a thousand years in Jerusalem."

The thousand years reign went current a long time among the Christians, and this period was in great repute among the Gentiles. At the end of a thousand years the souls of the Egyptians returned into their bodies; the souls in Virgil's purgatory underwent a purification for the same space of time, ET MILLE PER ANNOS. The Millenarian new Jerusalem was to have twelve gates, in remembrance of the twelve apostles, the form square, the length, breadth, and heighth, twelve thousand stades, that is five hundred leagues; so that the houses must have been five hundred leagues high: this could not but make it to those living in the upper ſtory ſomething troubleſome: but however, this is what the Apocalypſe ſays (G), chap. xxi.

Though Juſtin be the firſt who attributes the Apocalypſe to St. John, ſome perſons diſallow his teſtimony, ſeeing, in the ſame Dialogue with the Jew Tryphon, he ſays that, according to the apoſtle's narrative, at Jeſus Chriſt's going down into Jordan, the waters of that river boiled, and were all in a flame; yet not a jot of this is to be found in the apoſtolic writings.

The ſame St. Juſtin confidently cites the oracles of the Sybils, and farther pretends to have ſeen the remains of the little houſes in the Pharos of Egypt, where the ſeventy-two interpreters were ſhut up in Herod's time. For ſuch an aſſertion the author ſeems to have been himſelf a proper ſubject for confinement.

St. Irenæus, next in ſucceſſion, and who alſo held the Millennium, ſays, that he was informed by an old man, that St. John compoſed the Apocalypſe: but it has been objected to St. Irenæus, that he has written, there can be but four goſpels, as there are but four parts of the world, and four cardinal winds, and that Ezekiel ſaw only four beaſts. This reaſoning he calls a demonſtration; and it muſt be owned, that Irenæus' demonſtrating carries as much weight as Juſtin's ſeeing.

(G) The deſcription of the new Jeruſalem is entirely figurative; ſo that to take each metaphor in a literal ſenſe is ridiculous. The length, and the breadth, and the height of it are repreſented equal, to denote that in the new city all parts ſhall be equal in perfection. The deſign of the whole is only to ſhew, that the manſions of the bleſſed will be moſt glorious places.

Clement

Clement of Alexandria, in his ELECTA, mentions only an Apocalypse of St. Peter's, which was highly respected. Tertullian, a warm stickler for the Millennium, not only affirms that St. John has predicted this resurrection, and reign in the city of Jerusalem, but that this Jerusalem was then forming in the air; that all the Christians in Palestine, and the very Pagans, had seen it forty nights successively, but unluckily this city disappeared at day-light.

Origen, in his preface to St. John's Gospel, quotes the oracles of the Apocalypse, but he likewise quotes the oracles of the Sybils: yet St. Dionysius of Alexandria, who wrote about the middle of the third century, says in one of his fragments, preserved by Eusebius, that almost all the doctors rejected the Apocalypse, as a senseless book, that, instead of being written by St. John, the author of it was one Cerinthus, who borrowed a respectable name, to give the greater weight to his chimeras.

The council of Laodicea, held in 360, did not admit the Apocalypse among the canonical books; and it was something odd, that Laodicea, a church to which the Apocalypse was directed, should reject a treasure particularly appointed for it; and even the bishop of Ephesus, a member of the council, should also reject this book of St. John, though buried in his metropolis.

It was visible to all that St. John kept stirring in his grave, the earth continually heaving and falling; yet the same persons who were sure that St. John was not actually dead, were also sure that he did not write the Apocalypse. But the Millenarians tenaciously persisted in their opinions. Sulpicius Severus, in his Sacred History, Book IX. calls those who did not hold the Apocalypse, mad and impious. At length, after many doubts and controversies, and council clashing with council, Sulpicius's opinion prevailed; and the point having undergone a thorough discussion, the church (from whose judgment there lies no appeal) has decided the Apocalypse to have been indisputably written by St. John.

Every Christian sect has attributed to itself the prophecies contained in this book. The English have found in it the revolutions of Great Britain; the Lutherans the disturbances in Germany; the French Reformed the reign of Charles IX. and the regency of Catherine de Medicis; and they are all equally in the right. Bossuet and Newton have both commented on the Apocalypse: but, after all, the eloquent declamations of the former, and the sublime discoveries of the latter, have done them much greater honour than their comments.

ATHEIST, ATHEISM.

FORMERLY he who was possessed of any secret in an art, ran great risque of being looked upon as a sorcerer; every new sect was accused of murdering infants in the celebration of its mysteries; and every philosopher who departed from the jargon of schools, fanatics and cheats never failed to charge with atheism, and ignorant and weak judges so surely passed sentence on them.

Anaxagoras took upon him to affirm, that the sun is not guided by Apollo, sitting in a car drawn by four mettlesome steeds; on this he is exclaimed against as an atheist, and obliged to fly his country.

Aristotle being accused of atheism by a priest, and not able to procure justice against his accuser, withdraws to Chalcis. But in all the history of
Greece

Greece there is not a more heinous tranfaction than the death of Socrates.

Aristophanes (he whom commentators admire becaufe he was a Greek, not confidering that Socrates was alfo a Greek) Ariftophanes was the firft who brought the Athenians to account Socrates an atheift.

This comic poet, who is neither comic nor a poet, would not have been allowed among us to have exhibited farces at St. Laurence's fair. To me he feems more contemptible, more low-lived, and fcurrilous than Plutarch makes him, who fpeaks of him in this manner: "Ariftophanes's "language is, indeed, that of a wretched quack, "full of the loweft and moft difagreeable points and "quirks; he cannot raife a laugh among the very "vulgar, and to perfons of judgment and honour "he is quite infupportable; his arrogance is be- "yond all bearing, and all good people deteft his "malignity."

So this, by the bye, is the buffoon whom Madam Dacier, amidft all her admiration of Socrates, can find in her heart to admire. This is the man who remotely prepared the poifon by which infamous judges put an end to the exiftence of the moft vir- tuous man then living in Greece.

The tanners, the fhoe-makers, and fempftreffes of Athens were hugely diverted with a farce, where Socrates being haled up into the air in a bafket, proclaims that there is no god, and makes his boaft, that he had ftole a cloak, whilft he was teaching philofophy. Such a people, and whofe bad govern- ment could countenance fuch fcandalous licenti- oufnefs, well deferved what has happened to them, to be brought under fubjection to the Romans, and to be at prefent flaves to the Turks.

We fhall pafs over the common fpace of time be- tween the Roman commonwealth and our days;

observing

observing only, that the Romans, who were much wiser than the Greeks, never molested any philosopher for his opinion. It was not so among the barbarous nations who seated themselves in the Roman empire. The emperor Frederic II. having some difference with the popes, was immediately arraigned of atheism, and reported to have been, jointly with his chancellor de Vineis, the author of the book intitled THE THREE IMPOSTORS.

Our chancellor de l'Hopital, that excellent man, was branded as an Atheist, because he opposed persecutions, "Homo doctus sed verus atheos*." A Jesuit, Garasse, as much below Aristophanes as the latter was below Homer; a wretch whose name is become ridiculous among the very fanatics, makes every body atheists; at least this is the appellation he gives to. all who have incurred his displeasure. With him Theodore de Beze is an atheist, and he it is who led the people into an error concerning Vanini.

Vanini's wretched end raises no indignation or pity like that of Socrates. This Italian was only an insignificant pedant: yet was he no atheist, for which he suffered, but as far from it as man could be.

He was a poor Neapolitan churchman, a kind of preacher and professor of divinity, a vehement disputer in quiddities and universals; "et utrum chimera bombinans in vacuo possit comedere secundas intentiones." There was nothing in him which looked toward atheism; and his ideas of God are perfectly agreeable to the most sound and most approved theology. "God is his beginning and
" end, the Father of both, in no need of either;

---

* Commentarium Rerum Gallicarum. L. XXVIII.

" eternal

" eternal without existing in time, every-where
" present without being in any place. To him there
" is neither past nor future, space nor time; the
" Creator and Governor of all things; immutable,
" infinite without parts; his power is his will, &c."

Vanini was for reviving the fine thought of Plato, espoused by Averroes, that God had created a chain of beings from the most minute to the largest, and the last link of which is fastened to his eternal throne; a notion which, though it has more of sublimity than truth, is as far from atheism as something from nothing.

He travelled to dispute and make his fortune; but unluckily, disputing is the very opposite road to fortune, every person against whom one enters the list being thus made a rancorous and irreconcileable enemy. Hence Vanini's misfortunes; his heat and rudeness in disputing brought on him the hatred of some divines; and having a quarrel with one Francon, or Franconi, this man, being connected with his enemies, charged him with being an atheist, and teaching atheism.

This Francon, or Franconi, supported by some witnesses, had the barbarity, when confronted with Vanini, to maintain, with aggravations, the whole of what he had advanced; whereas Vanini being interrogated, what he thought of the existence of God, made answer, That, agreeably to the church, he worshipped one God in three Persons; and taking up a straw, which lay on the ground, " This," says he, " sufficiently proves that there is a Creator;" then made a very fine speech on vegetation and motion, and the necessity of a Supreme Being, without whom there could be neither motion or vegetation.

The President Gramont gives us an account of this speech in his history of France, now scarce known; and this historian, from an inconceivable prepoſſeſſion, will have it that Vanini ſpoke only out of "vanity or fear, and not from a ſincere perſuaſion."

What grounds could the Preſident Gramont have for ſuch a raſh and ſanguinary judgment? It is manifeſt, that, on Vanini's anſwer, he ought to have been cleared of the charge of atheiſm. But what was the iſſue? This unhappy foreign prieſt dabbled likewiſe in phyſic: a large living toad, which he kept in a veſſel of water, being found at his houſe, was made uſe of to charge him with ſorcery, and the toad was ſaid to be the only deity he worſhipped. Several paſſages of his books were wreſted to an impious meaning, than which nothing is more eaſy and more common, taking the objections for anſwers, putting a malicious conſtruction on every ambiguous phraſe, and miſrepreſenting innocent expreſſions. At length his enemies extorted from the judges a capital ſentence againſt him.

This death could not be juſtified without accuſing this unfortunate creature of moſt horrid crimes; and one Merſenne, a Minim, a name quite ſuitable to his character, has been ſo mad as to affirm in print, that Vanini ſet out from Naples with ten of his apoſtles, to go and convert all nations to atheiſm. Such incongruity! How could a poor prieſt have twelve men in his pay? how ſhould he have prevailed with twelve Neapolitans to undertake an expenſive journey, and at the hazard of their lives, for the ſake of diſſeminating this abominable doctrine? Could a king afford to hire twelve preachers of atheiſm? This is ſuch an abſurdity as never came into any one's mind but Father Merſenne. But from him the tale has been repeated over and over; the journals and hiſtorical dictionaries have been ſtained and ſullied with it; and the public,

who

who are fond of extraordinary things, have greedily swallowed it.

Bayle himself, in his Miscellaneous Thoughts, speaks of Vanini as an atheist, making use of him in support of his paradox, "That a society of "atheists can subsist." He affirms that Vanini was a man of very regular morals, and died a martyr to his philosophical opinions. Now, in both, is he mistaken; Vanini, though a priest, in his dialogue written in imitation of Erasmus, does not hide from us that he had a mistress, named Isabella; he was both a free liver and a free writer, but he was no atheist.

A century after his death, the learned La Croze, and another under the name of Philalethes, wrote a vindication of him; but the memory of a poor Neapolitan being what few give themselves any concern about, these ingenious persons might have saved themselves that trouble.

The Jesuit Hardouin, with all Garasse's rashness, but much more learning, in his ATHEI DETECTI, accuses the Descartes, the Arnaulds, the Paschals, the Nicolas, the Malbranches, of atheism; but it was their good fortune to come to a better end than poor Vanini.

From all these facts, I now proceed to Bayle's moral question, "Whether a society of atheists could subsist?" And here let us previously observe, the enormous contradiction of men in disputes; they who most furiously inveighed against Bayle's opinion, they who have with the greatest rancour denied the possibility of a society of atheists, have since as confidently maintained, that atheism is the established religion in China.

They are certainly very little acquainted with China; for had they only read an edict of the emperors of that vast country, they would have seen that these edicts are like sermons, frequently making mention of the Supreme Being, as governing, punishing, and rewarding.

At the same time they are not less mistaken concerning the impossibility of a society of atheists; and I wonder how Mr. Bayle came to overlook a striking example, which would have given a decisive victory to his cause.

Why is a society of atheists thought impossible? Because it is thought that men under no restraint could never live together; that laws avail nothing against secret crimes; and that there must be an avenging God, punishing in this world or the other those delinquents who have escaped human justice.

Though Moses's laws did not teach a life to come, did not threaten any punishments after death, and did not give the primitive Jews the least insight into the immortality of the soul, still the Jews, so far from being atheists, so far from denying a divine vengeance against wickedness, were the most religious men on the face of the earth. They not only believed the existence of an eternal God, but they believed him to be ever present among them; they dreaded being punished in themselves, in their wives, in their children, in their posterity to the fourth generation; and this was a very powerful restraint.

But, among the Gentiles, several sects had no curb; the Sceptics doubted of every thing; the Academics suspended their judgment concerning every thing; the Epicureans held that the Deity could not concern itself about human affairs, and, in reality, they did not allow of any Deity; they were persuaded that the soul is not a substance, but a faculty born and perishing with the body; consequently their only check was morality and honour. The Roman senators and knights were downright atheists,

atheists, as neither to fear or expect any thing from the gods amounts to a denial of their existence; so that the Roman senate, in Cæsar and Cicero's time, was, in fact, an assembly of atheists.

That great orator, in his speech for Cluentius, says to a full senate, "What hurt does death do to him? All the idle tales about hell none of us give the least credit to; then what has death deprived him of? Nothing but the feeling of pain."

Does not Cæsar, Cataline's friend, in order to save that wretch from an indictment brought against him by the same Cicero, object, that to put a criminal to death is not punishing him; that death is nothing, that it is only the end of our sufferings, that it is rather a happy than a fatal moment? And did not Cicero and the whole senate yield to these arguments? so that the conquerors and legislators of the known universe were evidently a society of men without any fear of God; and thus were real atheists.

Bayle afterwards examines whether idolatry be more dangerous than atheism; whether the disbelief of a deity be more criminal than the having unworthy opinions of him? and herein he is of Plutarch's mind, thinking a disbelief preferable to an ill opinion. But, with submission to Plutarch, nothing can be more evident than that it was infinitely better for the Greeks to stand in awe of Ceres, Neptune, and Jupiter, than to be under no manner of awe; the sacredness of oaths is manifest and necessary, and they who hold that perjury will be punished, are certainly more to be trusted than those who think that a false oath will be attended with no ill consequence. It is beyond all question, that in a policed city, even a bad religion is better than none.

Bayle,

Bayle, therefore, should rather have examined which is the more dangerous, fanaticism or atheism? Now fanaticism is certainly a thousand times more mischievous; for atheism stimulates to none of those sanguinary procedures for which fanaticism is notorious; if atheism does not suppress crimes, fanaticism incites to the commission of them. Allowing the author of COMMENTARIUM RERUM GALLICARUM, that chancellor de l'Hopital was an atheist, still the laws he made are wise and good, and all his counsels tended to moderation and concord. The fanatics committed the massacre of St. Bartholomew. Hobbs was accounted an atheist, yet he led a quiet harmless life, whilst the fanatics were deluging England, Scotland, and Ireland with blood. Spinosa was not only an atheist, but taught atheism; yet who can say he had any hand in the juridical murder of Barneweldt? It was not he who tore the two De Wits to pieces, and broiled and ate their flesh.

Atheists, for the most part, are men of study, but bold and erroneous in their reasonings, and not comprehending the creation, the original of evil, and other difficulties, have recourse to the hypothesis of the eternity of things, and of necessity.

The sensualist and the ambitious have little time for speculation, or to embrace a bad system; to compare Lucretius with Socrates is quite out of their way. Such is the present state of things among us!

It was otherwise with the senate of Rome, which almost totally consisted of atheists both in theory and practice, believing neither in Providence nor a future state. It was a meeting of philosophers, of votaries to pleasure and ambition; all very dangerous sets of men, and who, accordingly, overturned the republic.

I would

I would not willingly lie at the mercy of an atheistical prince, who might think it his interest to have me pounded in a mortar: I am very certain that would be my fate. And, were I a sovereign, I would not have about me any atheistical courtiers, whose interest it might be to poison me, as then I must every day be taking alexipharmics; so necessary is it both for princes and people, that the minds be thoroughly imbibed with an idea of a Supreme Being, the Creator, Avenger, and Rewarder.

There are atheistical nations, says Bayle, in his THOUGHTS ON COMETS. The Caffres, the Hottentots, the Topinamboux, and many other petty nations, have no god: that may be; but it does not imply that they deny the existence of a Deity; they neither deny nor affirm; they have never heard a word about him; tell them there is a God, they will readily believe it; tell them that every thing is the work of nature, and they will as cordially believe it: you may as well say, that they are Anti-Cartesians as to call them atheists. They are mere children, and a child is neither atheist nor theist; he is nothing.

What are the inferences from all this? That atheism is a most pernicious monster in sovereign princes, and likewise in statesmen, however harmless their life be, because from their cabinet they can make their way to the former; that if it be not so mischievous as fanaticism, it is almost ever destructive of virtue. I congratulate the present age, on there being fewer atheists now than ever; philosophers having discovered that there is no vegetable without a germ, no germ without design, &c. and that corn is not produced by putrefaction.

Some

Some unphilosophical geometricians have rejected final causes, but they are admitted by all real philosophers; and, to use the expression of a known author, "A catechist makes God known to children, and Newton demonstrates him to the learned."

BAPTISM.

BAPTISM, a Greek word, signifying immersion: men being ever led by their senses, easily came to fancy that what washed the body likewise cleansed the soul. In the vaults under the Egyptian temples were large tubs for the ablutions of the priests and the initiated. The Indians, from time immemorial, purified themselves in the Ganges, and the ceremony still subsists among them. The Hebrews adopted it, baptizing all proselytes who would not submit to be circumcised; especially the women, as exempt from that operation, except in Ethiopia only, were baptized; it was as regeneration; it imparted a new soul, among them, as in Egypt. Concerning this, see Epiphanius, Maimonides, and the Gemara.

John baptized in the Jordan; he baptized even Jesus Christ himself, who, however, never baptized any one, yet was pleased to consecrate this antient ceremony. All signs are of themselves indifferent, and God annexes his grace to such as he thinks fit to chuse. Baptism soon became the principal rite, and the seal of Christianity. The first fifteen bishops of Jerusalem were all circumcised, and there is no certainty of their having ever been baptized.

In the first ages of Christianity this sacrament was abused, nothing being more common than to delay

delay baptism till the agony of death; of this the emperor Constantine is no slight proof. This was his way of reasoning: Baptism washes away all sin, so that I may kill my wife, my son, and all my relations, then I'll get myself baptized, and so go to heaven; and he acted accordingly. Such an instance carried danger with it, and, by degrees, the custom of delaying the sacred laver till death, wore off.

The Greeks always adhered to baptism by immersion; but the Latins, towards the end of the eighth century, having extended their religion over Gaul and Germany, and seeing that immersion in cold countries did not agree with children, substituted in its stead aspersion, or sprinkling, for which they were often anathematized by the Greek church.

St. Cyprian, bishop of Carthage, being asked whether they whose bodies had been only sprinkled were really baptized; he answers, in his 70th letter, that several churches did not hold them to be Christians; that he does, but withal, what grace they have, is infinitely less than that of those who, according to the primitive rite, had been dipped three times.

After immersion a Christian became initiated; whereas before he was only a catechumen; but initiation required securities and sponsors, who were called by a name answerable to that of godfathers, that the church might be sure of the fidelity of the new Christians, and the sacred mysteries be not divulged. Wherefore during the first centuries, the Pagans, in general, knew as little of the Christian mysteries, as the Christians did of the mysteries of Isis and Eleusis.

Cyril of Alexandria, in a writing of his against the emperor Julian, delivers himself thus: " I
" would speak a word of baptism, did I not fear,
" that

"that what I say might come to those who are not initiated."

Children were baptized so early as the second century, it being, indeed, very natural that Christians should be solicitous for this sacrament to be administered to their children, as without it they would be damned; and, at length, it was concluded that the time of administration should be at the end of eight days, in imitation of the Jews administring circumcision. The Greek church still retains this custom. However, in the third century the custom prevailed of not being baptized till near death.

Those who died in the first week, some rigid fathers of the church held to be damned; but Peter Chrysologus, in the fifth century, found out Limbo, a kind of mitigated hell, or, properly, the borders, or suburbs, of hell, whither unbaptized children go; and the abode of the patriarchs before Jesus Christ descended into hell. And ever since it has been the current opinion, that Jesus Christ descended into Limbo, and not into hell itself.

It has been debated whether a Christian could, in the deserts of Arabia, be baptized with sand; but carried in the negative: whether rose-water might be used for baptism; it was decided that it must be pure water, yet muddy water would do on an emergency. Thus the whole of this discipline appears to depend on the prudence of the primitive pastors, by whom it was instituted.

BEASTS.

IS it possible any one should say, or affirm in writing, that beasts are machines, void of knowledge and sense, have a sameness in all their operations, neither learning nor perfecting any thing, &c.

How! this bird which makes a semicircular nest when he fixes it against a wall, who, when in an angle, shapes it like a quadrant, and circular when he builds it in a tree; is this having a sameness in its operations? Does this hound, after three months teaching, know no more than when you first took him in hand? Your canary-bird, does he repeat a tune at first hearing, or rather is it not some time before you can bring him to it? is he not often out, and does he not improve by practice?

Is it from my speaking that you allow me sense, memory, and ideas? Well; I am silent; but you see me come home very melancholy, and with eager anxiety look for a paper, open the bureau where I remember to have put it, take it up and read it with apparent joy. You hence infer, that I have felt pain and pleasure, and that I have memory and knowledge.

Make then the like inference concerning this dog, who, having lost his master, runs about every where with melancholy yellings, comes home all in a ferment, runs up and down, roves from room to room, till at length he finds his beloved master in his closet, and then expresses his joy in softer cries, gesticulations, and fawnings.

This dog, so very superior to man in affection, is seized by some barbarian virtuosos, who nail him down on a table, and diffect him while living, the better to fhew you the meferaic veins. All the fame organs of fenfation which are in yourfelf you perceive in him. Now, Machinift, what fay you? anfwer me, has nature created all the fprings of feeling in this animal, that it may not feel? Has it nerves to be impaffible? For fhame! charge not nature with fuch weaknefs and inconfiftency.

But the fcholaftic doctors afk what the foul of beafts is? This is a queftion I don't underftand. A tree has the faculty of receiving fap into its fibres, of circulating it, of unfolding the buds of its leaves and fruits. Do you now afk me what the foul of a tree is? It has received thefe properties as the animal above has received thofe of fenfation, memory, and a certain number of ideas. Who formed all thofe properties, who has imparted all thefe faculties? He who caufes the grafs of the field to grow, and the earth to gravitate towards the fun.

The fouls of beafts are fubftantial forms, fays Ariftotle, who has been followed by the Arabian fchool, and this by the Angelic fchool, and the Angelic fchool by the Sorbonne, and the Sorbonne by no body in the world.

The fouls of beafts are material, is the cry of other philofophers, but as little to the purpofe as the former; when called upon to define a material foul, they only perplex the caufe: they muft neceffarily allow it to be fenfitive matter. But whence does it derive this fenfation? From a material foul, which muft mean, that it is matter giving fenfation to matter; beyond this circle they have nothing to fay.

According to others, equally wife, the foul of beafts is a fpiritual effence, dying with the body; but where are your proofs? What idea have you of

this

this spiritual being ? which with its sensation, memory, and its share of ideas and combinations, will never be able to know so much as a child of six years. What grounds have you to think, that this incorporeal being dies with the body? But still more stupid are they who affirm this soul to be neither body nor spirit. A fine system truly! By spirit we can mean only something unknown, which is not body; so that the upshot of this wise system is, that the soul of beasts is a substance, which is neither body, nor something which is not body.

Whence can so many contradictory errors arise? From a custom which has always prevailed among men, of investigating the nature of a thing before they knew whether any such thing existed. The sucker, or clapper, of a bellows is likewise called the soul of the bellows. Well, what is this soul? it is only a name I have given to that sucker, or clapper, which falls down, lets in the air, and rising again, propels it through a pipe on my working the bellows.

Here is no soul distinct from the machine itself; but who puts the bellows of animals in motion? I have already told you: he who puts the heavenly bodies in motion. The philosopher who said "Deus est anima brutorum," was in the right: but he should have gone farther [*].

BEAUTY, BEAUTIFUL.

ASK a toad what is beauty, the supremely beautiful, the TO-KALON, he will answer you, that it is his female, with two large round eyes

---

[*] This is the Pythagorean system, "Quod Deus sit anima mundi." See Ruæus on Virg. Æn. lib. vi. ver. 726.

projecting out of its little head; a broad and flat neck, yellow belly, and dark brown back. Ask a Guinea Negro; and with him beauty is a greasy black skin, hollow eyes, and a flat nose.

Put the question to the devil, and he will tell you, that beauty is a pair of horns, four claws, and a tail. Consult the philosophers likewise, they will give you some unintelligible jargon for answer, they must have something correspondent to BEAUTY IN THE ABSTRACT, to the TO-KALON.

I once sat next to a philosopher at a tragedy; that's beautiful, said he! How beautiful? said I! because the author has attained his end. The next day he took a dose of physic, which had a very good effect; that's a beautiful physic, said I, it has attained its end: he perceived that a medicine is not to be called beautiful, and that the word beauty is applicable only to those things which give a pleasure accompanied with admiration; that tragedy, he said, had excited these two sensations in him, and that was the TO-KALON, the beautiful.

We went to England together, and happened to be at the same play, perfectly well translated; but the spectators, one and all, yawned. Oh-ho! said he, the TO-KALON, I find, is not the same in England as in France; and, after several pertinent reflections, he concluded that beauty is very relative; that what is decent at Japan is indecent at Rome, and what is fashionable at Paris is otherwise at Pekin; and thus he saved himself the trouble of composing a long treatise on the beautiful.

BODY.

BODY.

AS we know nothing of spirit, so are we alike ignorant of body: we perceive some properties; but what is this subject in which these properties reside? All is body, said Democritus and Epicurus; there is no body at all, said the disciples of Zeno the Elæan.

Berkeley, bishop of Cloyne, is the last who has gone about to prove the non-existence of bodies; and he deals chiefly in captious sophisms: there is, says he, neither colour, smell, nor heat, in them; these modalities are in your sensations and not in the objects; a truth, which being before sufficiently known, he needed not to have taken the trouble of proving. But from thence he proceeds to extension and solidity, which are essential to body, and is for proving that there is no extension in a piece of green cloth, because this cloth, in reality, is not green; this sensation of green is only in you, therefore the sensation of extension is likewise only in you: and having overthrown extension, he concludes, that solidity being annexed to it, falls of itself, and thus there is nothing in the world but our ideas. So that, according to this philosopher, ten thousand men killed by as many cannon shot, are, in reality, only ten thousand conceptions of our minds.

My lord of Cloyne might have avoided exposing himself to such ridicule; he fancies that he proves that there is no such thing as extension, because a body through a glass appeared to him four times larger than to his naked eye, and four times smaller through another glass: thence he concludes, that as the extension of a body cannot, at the same time, be four feet, six feet, and only one foot, such extension tenfion exifts not; then there is nothing. He needed only to have taken a meafure, and fay, however extended a body may appear to me, its actual extenfion is fo many of thefe meafures.

He might eafily have feen that extenfion and folidity are very different from founds, colours, taftes, and fmells, &c. Thefe are manifeftly fenfations excited by the configuration of the parts. But extenfion is not a fenfation: though on the going out of a fire I no longer feel heat; on the agitation of the air ceafing I hear nothing; and from a withered rofe I fmell nothing; yet the fire, the air, and the rofe, have all their extenfion, without any relation to me. Berkeley's paradox really does not deferve a formal refutation.

But the cream of the jeft is to know what led him into this paradox. A long time ago I had fome talk with him, when he told me, that his opinion originally proceeded from the inconceivablenefs of what the fubject of extenfion is; and indeed he triumphs in that part of his book, where he afks Hilas what this fame fubject, this SUBSTRATUM, this fubftance, is? It is, anfwers Hilas, the body extended; then the bifhop, under the name of Philonoüs, laughs at him; and poor Hilas, perceiving that he had faid extenfion was the fubject of extenfion, and thus had talked fillily, is quite abafhed, and owns that it is utterly inconceivable to him; that there is no fuch thing as body; that the world, inftead of being material, as commonly thought, is intellectual.

It would have become Philonoüs only to have faid to Hilas, we know nothing concerning the conftitution of this fubject, of this extended, folid, divifible, moveable, figured, fubftance, &c. We know no more of it than of the thinking, feeling, and willing fubject; ftill this fubject certainly exifts, fince

it

it has effential properties from which it cannot be feparated.

We are all, like the Paris ladies; they live high without knowing the ingredients in ragouts; fo we make ufe of bodies without knowing the compofition of them. What is body made of? of parts, and thefe parts are reducible to other parts. What are thofe laft parts? ftill bodies; fo you go on dividing, and are never nearer the mark.

At length, a fubtile philofopher, obferving that a picture is made of ingredients, none of which is a picture, and a houfe of materials of which none is a houfe, fancied bodies to be conftructed of innumerable little beings, which are not bodies, and thefe are the MONADES fo much talked of. This fyftem, however, has its fair fide, and, had it been confirmed by Revelation, I fhould think it very poffible. All thefe minute beings would be mathematical points, fpecies of fouls waiting only for a tegument to put themfelves into it; this would make a continual metempfychofis, a monade entering fometimes nto a whale, fometimes into a tree, and fometimes into a juggler. This fyftem is full as good as another; I can relifh it full as well as the declenfion of atoms, the fubftantial forms, verfatile grace, and Don Calmet's vampires.

CHINESE CATECHISM;

Or, DIALOGUES between Cu-su, a disciple of CONFUCIUS, and Prince Kou, son to the King of Lou, tributary to the CHINESE emperor GNENVAN, four hundred and seventeen years before our common æra.

Translated into LATIN by Father FOUQUET, formerly a Jesuit. The manuscript is in the VATICAN library, Number 42759.

K o u.

WHAT is meant by my duty to worship heaven (Chang-ti)?

Cu-su. Not the material heaven, which we see with our eyes; for this heaven is nothing but the air, and the air is composed of every kind of earthly exhalations. Now what a folly would it be to worship vapours?

Kou. It is, however, what I should not much wonder at; men, in my opinion, have given into greater follies.

Cu-su. Very true; but you being born to rule over others, it becomes you to be wise.

Kou. There are whole nations who worship heaven and the planets.

Cu-su. The planets are only so many earths like ours; the moon, for instance, might as well worship our sand and dirt, as we prostrate ourselves before the moon's sand and dirt.

Kou. What is the meaning of what we so often hear; heaven and earth, to go up to heaven, to be deserving of heaven?

Cu-

Cu-su. It is talking very fillily; there is no such thing as heaven *; every planet is environed with its atmofphere as with a fhell, and rolls in the fpace round its fun; every fun is the center of feveral planets, which are continually going their rounds; there is neither high nor low, up nor down. Should the inhabitants of the moon talk of going up to the earth, of making one's felf deferving of the earth, it would be talking madly; and we are little wifer in talking of deferving heaven. We might as well fay a man muft make himfelf deferving of the air, deferving of the conftellation of the dragon, deferving of fpace.

Kou. I believe I underftand you; we are only to worfhip God who made heaven and earth.

Cu-su. To be fure, we are to worfhip God alone. But in faying that he made heaven and earth, however devout our meaning may be, it is talking very fillily. For if by heaven we mean the prodigious fpace in which God kindled fo many funs, and fet fo many worlds in motion, it is much more ridiculous to fay, "Heaven and earth," than to fay, "the mountains and a grain of fand." Our globe is infinitely lefs than a grain of fand, in comparifon of thofe millions of ten thoufands of millions of worlds, among the infinitude of which we are loft. All that we can do, is to join our feeble voice to that of the innumerable beings, which, throughout the abyfs of expanfion, afcribe homage and glory to their adorable Creator.

Kou. It was, then, a great impofition to tell us, that Fo came down among us from the fourth heaven, affuming the form of a white elephant.

---

* This is only difputing about words; a place of future rewards, which the Chinefe philofopher feems to allow, is Heaven, wherever it be.

Cu-su. These are tales which the bonzes tell to old women and children. The eternal Author of all beings is alone to be worshipped.

Kou. But how can one being make the other beings?

Cu-su. You see yonder star: it is fifteen hundred thousand millions of Lis from our globe, and emits rays which on your eyes form two angles equal at the top; and the like angles they form on the eyes of all animals; is not this manifest design? Is not this an admirable law? and is it not the workman who makes a work? and who frames laws but a legislator?. Therefore there is an eternal Artist, an eternal Legislator.

Kou. But who made this Artist, and what is he like?

Cu-su. My dear prince, as I was yesterday walking near the vast Palace, lately built by the king your father, I over-heard two crickets; one said to the other, What a stupendous fabric is here! Yes, said the other; and though I am not a little proud of my species, he who has made this prodigy, must be something above a cricket; but I have no idea of that being; such a one I see there must be, but what he is I know not.

Kou. You are a cricket of infinitely more knowledge than I; and what I particularly like in you, is your not pretending to know what you really do not know.

Second Dialogue.

Cu-su. You allow, then, that there is an Almighty Being, self-existent, supreme Creator, and Maker of all nature.

Kou. Yes; but if he be self-existent he is illimited, consequently he is every-where, he exists throughout all matter, and in every part of myself.

Cu-su. Why not?

Kou.

Kou. I should then be a part of the Deity.

Cu-su. Perhaps that may not be the consequence; behold this piece of glass, you see the light penetrates it every-where, yet will you say it is light? It is mere sand, and nothing more: unquestionably every thing is in God; that by which every thing is animated must be every-where. God is not like the emperor of China, who dwells in his palace, and sends his orders by kolaos. As exifting he must necessarily fill the whole of space, and all his works; and since he is in you, this is a continual document never to do any thing to raise shame or remorse.

Kou. But for a person serenely to consider himself before the Supreme Being without shame or difguft, what must he do?

Cu-su. Be juft.

Kou. And what further?

Cu-su. Be juft.

Kou. But Laokium's fect says, there is no such thing as juft or unjuft, vice or virtue.

Cu-su. And does Laokium's fect say there is no such thing as health nor fickness?

Kou. No, to be sure; what egregious nonsense that would be!

Cu-su. And let me tell you, that to think there is neither health nor fickness of foul, nor virtue nor vice, is as egregious an error, and much more mischievous. They who have advanced that every thing is alike, are monfters: is it alike, carefully to bring up a son, or, at his birth, to dash him against the stones; to relieve a mother, or to plunge a dagger into her heart?

Kou. That is horrible! I detest Laokium's fect; but juft and unjuft are oftentimes so interwoven, that one is at a loss. Who can be said precisely to know what is forbidden and what is allowed?

lowed? Who can safely set limits to good and evil? I wish you would give me a sure rule for this important distinction.

Cu-su. There can be no better than that of Confutzee, my master, "Live as thou wouldst have lived when thou comest to die; use thy neighbour as thou wouldst have him use thee."

Kou. Those maxims, I own, should be mankind's standing law. But what am I the better for my good life, when I come to die? What mighty advantage shall I get by my virtue? That clock goes as well as ever clock did; but when it comes to be worn out, or should it be destroyed by accident, will it be happy for having struck the hours regularly?

Cu-su. That clock is without thought or feeling, and incapable of remorse, which you sharply feel on the commission of any crime.

Kou. But what if by frequent crimes I come to be no longer sensible of remorse.

Cu-su. Then it is high time an end should be put to your being; and take my word for it, that, as men do not love to be oppressed, should that be the case, one or another would stop you in your career, and save you the committing any more crimes.

Kou. At that rate God, who is in them, after allowing me to be wicked, would allow them likewise to be so.

Cu-su. God has endued you with reason, neither you nor they are to make a wrong use of it; as otherwise you will not only be unhappy in this life, but how do you know but you may likewise be so in another?

Kou. And who told you there is another life?

Cu-su. The bare uncertainty of it should make you behave as if it was an undoubted certainty.

Kou.

Kou. But what if I am sure there is no such thing?
Cu-su. That I defy you to make good.

Third Dialogue.

Kou. You urge me home, Cu-su; my being rewarded or punished after death, requires that something which feels and thinks in me, must continue to subsist after me; now as no part in me had any thought or sense before my birth, why should it after my death? What can this incomprehensible part of myself be? Will the humming of that bee continue after the end of its existence? or the vegetation of this plant, when plucked up by the roots? Is not vegetation a word made use of to express the inexplicable mode appointed by the Supreme Being, for the plants imbibing the juices of the earth? So the soul is an invented word, faintly and obscurely denoting the spring of human life. All animals have a motion, and this ability to move is called active force; but this force is no distinct being whatever. We have passions, memory, and reason; but these passions, this memory, and reason, are surely not separate things, they are not beings existing in us, they are not diminutive persons of a particular existence, they are generical words invented to fix our ideas. Thus the soul itself, which signifies our memory, our reason, our passions, is only a bare word. Whence then motion in nature? from God. Whence vegetation in the plant? from God. Whence motion in animals? from God. Whence cogitation in man? from God[*].

Were the human soul a diminutive person, inclosed within our body, to direct its motions and

---

[*] This opinion of the Chinese is the Pythagorean dogma of the "Anima Mundi," which has been fully refuted by Cudworth, Dr. Clarke, and several other learned divines.

ideas, wou'd not that betray in the eternal Maker of the world an impotence and an artifice quite unworthy of him? He then muſt have been incapable of making automata, which ſhall have the gift of motion and thought in themſelves. When I learned Greek under you, you made me read Homer, where Vulcan appears to me an excellent ſmith, when he makes golden tripods, going of themſelves to the council of the gods; but had this ſame Vulcan concealed within thoſe tripods one of his boys, to make them move without being perceived, I ſhould think him but a bungling cheat.

Some low-thoughted dreamers have been charmed with the fancy of the planets being rolled along by genii, as ſomething very grand and ſublime; but God has not been reduced to ſuch a paltry ſhift: in a word, wherefore put two ſprings to a work when one will do? That God can animate that ſo little known being which we call matter, you dare not deny; why then ſhould he make uſe of another agent to animate it?

Farther; what may that ſoul be which you are pleaſed to give to our body? From whence did it come? When did it come? Muſt the Creator of the univerſe be continually watching the copulation of men and women? cloſely obſerve the moment when a germ iſſues from a man's body and paſſes into that of a woman, and then quickly inject a ſoul into this germ? And if this germ dies, what becomes of its ſoul? either it muſt have been created ineffectually, or muſt wait another opportunity.

This is really a ſtrange employment for the Sovereign of the world; and it is not only on the copulation of the human ſpecies, that he muſt be continually intent, but muſt obſerve the like vigilance and celerity with all animals whatever; for, like us,

they

they have memory, ideas, and paffions; and if a
foul be neceffary for the formation of thefe fentiments, thefe ideas, thefe paffions, and this memory, God muft be perpetually at work about fouls
for elephants and fleas, for fifh and for bonzes.

What idea does fuch a notion give of the Architect of fo many millions of worlds, thus obliged to
be continually making invifible props for perpetu-
ating his work?

Thefe are fome, though a very fmall fample, of
the reafons for queftioning the foul's exiftence.

Cu-su. You reafon candidly; and fuch a virtuous turn of mind, even if miftaken, cannot but be
agreeable to the Supreme Being. You may be in
an error, but as you do not endeavour to deceive
yourfelf, your error is excufable. But confider
what you have propofed to me are only doubts, and
melancholy doubts; liften to probabilities of a fo-
lacing nature: to be annihilated is difmal; hope then
for life. A thought you know is not matter, nor has
any affinity with it. Why then do you make fuch
a difficulty of believing that God has put a divine
principle into you, which being indiffoluble, cannot be fubject to death? Can you fay that it is impoffible that you fhould have a foul? No, certainly: and if it be poffible that you have one, is it
not alfo very probable? How can you reject fo
noble a fyftem, and fo neceffary to mankind? Shall
a few flender objections with-hold your affent?

Kou. I would embrace this fyftem with all my
heart, on its being proved to me; but it is not in
my power to believe without evidence. I am always ftruck with this grand idea, that God has
made every thing, that he is every-where, that he
penetrates all things, and gives life and motion to
all things; and if he is in all the parts of my being, as he is in all the parts of nature, I do not fee
any

any need I have of a foul. Where is the ufe or importance of this little fubaltern being to me who am animated by God himfelf? of what improvement can it be? It is not from ourfelves that we derive our ideas, they generally obtrude themfelves on us againft our wills; we have them when locked in fleep; every thing paffes in us without our intervention. What would it fignify to the foul, were it to fay to the blood and animal fpirits, be fo kind as to gratify me in running this way, they will ftill circulate in their natural courfe. Let me be the machine of a God whofe exiftence all things proclaim aloud, rather than of a foul whofe exiftence is a very great uncertainty.

Cu-su. Well, if God himfelf animates you, be very careful of committing any crime as defiling that God, who is within you; and if he has given you a foul, never let it offend him. In both fyftems you have a volition, you are free, that is, you have a power of doing what you will; make ufe of this power in ferving that God who gave it you. If you are a philofopher, fo much the better, but it is neceffary for you to be juft; and you will be more fo when you come to believe that you have an immortal foul.

Be pleafed to anfwer me, Is not God fovereign and perfect juftice?

Kou. Doubtlefs; and could he ceafe to be fo (which is blafphemy to think) I would myfelf act equitably.

Cu-su. Will it not be your duty, when on the throne, to reward virtue and punifh vice? and can you think of God's not doing what is incumbent on yourfelf to do? You know that there are, and ever will be, in this life, good men diftreffed, whilft wicked men profper: therefore good and evil muft be finally judged in another life. It is this so simple, so general, and so natural, opinion which has introduced and fixed among so many nations the belief of the immortality of our souls, and their being judged by divine justice, on their quitting this mortal tenement. Is there, can there be, a system more rational, more suitable to the Deity, and more beneficial to mankind *?

Kou. Why then have so many nations rejected this system? You know, that in our province we have about two hundred families of the old Sinous, who formerly dwelt in part of Arabia Petrea; and neither they nor their ancestors ever believed any thing of the immortality of the soul: they have their five books as we have our five KING; I have read a translation of them; their laws, which necessarily correspond with those of all other nations, enjoin them to respect their parents, not to steal nor lye, to abstain from adultery and bloodshed; yet these laws are wholly silent as to rewards and punishments in another life.

Cu-su. If this truth has not yet been made known to those poor people, unquestionably their eyes will one day be opened. But what signifies a small obscure tribe, when the Babylonians, the Egyptians, the Indians, and all policed nations, have subscribed to this salutary doctrine? If you were sick, would you decline making use of a remedy approved by all the Chinese, because some barbarous mountaineers had expressed a dislike of it? God has endued you with reason, and this reason tells you that the soul must be immortal, therefore it is God himself who tells you so.

Kou. But how can I be rewarded or punished, when I shall cease to be myself, when nothing

---

* Our author has omitted the natural proofs of the immortality of the soul, which the reader may see in Dr. Clarke's Evidences of Natural and Revealed Religion, p. 265. See also our remarks on the word SOUL.

which had conſtituted my perſon will be remaining; it is only by my memory that I am always myſelf: now my memory I loſe in my laſt illneſs; ſo that, after my death, nothing under a miracle can reſtore it to me, and thus replace me in my former exiſtence.

Cu-su. That is as much as to ſay, ſhould a prince, after making his way to the throne by the murder of all his relations, play the tyrant over his ſubjects, he need only ſay to God, It is not I; I have totally loſt my memory; you miſtake, I am no longer the ſame perſon. Think you God would be very well pleaſed with ſuch a ſophiſm?

Kou. Well, I acquieſce; I was for living irreproachable for my own ſake, now I will do ſo to pleaſe the Supreme Being. I thought the whole matter was for my ſoul to be juſt and virtuous in this life; but I will now hope that it will be happy in another: this opinion, I do perceive, makes for the good both of ſubjects and ſovereigns; ſtill the worſhip of the Deity perplexes me.

Fourth Dialogue.

Cu-su. Why, what is there that can offend you in our Chu-king, the firſt canonical book, and which all the Chineſe emperors have ſo greatly reſpected. You plough a field with your own royal hands, by way of ſetting an example to the people, and the firſt fruits of it you offer to the Chang-ti, to the Tien, to the Supreme Being, and ſacrifice to him four times every year. You are king and high-prieſt, you promiſe God to do all the good which ſhall be in your power; is there any thing in this which you cannot digeſt?

Kou. I am very far from making any exceptions; I know that God has no need either of our ſacrifices or prayers, but the offering them to him is very needful for us; his worſhip was not inſtituted

for

for himself but on our account. I am very much delighted with praying, and am particularly careful that there shall be nothing ridiculous in my prayers; for were I to cry out till my throat is flead, " That the mountain of the Chang-ti is a " fat mountain, and that fat mountains are not to " be looked on;" though I should have put the sun to flight, and dried up the moon, will this rant be acceptable to the Supreme Being, or of any benefit to my subjects or myself?

Especially, I cannot bear with the silliness of the sects about us; on one side is Laotze, whom his mother conceived by the junction of heaven and earth, and was fourscore years pregnant with him. I as little believe his doctrine of universal deprivation and annihilation, as his being born with white hair, or his going to promulgate his doctrine on a black cow.

The god Fo I put on the same footing, notwithstanding he had a white elephant for his father, and promises immortal life.

One thing, at which I cannot forbear taking great offence, is the bonzes continually preaching such chimeras, thus deceiving the people in order the better to sway them; they gain to themselves respect by mortifications, at which indeed nature shudders. Some deny themselves, during their whole lives, the most salutary foods, as if there was no way of pleasing God but by a bad diet. Others carry a pillory about their necks, and sometimes they richly deserve it; they drive nails into their thighs as into boards; and for these things the people follow them in crowds. On the king's issuing any edict which does not suit their humour, they coolly tell their auditors that this edict is not to be found in the commentary of the god Fo, and that god is to be obeyed preferably to men. Now, how to remedy this popular distemper, which is extravagant to the highest degree, and not less dangerous? Toleration, you know, is the principle of the Chinese, and indeed of all Asiatic governments; but such an indulgence must be owned highly mischievous, as exposing an empire to be overthrown on account of some fanatical notions.

Cu-su. God forbid that I should go about to extinguish in you the spirit of toleration, that quality so eminently respectable, and which to souls is what the permission of eating is to bodies. By the law of nature, every one may believe what he will, as well as eat what he will. A physician is not to kill his patients for not observing the diet which he had prescribed to them; neither has a sovereign a right to hang his subjects for not thinking as he thinks; but he has a right to prevent disturbances, and with prudent measures he will very easily root out superstitions of all kinds. You know what happened to Daon, the sixth king of Chaldea, about four thousand years ago.

Kou. No. I pray oblige me with an account of it.

Cu-su. The Chaldean priests had taken it into their heads to worship the pikes of the Euphrates, pretending that a famous pike called Oannes, had formerly taught them divinity; that this pike was immortal, three feet in length, and a small crescent on the tail. In veneration to this Oannes, no pikes were to be eaten. A mighty dispute arose among the divines, whether the pike Oannes had a soft or hard roe. Both parties not only fulminated excommunications, but they several times came to blows. To put an end to such disturbances, king Daon made use of this expedient.

He ordered a strict fast for three days to both parties; and at the expiration of it, sent for the sticklers for the hard roed pike, who accordingly went

were present at his dinner; a pike was brought to him three feet in length, and on the tail a small crescent had been put. Is this your god, said he to the doctors? Yes, Sir, answered they; we know him by the crescent on the tail, and make no question but he is hard-roed. On this the king ordering the pike to be opened, it was found to have the finest melt that could be. Now, said the king, you see this is not your god, it being soft-roed; and the king and his nobles ate the pike, and the hard-roed divines were not a little pleased that the god of their adversaries had been fried.

Immediately after the doctors of the opposite side were sent for, and a pike of three feet, with a crescent on his tail, being shewn to them, they, with great joy, assured his majesty, that it was the god Oannes, and that he had a soft roe; but behold! on being opened, it was found hard-roed. At this the two parties, equally out of countenance, and still fasting, the good-natured king told them that he could only give them a dinner of pikes, and they greedily fell to eating both hard and soft-roed without distinction. This closed the civil war, with great applauses of king Daon's wisdom and goodness; and since that time the people have been allowed to eat pikes as often as they pleased.

Kou. Well done, king Daon! and I give you my word I will follow his example on every occasion, and as far as I can, without injuring any one; there shall be no worshipping of Fo's and pikes.

I know that in the countries of Pegu and Tonquin, there are little gods and little Talapoins which bring down the moon, when in the wane, and clearly foretel what is to come, that is, they clearly see what is not, for futurity is not. I will take care that the Talapoins shall not come within my reach, to make futurity present, and bring down the moon.

It is a shame that there should be sects rambling from town to town, propagating their delusions, as quacks their medicaments. What a disgrace is it to the human mind, for petty nations to think that truth belongs to them alone, and that the vast empire of China is given up to error? Is then the Eternal Being only the god of the island of Formosa or Borneo? Has he no concern for the other parts of the universe? My dear Cu-su, he is a father to all men, he allows every one to eat pike: the most acceptable homage which can be paid to him is being virtuous; the finest of all his temples, as the great emperor Hiao used to say, is a pure heart.

FIFTH DIALOGUE.

Cu-su. Since you love virtue, in what manner do you propose to practise it when you come to be king?

Kou. In not being unjust to my neighbours or my subjects.

Cu-su. To do no harm does not come up to virtue. I hope my prince will do good, will feed the poor by employing them in useful labour, and not endow sloth; mend and embellish the highways, dig canals, build public edifices, encourage arts, reward merit of every kind, and pardon involuntary faults.

Kou. This I call not being unjust; those things are plain duties.

Cu-su. Your way of thinking becomes a king; but there is the king and the man; the public life and private life. You will be married; how many wives do you think of having?

Kou.

Kou. Why, a dozen, I think, will do: a greater number might be an avocation from bufinefs; I don't approve of kings with their three hundred wives and feven hundred concubines, and thoufands of eunuchs to wait on them. This humour of having eunuchs, efpecially, appears to me a moft execrable infult and outrage to human nature. The caftrating of cocks I can forgive, as eating the better for it; but I never have heard of eunuchs being roafted. What is the ufe of their being thus mutilated? It improves their voices; the Dala-i Lama has fifty of them purely to fing in his pagod. Let him tell me whether the Chang-ti is much delighted with the clear pipes of thefe fifty geldings.

Another moft ridiculous thing is the bonzes not marrying. They boaft of being wifer than the other Chinefe; well then, let them fhew their wifdom in getting wife children. An odd manner of worfhipping the Chang-ti, to deprive him of worfhippers; and, to be fure, they muft have a great affection for mankind, who go the way to extinguifh the fpecies! The good little Lama called STELCA ISANT EREPI, ufed to fay, " That every prieft " ought to get as many children as he could:" what he preached he practifed, and was very ufeful in his generation. For my part, I fhall marry all the lamas and bonzes, and lamaffes and bonzeffes, who fhall appear to have a call to this holy work; befides making them better patriots, I fhall think it no fmall fervice to my dominions.

Cu-su. What an excellent prince fhall we have in you! I cannot forbear weeping for joy. But you will not be fatisfied with having wives and fubjects, for, after all, one cannot be perpetually drawing up edicts, and getting children; you will likewife make yourfelf fome friends.

Kou. I am not without some already, and those good ones, putting me in mind of my faults, and I allow myself the liberty of reproving theirs; we likewise mutually comfort and encourage one another; friendship is the balm of life, it excels that of the chemist Eruil, and even all the nostrums of the great Ranoud are not comparable to it. I think friendship should have been made a religious precept. I have a good mind to insert it in our ritual.

Cu-su. By no means; friendship is sufficiently sacred of itself. Never enjoin it; the heart must be free: besides, were you to make a precept, a mystery, a rite, a ceremony, of friendship, it would soon become ridiculous through the fantastical preachings and writings of the bonzes: let it not be exposed to such profanation.

But how will you deal with your enemies? Confutzee, I believe, in not less than twenty places, directs us to love them: does not this appear something difficult to you?

Kou. Love one's enemies! Oh, dear doctor! nothing is so common.

Cu-su. But what do you mean by love?

Kou. Mean by it what it really is. I was a volunteer under the prince of Decon against the prince of Vis-brunk; when a wounded enemy fell into our hands we took as much care of him as if he had been our brother: we have often parted with our beds to them, and we lay by them on tygers skins spread on the bare ground; we have tended and nursed them ourselves: Is not this loving our enemies? You would not have us love them as a man loves his mistress?

Cu-su. I am exceedingly pleased with your talk, and wish that all nations could hear you, for

I have been informed of some so very conceited and impertinent as to say that we know nothing of true virtue; that our good actions are only specious sins; that we stand in need of their Talapoins to instruct us in right principles. Poor creatures! A few years ago there was no such thing as reading or writing among them, and now they are for teaching their masters.

Sixth Dialogue.

Cu-su. I shall not repeat to you the commonplaces, which for these five or six thousand years past, have been retailed among us, relating to all the several virtues. Some there are which only concern ourselves, as prudence in the guidance of our soul, temperance in the government of our bodies; but these are rather dictates of policy, and care of health: the real virtues are those which promote the welfare of society, as fidelity, magnanimity, beneficence, toleration, &c. and, thank heaven, these are the first things which every woman, among us, teaches her children; they are the rudiments of the rising generation, both in town and country; but I am sorry to say it, there is a great virtue which is sadly on the decline among us.

Kou. Quickly name it, and no endeavour of mine shall be wanting to revive it.

Cu-su. It is hospitality; for since inns have got footing among us, this so social virtue, this sacred tie of mankind, becomes more and more relaxed: that pernicious institution, I am told, we have borrowed from some western savages; who, probably, have no houses to entertain travellers. My heart melts with delight when I have the happiness of entertaining, in the vast city of Lou, in Honcham,

cham, that superb square, or my delicious seat of Ki, some generous stranger come from Samarcande, to whom, from that moment, I become sacred, and who, by all laws human and divine, is bound to entertain me, on any call I may have into Tartary, and to be my cordial friend.

The savages I am speaking of do not admit strangers into their huts, filthy as they are, without their paying, and dearly too, for such sordid reception; and yet those wretches, I hear, think themselves above us, and that our morality is nothing in comparison of theirs. Their preachers excel Confutzee himself; in a word, they alone know what true justice is, and a sign of it is, they sell on the roads some sophisticated stuff for wine, and their women, as if mad, rove about the streets, and dance, whilst ours are breeding silk-worms.

Kou. I very much approve of hospitality, and the practice of it gives me pleasure; but I am afraid it will be much abused. Near Thibet dwells a people, who, besides the badness of their habitations, being of a roving disposition, will, on any trifle, go from one end of the world to the other; and, on your having occasion to go to Thibet, so far from returning your hospitality, they have nothing to set before you, nor so much as a bed for you to lie on; this is enough to put one out of conceit with courtesy.

Cu-su. These disappointments may easily be remedied, by entertaining such persons only as come well recommended. Every virtue has its difficulties and dangers, and without them the practice of virtue would want much of its glory and excellence. How wise and holy is our Confutzee? There is not a virtue which he does not inculcate; every sentence of his is pregnant with the happiness of mankind:

mankind: one, at present, recurs to me, I think it is the fifty-third:

> "Kindnesses acknowledge with kindness, and never revenge injuries."

What maxim, what law, can the western people bring in competition with such exalted morality? Then in how many places, and how strongly, does he recommend humility? Did this amiable virtue prevail among men, there would be a total end of all quarrels and broils.

Kou. I have read all that Confutzee, and the sages before him, have said about humility; but none of them, I think, have been sufficiently accurate in their definition of it. There may, perhaps, be but little humility in taking on one to censure them; but, with all due humility, I own that they are beyond my comprehension. What is your idea of humility?

Cu-su. Humility I take to be mental modesty; for as to external modesty, it is no more than civility. Humility cannot consist in denying to one's self that superiority which we may have acquired above another. An able physician cannot but be sensible that he is possessed of a knowledge infinitely beyond his delirious patient. The teacher of astronomy must necessarily think himself more learned than his scholar; but they must not pride themselves in their superior talents. Humility is not debasement, but a corrective to self-love, as modesty is the temperament to pride.

Kou. Well, it is in the practice of all these virtues, and the worship of one simple and universal God, that I propose to live, far from the chimeras of sophists, and the illusion of false prophets. The love of mankind shall be my virtue, and the love of God my religion. As to the god Fo, and Laotzee,

Laotzee and Vitſnou, who has ſo often become incarnate among the Indians, and Sammonocodom, who came down from heaven to fly a kite among the Siameſe, together with the Camis, who went from the moon to viſit Japan; I cannot endure ſuch impious fooleries.

How weak, and at the ſame time how cruel, is it for a people to conceit that there is no god but with them only! it is downright blaſphemy. The light of the ſun irradiates all nations, and the light of God ſhines only in a little inſignificant tribe in a corner of this globe. That ever ſuch a thought could enter the mind of man! The Deity ſpeaks to the heart of all men of all nations, and they ſhould, from one end of the univerſe to the other, be linked together in the bonds of charity.

Cu-su. O wiſe Kou! you have ſpoke like one inſpired by the Chang-ti himſelf; you will make a worthy prince. From being my pupil you are become my teacher.

The JAPANESE CATECHISM.

The INDIAN.

IS it ſo, that formerly the Japaneſe knew nothing of cookery; that they had ſubmitted their kingdom to the great Lama; that this great Lama arbitrarily preſcribed what they ſhould eat and drink; that he uſed, at times, to ſend to you an inferior Lama for receiving the tributes, who, in return, gave you a ſign of protection, which he made with his two fore-fingers and thumb?

The JAPANESE.

Alas! it is but too true; nay, all the places of the Canuſi, or the chief cooks of our iſland, were

diſpoſed

disposed of by the Lama, and the love of God was quite out of the question. Farther, every house of our seculars paid annually an ounce of silver to this head-cook of Thibet, whilst all the amends we had was some small plates of RELICKS, and these none of the best tasted ; and on every new whim of his, as making war against the people of Tangut, we were saddled with fresh subsidies. Our nation frequently complained, but all we got by it was to pay the more for presuming to complain. At length love, which does every thing for the best, freed us from this galling thraldom. One of our emperors quarrelled with the great Lama about a woman ; but it must be owned that they who in this affair did us the best turn, were our Canusi, or Pauxcospies; it is to them that, in fact, we owe our deliverance, and it happened in this manner:

The great Lama, forsooth, insisted on being always in the right; our Dairi and Canusi would have it that sometimes, at least, they might be in the right. This claim the great Lama derided, as an absurdity; on which our gentry, being as stiff as he was haughty, broke with him for ever.

IND. Well, ever since you have had golden days, I suppose ?

JAP. Far from it ; for near two hundred years there was nothing but persecutions, violences, and bloodshed among us. After all our Canusis pretending to be in the right, it is but an hundred years since they have had their right reason ; but since this time, we may boldly esteem ourselves one of the happiest nations on the earth.

IND. How can that be, if, as reported, you have no less than twelve different sects of cookery among you ? Why you must always be at daggers drawing.

JAP.

Jap. Why so? If there are twelve cooks, and each has a different receipt, shall we, instead of dining, cut each other's throats? No: every one may regale himself at that cook's whose manner of dressing victuals he likes best.

Ind. True; tastes are not to be disputed about: yet people will make them a matter of contention, and all sides grow hot.

Jap. After long disputing, men come to see the mischiefs of these jarrings, and at length agree on a reciprocal toleration; and certainly they can do nothing better.

Ind. And pray what are these cooks who make such a stir in your nation about the art of eating and drinking?

Jap. First, there's the Breuxehs, who never allow any pork or pudding; they hold with the old-fashioned cookery; they would as soon die, as lard a fowl; then they deal much in numbers, and if an ounce of silver be to be divided between them and the eleven other cooks, they instantly secure one-half to themselves, and the remainder take who will.

Ind. I fancy you do not often foul a plate with these folks.

Jap. Never. Then there's the Pispates, who, on some days of the week, and even for a considerable time of the year, will gormandize on turbot, trouts, foals, salmon, sturgeon, be they ever so dear, and would not for the world touch a sweetbread of veal, which may be had for a groat.

As for us Canusi, we are very fond of beef and a kind of pastry ware, in Japanese called pudding. Now all the world allows our cooks to be infinitely more knowing than those of the Pispates: nobody has gone farther than we in finding out what

was

was the garum of the Romans; we surpass all others in our knowledge of the onions of antient Egypt, the locust paste of the primitive Arabs, the Tartarian horse-flesh; and there is always something to be learned in the books of those Canusi commonly known by the name of Pauxcospies.

I shall omit those who eat only in Tarluh, those who observe the vincal diet, the Batistans, and others; but the Quekars deserve particular notice. Though I have very often been at table with them, I never saw one get drunk, or swear an oath. It is a hard matter to cheat them, but then they never cheat you. The law of loving one's neighbour as one's self seems really peculiar to them; for, in good truth, how can an honest Japanese talk of loving his neighbour as himself, when, for a little pay, he goes as a hireling, to blow his brains out, and hew him with a four inch broad sabre, and all this in form; then he, at the same time, exposes himself to the like fate, to be shot or sabred: so he may with more truth be said to hate his neighbour as himself. This is a phrenzy the Quekars were never possessed with. They say, and very justly, that poor mortals are earthen vessels, made to last but a very short time, and that they should not wantonly go and break themselves to pieces one against another.

I own, that were I not a Canusi, I should take part with the Quekars; for you see, that there can be no wranglings nor blows with such peaceable cooks. There is another and very numerous branch of cooks called Diestó; with these every one, without distinction, is welcome to their table, and you are at full liberty to eat as you like; you have larded or barded fowls, or neither larded nor barded, egg sauce, or oil; partridge, salmon, white or red wines; these things they hold as matters of
indifference,

indifference, provided you say a short prayer before and after dinner, and even without this ceremony before breakfast; and with good-natured worthy men they will banter about the great Lama, the Turlah, Vincal, and Memnon, &c. only these Diestos must acknowledge our Canusi to be very profound cooks; and especially let them never talk of curtailing our incomes; then we shall live very easily together.

IND. But still there must be cookery by law established, or the king's cookery.

JAP. There must so.; but when the king of Japan has regaled himself plentifully, he should be chearful and indulgent, and not hinder his good subjects from having their repasts.

IND. But should some hot-headed people take on themselves to eat sausages close to the king's nose, when the king is known to have an aversion to that food; should a mob of four or five thousand of them get together, each with his gridiron, to broil their sausages, and insult those who are against eating them—

JAP. In such a case they ought to be punished as turbulent drunkards. But we have obviated this danger; none but those who follow the royal cookery are capable of holding any employment; all others may, indeed, eat as they please, but this humour excludes them from some emoluments. Tumults are strictly forbidden, and instantly punished without mercy or mitigation; all quarrels at table are carefully restrained by a precept of our great Japanese cook, who has written in the sacred language, " Suti rho, cus flat, natis in usum lætitiæ scyphis pugnare tracum est:" that is, " the intent of feasting is a sober and decent mirth; but to throw glasses at one another is savage."

Under

DICTIONARY. 61

Under thefe maxims we live very happily; our liberty is fecured by our Taicofemas; we are every day growing more and more opulent; we have two hundred junks of the line, and are dreaded by our neighbours.

IND. Why then has the pious rhymer Recna (fon to the fo juftly celebrated Indian poet Recna) faid in a didactic work of his, intitled Grace, and not the Graces,

Le Japon où jadis brilla tant de lumiere,
Ne'eft plus qu'un trifte amas de folles vifions.

" Japan, once famed for intellectual light,
" lies now involved in error and chimerical
" vifion."

JAP. That Recna is himfelf an arrant vifionary. Does not that weak Indian know, that it is we who have taught his countrymen what light is? That it is to us India owes its knowing the courfe of the planets; that it is we who have made known to man the primitive laws of nature, and the doctrine of fluxions? To defcend to things of more common ufe; by us his countrymen were taught to build junks in mathematical proportions; they are beholden to us for thofe coverings of their legs which they call wove ftockings. Now is it poffible that, after fuch admirable and ufeful inventions, we fhould be madmen? And if he has rhimed on the follies of others, does that make him the only wife man? Let him leave us to our own cookery, and, if he muft be verfifying, I would advife him to chufe more poetical fubjects.

This Recna, trufting to the vifionaries of his country, has advanced, " That no good fauces were
" to

"to be made unless Brama himself, out of his par-
"ticular favour, taught his favourites to make the
"sauce; that there was an infinite number of
"cooks, who, with the best intentions and most
"earnest endeavours, were under an impossibility
"of making a ragout; Brama, from mere ill will,
"disabling them." Such stuff will not go down
in Japan, where the following sentence is esteemed
an indisputable truth:

"God never acts by partial will, but by general
laws."

IND. What can be said! He is full of his country's prejudices, those of his party, and his own.

JAP. A world of prejudices indeed!

The COUNTRY PRIEST's CATECHISM.

ARISTUS.

SO, my dear Theotimus, you are going to be a country parson.

THEOTIMUS.

Yes, I have had a small parish conferred on me; and I like it better than a larger; it is more suited both to my parts and my activity; having but one soul myself, the superintendance and direction of seventy thousand would certainly be too much for me; and I have ever wondered at the daringness of those who have taken on them the care of those immense districts. I cannot, in any tolerable measure, find myself equal to such a charge; a large flock really frightens me, but with a small one I may perhaps do some good. I have a smattering of the law, enough, with my careful endeavours, to prevent my poor parishioners from ruining one another by litigations; I am so far a physician as to prescribe to them in common cases; and I have so far looked into our best treatises on agriculture, that my advice may sometimes be of service to them. The lord of the manor and his lady are mighty good sort of people, and no devotees; they will second my endeavours to do good, so that I promise myself a very happy time of it, and that those among whom I am to live will not be the worse for my company.

ARIST. But could you not like to have a wife? It would be a great comfort after preaching, singing, confessing, communicating, baptizing, and burying, to be welcomed at your return home by an affectionate, cleanly, and virtuous wife; she would take care of your linen and person, divert you when in health, tend you in sickness, and make you the father of pretty children, the good education of whom would be of public advantage. I really pity your order, whose whole time is spent in the most valuable service of mankind, yet are debarred of a comfort and solacement so delectable, and withal so necessary.

THEOT. The Greek church makes a point of encouraging marriage in their priests; the church of England and the Protestants universally act with the like wisdom; but the policy of the Latin church is quite opposite, and I must submit to it. Perhaps in the present prevalence of a philosophical spirit, were a council convened, its decrees would be more favourable to human nature than those of the council of Trent; but till that happy time, I must conform to the present laws; I am no stranger to its difficulties, but so many of my betters having taken the yoke on them, it is not for me to murmur.

ARIST.

ARIST. You have a great share of learning, and are likewise master of a nervous eloquence; how do you intend to preach before a congregation of villagers?

THEOT. As I would before kings. I will insist on morality, and never meddle with controversy. God forbid that I should go about diving into concomitant grace, effectual grace which may be resisted, sufficient grace which does not suffice; or examining whether the angels who came to Lot had a body, or only feigned to eat. A thousand things there are, which my congregation would not understand, nor I neither: my endeavour shall be to make them good, and to be so myself; but I shall make no divines, nor be so myself, no more than shall be absolutely necessary.

ARIST. You will make a good priest, indeed! I think I must purchase a country-house in your parish. But be so kind as to tell me how you will manage confession.

THEOT. Confession is highly beneficial, a strong curb to vice, and a very early institution. It was antiently practised at the celebration of all the mysteries of the church; and we have imitated and sanctified so devout an observance: it avails greatly, turning resentment and hatred into forgiveness and friendship; by it the petty rogues are induced to restore what they had stolen. I own it has also its inconveniences. There are too many indiscreet confessors, chiefly among the monks, who sometimes teach girls more fooleries than they learn among the young men. In confession there should be no particulars; it is no juridical interrogatory, but only a sinner's acknowledgment of his faults to the Supreme Being, before another sinner, who is soon to make the like acknowledgment. This salutary avowal is not made to gratify a frivolous curiosity.

ARIST.

ARIST. And excommunications; will you ever proceed to such extremities?

THEOT. No; some rituals excommunicate grashoppers, sorcerers, and stage-players. Grashoppers I shall never exclude from my church, for they never come there; as little shall I excommunicate sorcerers, seeing there are none; and stage-players being authorized by the magistrates, and pensioned by his majesty, it would ill become me to brand them with infamy: and, to be ingenuous, I can with pleasure read a play, when kept within the limits of decency; such, for instance, as Athaliah and the Misanthrope, which contain a great deal of moral instruction. The lord of our manor has some such pieces acted at his seat by young people of a theatrical turn; these exhibitions lead to virtue through the attractive of pleasure, form the taste, and greatly contribute to a just elocution. Now, for my part, in all this I see nothing but what is very innocent, and even very useful; so that I intend, purely for my instruction, to be sometimes a spectator, but in a latticed box, to avoid giving offence to the weak.

ARIST. The more you let me into your way of thinking, the more desirous am I of becoming your parishioner; but one point remains, which I think of very great importance. How will you do to hinder the peasants from fuddling on the holidays, which, you know, is their chief way of keeping festivals? Some, overcome by a liquid poison, are seen with their heads drooping almost to their knees, their hands dangling, their sight and hearing lost, in a condition very much beneath beasts; led home reeling by their lamenting wives, incapable of going to work the next day, often sick, and sometimes irrecoverably besotted. Others, inflamed

F

ed by wine, raise quarrels, which soon come to furious blows; and these brutal scenes, a disgrace to human nature, have not seldom been known to end in a murder. It is a known truth, that the state loses more subjects by holidays than by wars; now how will you, if not eradicate this execrable custom out of your parish, at least bring it under some regulation?

THEOT. I have a remedy at hand; I shall not only give them leave, but exhort them to follow their occupations after divine service; and that I will take care to begin very early, for it is their being unemployed on such days which sends them to public-houses; on the working days we hear of no riot or bloodshed. Moderate labour is good both for soul and body: besides, the state wants their labour. Let us suppose, and the supposition is within bounds, five millions of men, one with another, doing ten pennyworth of work, and that these five millions of men are, by such a custom, rendered quite useless no less than thirty days in the year; consequently the state is deprived of work to the value of thirty times five millions of tenpences; now God never enjoined drunkenness, nor such detrimental observance of festivals.

ARIST. This will be reconciling devotion and business, and both are of God's appointment; thus you serve God, and do good to your neighbour. But amidst our ecclesiastical feuds, with which party will you side?

THEOT. With none. Virtue never occasions any disputes, because it comes from God; all these heart-burnings are about opinions, which are the inventions of men.

ARIST. Excellent! I wish all priests were like you.

CER-

CERTAIN, CERTAINTY.

HOW old may your friend Chriſtopher be? Twenty-eight. I have ſeen both his contract of marriage, and the regiſter of his birth: I have known him from a child; twenty-eight is his age. I am as certain of it as certain can be.

Soon after this man's anſwer, who was ſo ſure of what he ſaid, and of twenty others, in confirmation of the ſame thing, I happened to be informed that, for private reaſons, and by an odd contrivance, the regiſter of Chriſtopher's birth was antedated. They to whom I had ſpoken, knowing nothing of this, are ſtill in the greateſt certainty of what is not.

Had you, in Copernicus's time, aſked all the world, Did the ſun riſe, did the ſun ſet, to-day? they would, one and all, have anſwered, That's a certainty; we are fully certain of it: thus they were certain, and yet miſtaken.

Witchcraft, divinations, and poſſeſſions, were, for a long time, univerſally accounted the moſt certain things in the world. What numberleſs crowds have ſeen all thoſe fine things, and have been certain of them! but at preſent, ſuch certainty begins to loſe its credit.

A young man, juſt entered on geometry, and gone no farther than the definition of triangles, calls on me: Are not you certain, ſaid I to him, that the three angles of a triangle are equal to two right angles? He anſwers me, that, ſo far from being certain, he has not a clear idea of the propoſition; on which I demonſtrate it to him; this, indeed, makes him very certain of it, and he will be ſo as long as he lives.

Here is a certainty very different from the former: they were only probabilities, which, on being searched into, are found errors; but mathematical certainty is immutable and eternal.

I exist, I think, I feel pain; is all this as certain as a geometrical truth? Yes. And why? Because these truths are proved by the same principle, that a thing cannot, at the same time, be and not be. I cannot, at one and the same time, exist and not exist, feel and not feel. A triangle cannot have and not have a hundred and eighty degrees, the sum of two right angles.

Thus the physical certainty of my existence and my sensation, and mathematical certainty, are of a like validity, though differing in kind.

But this is by no means applicable to the certainty founded on appearances, or the unanimous relations of men.

How, say you, are not you certain that there is such a city as Pekin? Have you not some Pekin manufactures? Are you not certain of the existence of Pekin from the accounts of persons of different nations and different opinions, and writing violently against each other, when preaching the truth in that city. I answer, that it is highly probable there was such a city at that time, but I would not lay my life on its existence; whereas at any time will I stake my life that the three angles of a triangle are equal to two right angles.

The DICTIONAIRE ENCYCLOPEDIQUE has a very droll assertion, that should all Paris say that marshal Saxe is risen from the dead, a man ought to be as sure and certain of it, as he is that the marshal gained the battle of Fontenoy, on hearing all Paris say so. Excellent reasoning! I believe all Paris when it tells me a thing morally possible;

must I therefore believe all Paris when it tells me a thing which is both morally and naturally impossible?

The author of this article, I suppose, was in a bantering strain, and the other author against whom it was written, probably means no more by his extatic applauses at the end of it.

CHAIN OF EVENTS.

IT is an old supposition, that all events are linked together by an invincible fatality: this is destiny, which Homer makes superior to Jupiter himself. This sovereign of gods and men frankly declares that he cannot save his son Sarpedon from dying at the time appointed. Sarpedon was born at the very instant that he was to be born, at any other he could not be born; so he could not die any where but before Troy; he could be buried no where but in Lycia; his body was at the destined time to produce herbs and pulse, which were to be changed into the substance of some Lycians. His heirs were to institute a new form of government in his dominions; this new form was to affect the neighbouring kingdoms, and this put those who bordered on these neighbouring kingdoms on new measures of peace or war: thus the fate of the whole earth came gradually to be determined by that of Sarpedon, which depended on another event, and this by a chain of other events, was connected with the origin of things.

Had only one of these transactions been differently disposed, it would have caused a different universe; and that the present universe should exist and not exist is an impossibility, therefore it was not possible for Jupiter, with all his omnipotence, to save his son's life.

This system of necessity and fatality has, according to Leibnitz, been struck out by himself, under the appellation of SUFFICIENT REASON, but it is in reality of very antient date; that no effect is without a cause, and that, often, the least cause produces the greatest effects, is what the world is not to be aught at this time of day.

My lord Bolingbroke owns, that the trivial quarrel between the duchess of Marlborough and Mrs. Masham put him upon making the separate treaty between queen Anne and Lewis XIV. This treaty brought on the peace of Utrecht. This peace settled Philip V. on the Spanish throne. Philip V. dispossessed the house of Austria of Naples and Sicily; thus the Spanish prince, who is now king of Naples, evidently owes his sovereignty to Mrs. Masham: he would not have had it, perhaps he would not so much as have been born, had the duchess of Marlborough behaved with due complaisance towards the queen of England; his existence at Naples depended on a few follies committed at the court of London. Enquire into the situation of all the nations on the globe, and they all derive from a chain of events, apparently quite unconnected with any one thing, and connected with every thing. In this immense machine all is wheel-work, pully, cords, and spring.

It is the same in the physical system: a wind blowing from the south of Africa and the austral seas, brings with it part of the African atmosphere, which falls down again in rain among the vallies of the Alps, and these rains fructify our lands. Again our northern wind wafts our vapours among the Negroes: thus we benefit Guinea, and are benefited by by it; and this chain reaches from one end of the universe to the other.

But the truth of this principle, I think, has been stretched to a strange excess. Some will have it, that there is no atom ever so minute but its motion contributed to the present disposition of the whole world; and that every petty incident, whether among men or brutes, is an essential link in the great chain of fatality.

Let us understand one another: every effect has evidently its cause, recurring from cause to cause, up to the abyss of eternity; but every cause has not its effect traced forward to the end of time. That all events proceed from others I own; as the past has brought forth the present, the present produces the future; every thing has fathers, but every thing has not always children. This cannot be better elucidated than by a genealogical tree; every family is deduced from Adam, but many of its branches die without issue.

The events of this world are not without their genealogical tree: the inhabitants of Gaul and Spain are indisputably descended from Gomer, and the Russians from Magog, his younger brother, for so it is said in many huge books; then we are of course indebted to Magog for the sixty thousand Russians now in arms towards the confines of Pomerania, and the sixty thousand French in the neighbourhood of Franckfort. But I do not see how Magog's spitting to the right or left near Mount Caucasus, or his making two or three arches on the inside of a well, or his lying on his right or his left side, could have any considerable influence in the czarina Elizabeth's resolution of sending an army to the assistance of Mary Theresa, empress of the Romans. That my dog dreamed or did not dream in its sleep has any relation to the grand mogul's concerns, is what I cannot see into.

It must be considered, that all things are not full in nature; and that every motion is not communicated successively, so as to be continued round the world. On throwing into water a body of equal density, you easily conceive that in some short time the motion of such body, and that which it has caused in the water, will cease; motion is lost and recovered: thus the motion which might have been produced by Magog's spitting in a well, can have no affinity with what is now doing in Russia and Prussia; thus the present events are not issued from all the former events; they have their direct lines; but a thousand petty collateral lines do not in the least conduce to them: I say it again, every being has its fathers, but every being has not children. I may possibly enlarge on this head, when I come to speak of DESTINY.

CHAIN OF CREATED BEINGS.

AT my first reading Plato, I was charmed with his gradation of beings, rising from the slighteft atom to the supreme essence. Such a scale struck me with admiration; but, on a closer survey of it, this august phantom disappeared, as formerly ghosts used to hie away at the crowing of the cock.

Fancy is, at first, ravished in beholding the imperceptible ascent from senseless matter to organized bodies, from plants to zoophytes, from zoophytes to animals, from these to men, from men to genii, from these aetheral genii to immaterial essence, and lastly numberless different orders of these essences, fences, afcending through a fucceffion of increafing beauties and perfections, to God himfelf. The devout are mightily taken with this hierarchy, as reprefenting the pope and his cardinals, followed by the archbifhops and bifhops, and then by the reverend train of rectors, vicars, unbeneficed priefts, deacons, and fubdeacons; then come the Regulars, and the Capuclfins bring up the rear.

But from God to his moft perfect creatures the diftance is fomething greater than between the pope and the dean of the facred college; this dean may come to be pope, whereas the moft perfect of the genii never can be God. Infinitude lies between God and him.

Neither does this chain, this pretended gradation, exift any longer in vegetables and animals, fome fpecies of plants and animals being totally extinguifhed. The murex is not to be found; it was forbidden to eat the griffin, and ixion, which, whatever Bochart may fay, have, for ages paft, not been in nature; where then is the chain?

If no fpecies have been loft, yet it is manifeft they may be deftroyed, for lions and rhinocerofes are growing very fcarce.

It is far from being improbable that there have been breeds of men now no longer exifting; but I grant that they all have been preferved, as truly as the whites, the blacks, the Caffres, to whom nature has given a membraneous apron hanging from their belly half down their thighs; the Samoiedes, where one of the nipples of the women's breafts is of a fine ebony, &c.

Is there not a manifeft chafm between the monkey and man? Is it not eafy to conceive a two-legged animal without feathers, endowed with underftanding, but without fpeech or our fhape, which we might tame and inftruct, fo that it fhould anfwer

to

to our signs, and serve us to many purposes; and between this new species and that of man, might not others be contrived?

Farther, divine Plato, you quarter in the firmament a series of cœlestial substances. As for us, we believe the existence of some of these substances, being taught so by our faith. But what grounds can you have for such a belief? It is to be supposed, that you never conversed with Socrates's genius; and the good man Heres, who kindly rose from the dead, purely to communicate to you the mysteries of the other world, did not say a word to you about such substances.

This supposed chain is not less imperfect in the sensible universe.

What gradation, pray, is there between those planets of yours? The moon is forty times smaller than our globe. In your journey from the moon through the ether you meet with Venus, which is nearly as big as the earth. Whence you come to Mercury turning in an ellipsis, which is very different from Venus' orbits; he is twenty-seven times smaller than our planet, and the sun is a million times larger. Mars is five times smaller; the former performs his orbit in two years, Jupiter its neighbour in twelve, Saturn takes up thirty, and yet Saturn, the most distant of any, is not so large as Jupiter. Amidst these disproportions what becomes of the gradation?

And then, how can you think that, in such immense voids, there can be a chain whereby every thing is connected; if such a chain there be, it is certainly that discovered by Newton, and by which all the globes of the planetary world gravitate towards each other, throughout these immense spaces.

Oh!

Oh! Plato, though so much admired, your writings swarm with fables and fictions; and the Cassiterides, where, in your time, men went quite naked, has produced a philosopher, who have taught the world truths as great and sublime as your notions were erroneous and puerile.

CHARACTER

COMES from a Greek word, signifying Impression and Graving; it is what nature has engraven in us; then can we efface it? This is a weighty question. A mishapen nose, cats eyes, or any deformity in the features, may be hidden with a masque, and can I do more with the character which nature has given me? A man naturally impetuous and passionate comes before Francis I. king of France, to complain of an outrage: the prince's aspect, the respectful behaviour of the courtiers, the very place, make a powerful impression on him. With eyes cast down, a soft voice, and every sign of humility, he presents his petition, so that one would think he was naturally as mild and polite, as are (at least at that time) the courtiers, among whom he is even out of countenance; but if Francis I. be a physiognomist, he will easily discover by the sullen fire in his eyes, by the straining of the muscles in his face, and the compression of his lips, that this man is not really so mild as he is obliged to appear. The same man follows him to Pavia, is taken with him, and confined in the same prison at Madrid; here the impression made on him by Francis's aspect and grandeur ceases; he grows familiar with the object of his respect. One day drawing on the king's boots, and doing it wrong, the king, soured by his misfortune,

fortune, takes pet; on this my gentleman, shaking off all respect to his majesty, throws the boots out of the window.

Sixtus Quintus was naturally petulant, obstinate, haughty, violent, revengeful, and arrogant; this character, however, seems quite mollified amidst the trials of his noviciate. But no sooner has he attained to some consideration in his order, than he flies into a passion against his superior, and severely belabours him with his fists, till he lays him sprawling. On his being made inquisitor at Venice, his insolence became intolerable. On his promotion to the purple, he was immediately seized with the RABBIA PAPALE, which so far got the better of his natural character, that he affected obscurity, mortification, humility, and a very weak state of health. At length he is chosen pope, and now the spring recovers its whole elasticity, which had been so long under restraint: never was a more haughty and despotic sovereign known.

" Naturam expellas furca tamen ipsa redibit."

Religion and morality lay a check on the force of the natural temper, but cannot extirpate it. A sot, when in a convent, reduced to half a pint of cyder at each meal, will no longer be seen drunk, but his love of wine will ever be the same.

Age weakens the natural character; it is a tree which produces only some degenerate fruits, still are they of one and the same nature. It grows knotty, and over-run with moss, and worm-eaten: but amidst all this, it continues what it was, whether oak or pear-tree. Could a man change his character, he would give himself one; he would be superior to nature. Can we give ourselves any thing? What have we that we have not received?

Endeavour to rouze the indolent to a constant activity, to freeze the impetuous into an apathy, to give a taste for poetry and music to one who has neither taste or ears, you may as well go about washing the Blackmoor white, or giving sight to one born blind. We only improve, polish, and conceal, what nature has put into us; we have nothing of our own putting.

A country gentleman is told, there are too many fish in that pond, they will never thrive; your meadows are crowded with sheep, they have not grass sufficient, they fall away to nothing. Sometime after this advice, it so falls out, that the pikes devour half the carps, and the wolves thin his meadows, so that what sheep are left, fatten apace. Shall he pique himself on his management? Well, this country gentleman is no other than thyself: one of thy passions has swallowed up the rest, and thou boastest of self-conquest. How very few among us, who may not be compared to that decrepit general, ninety years old, who meeting some young officers making a little free with girls, said to them, quite in a passion, Fy, gentlemen, what do you mean! do I set you any such example?

CHINA.

WE go to fetch earth from China, as if we had none; stuffs, as if we were without stuffs; a small herb to infuse into water, as if our climates did not afford any simples. In return, which is a very commendable zeal, we are for converting the Chinese; but we should not offer to dispute their antiquity, and tell them that they are idolaters.

idolaters: for, indeed, what would be thought of a capuchin who, after being kindly entertained at a feat of the Montmorenci's, fhould go about to perfuade them that they were but new made nobles, like fecretaries of ftate, and accufe them of being idolaters, having obferved in this feat two or three of the conftable's ftatues, which they highly value.

The celebrated Wolff, mathematical profeffor in the univerfity of Halle, once made a judicious oration on the Chinefe philofophers; he praifed this antient race of men, though different from us in the beard, eyes, nofe, ears, and reafoning; he commended the Chinefe as adoring one Supreme God, and cherifhing virtue, thus doing juftice to the emperors of China, to the Kolaos, to the tribunals, to the literati: the juftice, which the bonzes deferve, is of a different kind.

This Wolff, you muft know, drew to Halle a great refort of fcholars from all nations: there was in the fame univerfity a profeffor of divinity named Engel, who had fcarce a fingle fcholar; this man exafperated at ftarving with cold in his empty auditory, conceived a defign, and, to be fure very juftly, to ruin the profeffor of mathematics, and, as ufual with fuch men, he charged him with not believing in God.

Some European writers, utter ftrangers to China, had affirmed, that all the men of any note or confideration at Pekin were atheifts; now Wolff had commended the Pekin philofophers; Wolff therefore was an atheift; envy and hatred never formed better fyllogifms. Yet this argument, with the help of a cabal and a protector, appeared fo conclufive to the king of the country, that he fent the mathematician a dilemma in form, the import of which was, either to leave Halle in twenty-four hours, or to

be

be hanged. As Wolff always reasoned very justly, he immediately left the city; but by his departure the king lost two or three hundred thousand crowns a year, which the great number of that philosopher's scholars brought into the kingdom.

May this be a document to sovereigns, not always to lend an ear to calumny, and sacrifice a great man to the rancour of a blockhead.

Let us return to China.

What do we mean here, at the farthest part of the west, thus virulently to dispute whether Fohi, emperor of China, was the fourteenth emperor or not, and whether Fohi lived three thousand, or two thousand nine hundred years before our common æra? I should laugh at two Irishmen wrangling at Dublin about who, in the twelfth century, was the owner of the estate which I now hold; is it not clear that they should be determined by me, as having the writings in my hands? The case, I think, is similar with regard to the first emperors of China; the tribunals of the country are the best judges.

After all your important altercations about the fourteen princes who reigned before Fohi, the result will be, that China was then very well peopled, and had laws and a political constitution. Now, let me ask you, whether a nation living in towns, and having laws and sovereigns, does not imply a prodigious antiquity? Consider the time that must have passed, and the concurrence of circumstances, before iron could be found out in the mines, and then fitted for agriculture; and likewise before the invention of the shuttle and all other trades.

Some who play the fool with their pens have contrived a whimsical sort of calculation; the Jesuit Petau, in his sagacious computation, at the
epocha

epocha of only two hundred and eighty-five years after the deluge, gives the earth a hundred times more inhabitants than can be supposed in it at present. Cumberland and Whiston are no less ridiculous in their calculations. Good men! Had they only consulted the registers of our American colonies, they would have been astonished. They would have seen how very slowly the human species multiplies, and very often, so far from increasing, diminishes.

Let us, therefore, we who are but of yesterday, descendants from the Celts, who have but just cleared our wild countries from the forests with which they were over-run; let us, I say, leave the Chinese and the Indians in the quiet enjoyment of their fine climate and their antiquity; especially let us forbear calling the emperor of China and the soubab of Decan idolaters: neither are we to be infatuated with Chinese merit. The constitution of their empire is, indeed, the best in the whole world, the only one which is intirely modelled from paternal power (the mandarins, however, chastise their children very severely) the only one where the governor of a province is punished, if, at the expiration of his office, the people do not shew their approbation of his conduct by loud acclamations; the only one which has instituted prizes for virtue, whilst every where else the laws only punish vice; the only one whose laws have recommended themselves to its conquerors, whilst we are still swayed by the customs of our conquerors, the Burgundians, the Franks, and the Goths. But it must be owned, that the commonalty who are bonze-ridden, are no less knavish than ours; that foreigners are extremely imposed on, as amongst us; that in sciences the Chinese are two hundred years behind us; that, like us, they have

a thou-a thousand ridiculous notions, that they give credit to talismans and judicial astrology, which was also our case for a long time.

It must farther be owned, that they were amazed at our thermometer, at our way of freezing liquors by salt-petre, and with Torricelli's and Ohto Gueric's experiments, just as we ourselves were at our first seeing their physical exhibitions: farther, their physicians do not cure mortal distempers any more than ours; and the slighter illnesses nature alone cures them, as here: notwithstanding all this, the Chinese, four thousand years ago, when we did not know our letters, were masters of all that is essentially useful in that knowledge which we so much value ourselves on at present.

CHRISTIANITY.

HISTORICAL DISQUISITIONS concerning CHRISTIANITY.

IN vain have several of the learned expressed their wonder, that in the historian Josephus (H) they meet with no trace of Jesus Christ, the little passage

---

(H) That the passage concerning Christ in Josephus's history is universally allowed to be interpolated, is not true; very learned men have maintained the contrary. Besides, this is but a negative argument, which can be of no manner of weight against the positive and undoubted authorities of Pagan writers, not one of whom is mentioned by our author. Nothing can be more disingenuous. The star that appeared at Christ's birth, and the journey of the Chaldean wisemen, are mentioned by Chalcidius the Platonist, " Est quoque alia sanctior & ve-
" nerabilior

sage relating to him in his history being now universally given up as interpolated. Yet Josephus's father

" nerabilior historia, quæ perhibet ortu stellæ cujusdam non
" morbos mortesque denunciatas, sed descensum Dei vene-
" rabilis ad humanæ conservationis, rerumque mortalium
" gratiam: quam stellam cum nocturno tempore inspexis-
" sent Chaldæorum profecto sapientes viri, & consideratione
" rerum cælestium satis exercitati, quæsisse dicuntur recentis
" ortum Dei, repertaque illa majestate puerili veneratos esse,
" & vota Deo tanto convenientia nuncupasse. In Commen-
" tario ad Timæum."——The slaughter of the innocents by
Herod is related by Macrobius, who, at the same time, has
given us a reflection made on that occasion by the emperor
Augustus: " Cum audisset inter pueros, quos in Syria Hero-
" des rex Judæorum intra bimatum jussit interfici, filium quo-
" que ejus occisum, ait, " Melius est Herodis porcum esse quam
" filium." Lib. ii. cap. 4.——Christ's crucifixion under
Pontius Pilate is related by Tacitus: " Tiberio imperitante,
" per procuratorem Pontium Pilatum supplicio affectus erat."
Lib. xv.——The earthquake and miraculous darkness attend-
ing it, are recorded by Phlegon, lib. xiii. Chronicorum sive
Olympiadum. Τῷ δ' ἔτει τῆς C. B. Ὀλυμπιάδος ἐγένετο ἔκλειψις
ἡλίε μεγίςη τῶν ἐγνωρισμένων πρότερον· κἂν νὺξ ὥρα της ἡμέρας ἐγένετο,
ὥςε καὶ ἀςέρας ἐν ᾽ὑρανῷ φανῆναι, σεισμός τε μέγας κατὰ Βιθυνίαν γενόμενος
τὰ πολλὰ Νικαίας κατέςεψε.——Besides, these very circumstances
were mentioned in the public Roman records, to which the
early writers of Christianity used to appeal, as of undoubted
authority with their adversaries. See Grotius de Ver. Rel. Chr.
lib. iii. Dr. Clarke on the Evidences of Natural and Revealed
Religion, p. 357. And Mr. Addison, in his little treatise on
the Christian Religion, sect. 2.

The difficulties in the history of the Evangelists are such
as may be easily removed by consulting the annotations of
learned expositors, or even by a diligent meditation of the
Scriptures. If the obscurity of a work were an argument
against its authority, there would be an end of all historical
credibility. We meet with difficulties in Polybius, Livy, Plutarch, and yet we doubt not of their veracity.

But

father muſt have been an eye-witneſs of Jeſus's miracles. This hiſtorian was of the prieſtly lineage, and being related to queen Mariamne, Herod's wife, is minutely particular on all that prince's proceedings, yet wholly ſilent as to the life and death of Chriſt. Though neither concealing nor palliating Herod's cruelties, not a word does he ſay about his ordering the children to be maſſacred,

---

But to come to the difficulties mentioned by our author : 1. The Zachariah mentioned by St. Matthew, is moſt probably concluded to be the ſon of Jehoiada, whom the Jews ſtoned to death in the very court of the temple, at the command of Joaſh (Chron. ii. 24.) And as for the father's name not agreeing, Jehoiada might have two names, which was not an uncommon thing among the Jews. Beſides, even if we could not find ſuch a Zachariah in the Jewiſh hiſtory, is it a proof that he never exiſted ? Is it to be ſuppoſed the Scripture has given us every tranſaction of that nation, and that nothing has been omitted by the ſacred hiſtorian ?

2. The difficulties about the genealogy of Chriſt have at all times been made uſe of as an argument by the adverſaries of our holy religion. St. Matthew and St. Luke have given us two genealogies, which differ in appearance, but agree in the main. The Jews were very exact in their genealogies, and no doubt but the evangeliſts took that of our Saviour from the public records. But it is ſuppoſed by very learned writers, and with the greateſt probability, that one of theſe genealogies is that of Mary, and the other that of Joſeph. St. Matthew made the genealogy of Joſeph, who was the laſt male of David's race deſcended from Solomon ; and St. Luke that of the Virgin Mary, by Nathan from David. There are other opinions in regard to the ſolution of this difficulty ; but this is ſufficient to ſhew that the two genealogies may be reconciled. To conclude, we may ſafely affirm, with the learned Dr. Clarke, that the evidence which God has afforded for the truth of our religion is abundantly ſufficient ; and that the cauſe of men's infidelity is not the want of better evidence, but the dominion of their paſſions, which prevents them from hearkening to any reaſonable conviction.

on an information that a king of the Jews was just born. According to the Greek calendar the number of children put to death on that occasion amounted to fourteen thousand.

Of all the cruelties ever committed by all the tyrants that ever lived, this was the most horrible; a like instance is not to be found in history.

Yet the best writer the Jews ever had, the only one of any account with the Romans and Greeks, makes no manner of mention of a transaction so very extraordinary, and so very dreadful. He says not a word of the new star which had appeared in the east at the Saviour's nativity; and a phœnomenon so singular could not escape the knowledge of such an accurate historian as Josephus: he is likewise silent as to the darkness, which, at noonday, covered the whole earth for the space of three hours, whilst the Saviour was on the cross; the opening of the tombs at that awful time, and the number of the just, who rose from the dead.

It is no less a matter of wonder to the learned that these prodigies are not taken notice of by any Roman historian, though they happened in the reign of Tiberius, under the very eyes of a Roman governor and garrison, who naturally would have sent the emperor and senate a circumstantial account of the most miraculous event ever heard of. Rome itself must for three hours have been involved in thick darkness, and surely such a prodigy would have been noted in the annals of Rome, and those of all other nations. But God, I suppose, would not allow that such divine things should be committed to writing by prophane hands (I).

The same learned persons likewise meet with some difficulties in the evangelical history. They

---

(I) Josephus's silence is very well accounted for by the bishop of Cloyne, in his MINUTE PHILOSOPHER, p. 313.

observe,

observe, that, in St. Matthew, Jesus Christ says to the Scribes and Pharisees, that upon them should come all the innocent blood shed on the earth, from the blood of righteous Abel to that of Zachariah the son of Barac, whom they slew between the temple and the altar.

In all the history of the Hebrews, say they, we meet with no such person as Zachariah killed in the temple before the coming of the Messiah, nor in his time; but Josephus, in his history of the siege of Jerusalem, (chap. xix. book iv.) mentions a Zachariah the son of Barachiah, who was killed in the middle of the temple, by the faction of the Zelotes. This has given rise to a suspicion that St. Matthew's gospel was not written till after the taking of Jerusalem by Titus. But if we consider the infinite difference there must be between books divinely inspired and such as are merely human, all these doubts, difficulties, and objections, immediately vanish. It was God's pleasure that his birth, life, and death, should be shrouded in a cloud of respectable darkness. His ways in all things are different from ours.

The learned are also at a great loss to reconcile the difference of the two genealogies of Christ. In St. Matthew, Joseph's father is Jacob, Jacob's Matthan, Matthan's Eleazar; whereas St. Luke says that Joseph was the son of Heli, Heli of Matthat, Matthat of Levi, Levi of Janna, &c. They cannot reconcile the fifty-six ancestors in Christ's genealogy from Abraham, mentioned by Luke, to the two and forty different ancestors in the genealogy from the same Abraham, given by St. Matthew; and they are shocked that Matthew, mentioning forty-two generations, enumerates no more than forty-one.

They likewise are at a stand about Jesus not being the son of Joseph but of Mary. They farther have their doubts concerning the miracles of our Saviour, and quote St. Austin, St. Hilary, and others, who interpret the account of these miracles, in a mystic and allegorical sense: as the cursing and withering the fig-tree for not bearing figs when it was not the time of figs; the sending the devils into the swine in a country where those creatures were not allowed of; the turning the water into wine towards the end of an entertainment, when the guests were already heated with liquor. But all these cavils of the learned are put to silence by faith, whose merit is enhanced by these difficulties. The scope of this article is purely to follow the historical clue, and give a just and precise idea of those facts which nobody offers to controvert.

First, Jesus was born under the Mosaic law; in conformity to this law he was circumcised; he conformed to all its precepts; he kept all its feasts, and preached only morality; he made no revelation of the mystery of his incarnation; he never told the Jews that he was born of a Virgin; he received John's benediction, being baptized by him in the river Jordan, a ceremony to which great numbers of Jews submitted; he said nothing about the seven sacraments, nor did he institute, in his life-time the ecclesiastical hierarchy. He concealed from his cotemporaries that he was the Son of God, generated from all eternity, consubstantial with God, and that the Holy Ghost proceeded from the Father and the Son; he did not inform them that his person was composed of two natures and two wills: these great mysteries were, in after-times to be declared to man by persons illuminated with the light of the Holy Ghost. During his whole life he did not in the least deviate from the law of his forefathers. He shewed himself to the world only as a just man, acceptable to God, persecuted by envious doctors, and condemned to die by prejudiced magistrates. It was his pleasure that all the rest should be done by the holy church which he established.

Josephus, in the 12th chapter of his history, mentions an austere sect of Jews then recently founded by one Judas Galileus, "They make "light," says he, "of all earthly evils. Such is "their resolution, that they brave tortures, and on "an honourable motive, prefer death to life. They "have chose to be burnt, to be slain, and even "their bones to be broken, rather than utter the "least word against their legislator, or eat any for- "bidden food."

This character seems to belong to the Judaites and not to the Essenes; for Josephus's words are, "Judas was the author of a new sect totally dif- "ferent from the other three, i. e. the Sadducees, "the Pharisees, and the Essenes." And further on, he says; "They are by nation Jews, they live "in a close union among themselves, and hold "all sensuality vicious and sinful." Now the natural import of this phrase shews the author to be speaking of the Judaites.

However it be, these Judaites were known before Christ's disciples began to make any considerable figure in the world.

The Therapeutes were a society differing both from the Essenians and the Judaites, and had some affinity to the Indian Gymnosophists and Bramins. "They have," says Philo, "impulses of heavenly "love, by which they kindle into all the enthusi- "asm of the Coribantes and the Bacchanalians, "and are raised to that state of contemplation af- "ter which they aspire. This sect had its rise in
"Alexan-

"Alexandria, where the Jews were very numer-
"ous, and spread exceedingly throughout Egypt."

John the Baptist's disciples likewise spread a little in Egypt, but especially in Syria and Arabia; Asia-minor also was not without them. The Acts of the Apostles, ch. xix. says that St. Paul met with several at Ephesus; and asking them, "Have you "received the Holy Ghost?" They answered, "We have not so much as heard that there is a "Holy Ghost:" he said to them, "What bap- "tism, then, have you received?" They answered him, "The baptism of John." For some little time after Jesus's death, there were several different sects and societies among the Jews; the Pharisees, the Sadducees, the Essenes, the Judaites, the Therapeutes, the disciples of John, and the disciples of Christ, whose little flock God led by paths unknown to human wisdom.

Believers first had the name of Christians at Antioch, about the sixtieth year of our common æra; but, as we shall see in the sequel, they were known in the Roman empire by other appellations. Before that time they distinguished themselves only by the name of Brothers, Saints, and Faithful. Thus God, who had come down on earth to be a pattern of meekness and self-denial, founded his church on very weak, and apparently mean beginnings, and kept it in the same humble and mortified condition in which it pleased him to be born. All the first believers were of low parentage, obscure men, working with their own hands. The apostle Paul intimates, that he supported himself by making of tents. St. Peter raised to life Dorcas a sempstress, who used to make garments for the brethren; and the believers of Joppa used to hold their meetings in the house of one Simon a tanner, as may be seen in chap. ix. of the Acts of the Apostles.

The faithful secretly spread themselves in Greece, and some went from thence to Rome, mingling with the Jews, to whom the Romans allowed a synagogue. At first they continued with the Jews, and so far practised circumcision, that, as we have elsewhere observed, the fifteen first bishops of Jerusalem were every one circumcised.

The apostle Paul, on taking with him Timothy, whose father was a Gentile, circumcised him himself, at the little town of Lystra; but Titus, his other disciple, would not submit to that ceremony. The disciples of Jesus continued in unity with the Jews, till Paul bringing strangers into the temple, the Jews raised a persecution against him, and charged him with an intent of subverting the Mosaic law by the doctrine of Jesus Christ. It was in order to clear himself from this accusation, that James proposed to Paul his having his head shaved, and purifying himself in the temple, along with four Jews, who had made a vow to be shaved: "Them take, and purify thyself with them," says James to him (Acts ch. xxi.) "that all may know, "that all things whereof they were informed con- "cerning thee are nothing, and that thou keepest "the law of Moses."

This did not in the least abate the charge of impiety and heresy against Paul, and his trial was of some continuance; but the very articles for which he was indicted evidently shew, that he was come to Jerusalem to observe the Jewish rites.

His own words to Titus (Acts chap. xxv.) are, " Neither against the law of the Jews, nor against " the temple, have I offended any thing at all."

The apostles promulgated Jesus Christ as a Jew, an observer of the Jewish law, and sent by God to
inforce

inforce the obfervance of it. "Circumcifion veri-
"ly profiteth," fays the apoftle Paul, (Rom. ii.)
"if thou keepeft the law; but if thou be a break-
"er of the law, thy circumcifion is made uncir-
"cumcifion. If the uncircumcifion keep the righ-
"teoufnefs of the law, fhall not his uncircumcifion
"be counted for circumcifion? He is a Jew
"who is one inwardly."

When this apoftle fpeaks of Jefus Chrift in his epiftles, he does not make known the ineffable myftery of his confubftantiality with God. "We "are," fays he, in the fifth chapter to the Romans, "delivered by him from the wrath of God; the "gift of God is come to us through the grace im-"parted to one only man, Chrift Jefus; Death has "reigned by the fin of one man, and the juft fhall "reign in life by one man, Jefus Chrift." And in chap. viii. "We are heirs of God, and co-heirs "with Chrift:" and in chap. xvi. "To God, who "alone is wife, be honour and glory through Jefus "Chrift."——"Ye are Chrift's, and Chrift is "God's." Cor. i. 3. And 1 Cor. xv. 27. "All "things are fubject to him, God certainly except-"ed who hath fubjected all things to him."

Some difficulties have occurred in explaining the following paffage in the epiftle to the Philip-pians: "Let nothing be done through vain glory; "but in lowlinefs of mind let each efteem other "better than themfelves; let this mind be in you "which was in Chrift Jefus, who, being in the "form of God, thought it not robbery to be "equal with God" (K). The fenfe of the paffage

---

(K) This paffage has been greatly ftrained by the Socinians, from whom our author feems to have borrowed his remark.

The

sage seems very well set forth in a most valuable monument of antiquity, a letter from the churches of Vienne and Lyon, written in the year 117; part of it turns on the modesty of some of the faithful: "They would not," says the letter, "take on "themselves the august title of martyrs (for a few "tribulations) imitating Jesus Christ, who bear- "ing the likeness or image of God, did not think "the title of God's equal belonged to him." Origen, likewise, in his commentary on John, says, "Christ's greatness has appeared more resplendent "in his humiliation, than if he had thought it no "robbery to be God's equal." And, in reality, the contrary explication is a palpable inconsistency. What can be meant by "believe others your bet- "ters, imitate Jesus, who thought it no robbery, "no usurpation, to make himself God's equal?"

The original is, Ὅς ἐν μορφῇ Θεῦ ὑπάρχων ἐφ᾽ ἁρπαγμὸν ἡγήσατο τὸ εἶναι ἴσα Θεῷ: which in our English Testament is almost literally rendered thus: "Who being in the form "of God, thought it not robbery to be equal with God." Now we grant it would be difficult to find the example of modesty and humility meant by St. Paul, and alluded to by the churches of Vienne and Lyon in the above lines alone; but we should take the whole passage together, and what follows will demonstrate the sense: "but made himself of no "reputation, and took upon him the form of a servant, "humbled himself, and became obedient unto death." That is, though in his divine form or nature, he thought it not robbery, or any usurpation, to be equal with God; yet condescended to take the form of a servant, that is, human nature, and to lessen himself for the salvation of his people. Is not this an unparallelled example of humility and modesty? and is not this the plain obvious sense of the above passage? And does not this shew how easy it is to wrest the meaning of any text of Scripture, as the Arians and Socinians have done in the present case, in order to evade a very strong proof of Christ's divinity.

This

This would be a flat contradiction, overthrowing what precedes; it is giving an example of ambition for a pattern of meekness; it is a trespass against common-sense.

Thus it was that the wisdom of the apostles founded the infant church, and this wisdom was not discomposed by the contest between the apostles Peter, James, and John, on one side, and Paul on the other. It happened at Antioch: the apostle Peter, alias Cephas, alias Simon Barjona, used to eat with the Gentile converts, overlooking the ceremonies of the law, and the distinctions of aliments: he and Barnabas, together with other disciples, made no manner of scruple to eat pork, things strangled, or animals which divide the hoof, but do not chew the cud; but a number of Jewish Christians coming there, St. Peter associated with them, returning to his former abstinence from forbidden meats, and the observance of the Mosaic ceremonies.

This procedure has an air of discretion; he was unwilling to give any offence to his Jewish brethren; but St. Paul declared against him with some harshness: "I withstood him," says he, " to " his face, for he was to blame." Gal. ii.

This quarrel appears the more extraordinary in St. Paul, who, as having at first been a persecutor, should have shewn more temper; besides, he himself had gone into the temple at Jerusalem to sacrifice, had circumcised his disciple Timothy, and had performed those Jewish rites for which he now upbraids Cephas. St. Jerom will have it that this bickering between Paul and Cephas was only a feint. In his first Homily, tome iii. he says, that they acted like two pleaders at the bar, who grow warm, and use keen language, only that their clients may have the higher opinion of them; that

DICTIONARY. 93

Peter Cephas being appointed to preach to the Jews, and the Gentiles being Paul's department, they affected a quarrel; Paul to gain the Gentiles, and Peter to gain the Jews. But St. Austin can by no means relish this opinion. "I am sorry," says he, in his epistle to Jerom, "that so great a "man should patronize a falsity, PATRONUM "MENDACII."

Farther, if Peter was appointed apostle to the Jews, and Paul to the Gentiles, it is very probable that Peter never came to Rome. The Acts of the Apostles make no mention of Peter's journey into Italy.

However that be, about the year 60 of our æra, the Christians began to separate themselves from the Jewish communion; and this was what drew on them such censures, invectives, and persecutions from the synagogues of Rome, Greece, Egypt, and Asia. Their Jewish brethren not only charged them with impiety and atheism, but formally excommunicated them three times in their synagogues, even on the sabbath-day: still God upheld them amidst all their trials and sufferings.

Several churches were gradually formed, and before the end of the first century, the separation between the Jews and Christians became total: but the Roman government knew nothing of this schism; neither the senate nor the emperors of Rome concerning themselves about the wranglings of a little party, which, till then, God had conducted in obscurity, and was raising by insensible degrees.

Let us take a view of the state of the religion of the Roman empire at that time. Mysteries and expiations were in vogue almost all over the earth. Though the emperors, the grandees, and philosophers, secretly made a jest of those mysteries, still

it

it behoved them outwardly to conform to the public worship, left they should irritate the people, who, in religious affairs, give law to their betters; or rather thefe, to chain them the fafter, appear to wear the fame chains. Cicero himfelf was initiated into the Eleufinian myfteries. The principal tenet fet forth in thefe myfteries and fplendid feftivals was the knowledge of one only God; and it muft be owned that Paganifm has nothing more pious, and, in every refpect, more admirable, than the prayers and hymns ufed in thofe myfteries, and of which fragments are ftill remaining.

The Chriftians likewife, worshipping only one God, paved the way to their fuccefs in converting Gentiles. Even fome philofophers of Plato's fect became Chriftians: hence it is, that the fathers of the church, for the three firft centuries, were all Platonics.

The inconfiderate zeal of fome did not affect the fundamental truths. St. Juftin, one of the firft fathers, is cenfured for faying, in his Commentary on Ifaiah, that the faints fhould reign a thoufand years on the earth, in full enjoyment of all fenfual delights; he has been blamed for a pofition in his Apology for Chriftianity, that God, after making the earth, left the care of it to angels, that thefe fell in love with the women, and that the iffue of this paffion are the devils. Lactantius and other fathers have been condemned for inventing Sybilline oracles; he affirmed that the Sybilla Erythrea made four Greek verfes, of which the literal interpretation is,

" With five loaves and two fifhes
He fhall feed five thoufand men in the defert,
And

And gathering up the remains,
With them shall fill twelve baskets."

It has likewise been made a crime to the first Christians, that they were for palming on the world some acrostics, as written by an old Sybil, all beginning with the initial letters of the name of Jesus Christ, each in its order.

But, notwithstanding this zeal of some Christians, which was not according to knowledge, the church, under a divine superintendency, was daily increasing. At first the Christians used to celebrate their mysteries in lonely houses and taverns, and in the night time; from which practice, according to Minutius Felix, they got the appellation of Lucifugaces; Philo calls them Gesseans; but, during the four first centuries, they were most commonly known to the Gentiles by the name of Galileans and Nazarenes; that of Christians has, however, obtained beyond any other.

Neither the hierarchy, nor the rites and usages, were established all at once; the apostolic times were different from the succeeding. St. Paul, in his first epistle to the Corinthians, directs them, that, in a public assembly of the brethren, whether circumcised or uncircumcised, when several prophets were for speaking, only two or three should speak; and in the mean time, if any one had a revelation, the prophet who had begun to speak was to be silent.

It is owing to this custom of the primitive church that to this day, some Christian sects hold their assemblies without any hierarchy. Every one was then allowed to speak in the church, women excepted; what we call the sacred mass, and celebrate in the morning, was the Lord's Supper, originally administered in the evening;

these usages altered as the church gathered strength. A more extended society required more regulations, and the prudent pastors conformed to times and places.

According to St. Jerom and Eusebius, when the churches had received a form, they gradually came to consist of five different classes. The superintendents, episcopi, whence are derived the bishops; the elders of the society, presbyteroi, the priests, ministers, or deacons; the Pistoi, believers, or initiated, that is, the baptized, who were admitted to the Agapæs, or feasts of charity; and the Catechumens and Energumenes, who were candidates for baptism. None of these five orders were distinguished by any particular vesture or garb, nor was any of them bound to celibacy; witness Tertullian's dedicating a book to his wife; witness the example of the apostles. No painting or sculpture was seen in their assemblies during the first three centuries. The Christians used carefully to conceal their books from the Pagans, and trusted none with them except the initiated; the catechumens were not permitted to say the Lord's Prayer.

But what most distinguished the Christians, and continued down to our times, was the power of driving out devils with the sign of the cross. Origen, in his treatise against Celsus, owns, Numb. 133, that Antinous, who had been deified by the emperor Adrian, wrought miracles in Egypt, by charms and prestiges; but the devils, says he, quit the body of the possessed, on the bare pronunciation of the name of Jesus.

Tertullian goes still farther, and from the remote part of Africa where he was, says, in chap. 33. of his Apologeticon, " If your gods do not, in
" the presence of a true Christian, own themselves
" to be devils, we freely consent that you put
" that

"that Christian to death. Can there be a more
"evident demonstration?"

Jesus Christ, indeed, sent his apostles to drive out devils. The Jews, likewise, in his time, had this power; for, when Jesus had relieved some demoniacs, and sent the devils into the body of a herd of swine, and performed many other such cures, the Pharisees said, It is by the power of Belzebub he drives out devils: but Jesus answers, "If I drive them out by Belzebub, by whom do "your sons drive them out?". That the Jews boasted of such a power is indisputable; they had exorcists and exorcisms. On these occasions they called on the name of the God of Jacob and of Abraham, and consecrated herbs were put up the demoniac's nose (Josephus gives some account of these ceremonies). This power over the devils was taken away from the Jews, and transferred to the Christians, who, for some time past, seem likewise to have lost it.

This exorcising power comprehended that of preventing or defeating magical operations; for magic was ever in repute among all nations. All the fathers of the church bear witness to it. St. Justin owns, in his Apologetic, book iii. that the souls of the deceased are often evoked, and from thence draws an argument in favour of the soul's immortality. Lactantius, book vii. of his Divine Institution, says, "Should any one dare to deny "the existence of souls after death, the magician "will soon convince him by making it appear." Ireneus, Clement Alexandrinus, Tertullian, St. Cyprian, all affirm the like. At present, indeed, it is otherwise, and we hear no more of magicians or demoniacs; yet such there will be, when it so pleases God.

When the congregations of Christians were become considerable, and several presumed to insult the Roman worship, the civil power exerted itself against them, and the commonalty, especially, were most violent in persecuting this new religion. The Jews, who confined themselves to their synagogues, so far from being persecuted, had particular privileges, and were allowed the exercise of their religion at Rome, as they are at present; all the different worships in the several parts of the empire were tolerated, though the senate did not adopt them: but the Christians making no secret of their detestation of all those worships, and especially that of the empire, were several times exposed to cruel trials.

One of the first and most celebrated martyrs was Ignatius bishop of Antioch; he was condemned by the emperor Trajan himself, then in Asia, and, by his order, sent to Rome to be exposed to beasts, at a time when other Christians were under no open molestation in that city. His accusation is not known; but that emperor being otherwise famous for clemency, St. Ignatius's enemies must have been very violent in their prosecution. The history of his martyrdom relates that the name of Jesus Christ was found engraven on his heart in golden characters; and thence it is, that the Christians, in some places, took the name of the Theophori, which Ignatius had given to himself.

We have still a letter of his, in which he intreats the bishops and Christians not to oppose his martyrdom; whether that, even then, the Christians were strong enough to attempt a rescue, or that some of them might have interest to obtain his pardon. Another very remarkable circumstance is, that the Christians of Rome were allowed to go and meet him, when he was brought thither;

which

which evidently proves, that the man and not the sect was punished.

The persecutions were so far from being continued, that Origen, in his third book against Celsus, says, "It is easy to compute what number of Christians have died for their religion; few, and only from time to time, and by intervals, having died on that account."

So careful was God of his church, that, in spite of all its enemies, five councils were held in the first century, sixteen in the second, and thirty in the third; all tolerated: though sometimes they were forbidden, the magistrates, in their mistaken timidity, fearing that they might produce disturbances. Few of the reports of the proconsuls and prætors who pronounced sentence on the Christians are now remaining, and those are the only vouchers for ascertaining the accusations brought against them, and their punishments.

We have a fragment of Dionysius of Alexandria, containing an extract of a pro-consul of Egypt, under the emperor Valerian, which is as follows: "Dionysius, Faustus, Maximus, and Cheremon, being brought into court, the prefect Emilian thus addressed them: From my discourse with you, and from the many particulars I wrote to you, you must have been sensible that our princes have shewn you great lenity and indulgence; I again repeat it to you, they refer your life and safety to yourselves, and put your fate into your own hands: they require of you only one thing, and that no more than what reason requires, which is to worship the patron gods of their empire, and to forsake that other worship, which is so contrary to nature and good sense.

"Dionysius

"Dionyſius anſwered: Every one has not the ſame gods, and every one worſhips thoſe whom he believes to be really ſuch.

"The prefect Emilian replied; I ſee you are a ſet of ungrateful people, obſtinately ſlighting the kindneſs which the emperors would ſhew you. Aſſure yourſelves, no longer ſhall you ſtay here; I will order you away to Cephro, in the farther part of Lybia; that, by the emperor's command, is to be the place of your baniſhment: farther, do not imagine you ſhall be allowed there to hold your meetings, or to go to pray in thoſe places, which you call Cemeteries; any ſuch thing is abſolutely forbidden you, and what I will not allow."

Nothing bears more evident marks of truth than this trial, and it ſhews that theſe meetings were occaſionally prohibited; as with us, the Calviniſts are not allowed to hold any meeting whatever in Languedoc; and miniſters and preachers have been hanged, and even broke upon the wheel, for their diſobedience. Likewiſe in England and Ireland, the Roman Catholics lie under the ſame prohibition, and, on ſome occaſions, the delinquents have been condemned to die.

Amidſt all the ſeverity of the Roman laws, God inſpired ſeveral emperors with indulgence towards the Chriſtians. Diocleſian himſelf, whom ignorant people reckon a perſecutor, and the firſt year of whoſe reign is ſtill the epocha of martyrdoms, for above eighteen years openly countenanced Chriſtianity, and the moſt important poſts about his perſon were filled by Chriſtians. He even allowed a ſtately church to be built oppoſite his palace at Nicomedia, where he frequently reſided; and, to crown all, he married a Chriſtian lady.

Galerius

Galerius Cæsar, from some unhappy prejudices against the Christians, by whom he imagined himself ill used, induced Dioclesian to demolish the cathedral at Nicomedia. A Christian of more zeal than wisdom tore to pieces the emperor's edict, and this gave rise to that so famous persecution, in which, throughout the whole extent of the Roman empire, above two hundred persons were sentenced to die, exclusive of those whom the populace, ever fanatic and inhuman, might massacre, without any form of law.

So great was the number of martyrs at different times, that much circumspection is requisite, to avoid weakening the truth of the history of the real confessors of our holy religion, by a dangerous mixture of fables and false martyrs.

The Benedictine Don Ruinart, otherwise a person of learning equal to his zeal, should have chosen his authentic acts with more discretion. A manuscript for being taken from the abbey of St. Benedict on the Loire, or from a convent of Cælestines at Paris, and its agreement with a manuscript of the Feuillans, is not the more authentic; its antiquity must be evident, it must have been written by persons living at the time of the event, and farther must bear all the marks of truth and genuineness.

He might very well have omitted the story of Romanus, which happened in 303. This young man, it seems, had obtained Dioclesian's pardon at Antioch; yet, as he says, the judge Asclepiades condemned him to be burnt. The Jews, who had flocked to the execution, mocked young St. Romanus, and floutingly asked the Christians how their God, who had delivered Shadrach, Meshach, and Abednego, should suffer them to be burnt; on this, though the day was remarkably fine, such a tempest arose as immediately quenched the fire: then the judge ordered young Romanus's tongue to be cut out; and the emperor's first physician being present, officiously performed the operation, cutting his tongue off at the root. The young man, who before stammered, now spoke very fluently. The emperor was very much surprized at any one's speaking so well without a tongue; and the physician, to repeat the experiment, cut out the tongue of a man who happened to be passing by, but he died immediately after the operation.

Eusebius, from whom the credulous Ruinart has taken this tale, should have had so much respect for the real miracles performed in the Old and New Testament, which no body will ever call in question, as not to foist among them such suspicious stories, which may give offence to the weak.

This last persecution did not spread throughout the whole empire. England had at that time some glimmerings of Christianity, which, however, soon were smothered, but appeared again under the Saxon kings. The southern parts of Gaul and Spain swarmed with Christians. Cæsar Constantius Chlorus shewed them very great favour in all those provinces. He had a concubine who was a Christian, and this no less a person than Constantine's mother, or St. Helena, for they were never openly married; and he even dismissed her in the year 292, on his marrying the daughter of Maximian Hercules; but she retained her ascendency, and made use of it to inspire him with a strong affection for our holy religion.

Divine Providence, by means apparently human, now brought about the establishment and superiority of this church. Constantius Chlorus dying at York in 306, and his children by the daughter of a

Cæsar

Cæsar not being of age to claim the empire, Constantine boldly got himself chosen at York by a body of soldiers, mostly Germans, Gauls, and Britons. It was not likely that such an election, made without the consent of the city of Rome, the senate, and the army could subsist; but God gave him a complete victory over Maxentius, who had been chosen at Rome, and at length rid him of all his colleagues. It must be owned that, at first, he rendered himself utterly unworthy of the Divine favour, murdering his wife, his son, and all his near relations.

What Zozimus relates on this head may be questioned: he says, that Constantine, tortured with remorse, after so many crimes, enquired of the pontiffs of the empire, if they had any expiations for him; and their answer was, that they knew of none. Indeed there had been none for Nero, for in Greece he did not presume to assist at the sacred mysteries. Yet the Tauroboli were then in use, and it is not easy to believe, that a despotic emperor should not have found one priest to grant him expiatory sacrifices. Perhaps, it is still less to be believed, that Constantine, being taken up with war, actuated by ambition, and surrounded with flatterers, could be at leisure for remorses. Zozimus adds, that an Egyytian priest, who came from Spain, having gained admittance to him, assured him of an expiation of all his crimes in the Christian religion. Osius, bishop of Corduba, is suspected to have been this priest.

However that be, Constantine openly communicated with the Christians, though he never was above a catechumen, deferring his baptism to the hour of death. He built the city of Constantinople, which became the center of the empire, and of the Christian religion. Now the

the church begins to assume an august appearance.

It is to be observed, that from the year 314, before Constantine resided in his new city, the Christians smartly revenged themselves on their persecutors. They threw Maximian's wife into the Orontes, they murdered all his relations in Egypt and Palestine, they massacred all the magistrates who had distinguished themselves by their zeal against Christianity. Dioclesian's widow and daughter, who had concealed themselves at Thessalonica, were discovered, and their bodies thrown into the sea. It were to be wished that the Christians had not given way so much to the spirit of revenge; but God, in his vindictive justice, was pleased that the hands of the Christians, as soon as they were at liberty to act, should be dyed with the blood of their unjust persecutors.

Constantine convened at Nicea, opposite to Constantinople, the first oecumenical council; and in which Osius presided. There was determined the great question, which disturbed the church concerning Christ's divinity: one side availing themselves of the opinion of Origen, who, in chap. 6. against Celsus, says, "We offer up our "prayers to God, through Jesus, who holds the "middle place between created natures and the "uncreated nature, who brings to us his Father's "grace, and presents our prayers to the great God "as our high priest." They also pleaded several passages of St. Paul, some of which have been mentioned; but their capital foundation was these words of Jesus Christ himself: "My Father "is greater than I;" and they held Jesus, as the first-born of creation, as the most pure emanation from the Supreme essence, but not precisely as God.

The other side, who were the orthodox, produced passages more suitable to the eternal deity of Jesus, as this: "My Father and I are the same thing;" words which the adversaries make to mean no more than "My Father and I have the same design, the same will; I have no other desires than those of my Father." Alexander bishop of Alexandria, and after him Athanasius, headed the orthodox: in the opposite party were Eusebius bishop of Nicomedia, seventeen other bishops, the priest Arius, and many other priests. The quarrel immediately was inflamed, St. Alexander having called his adversaries Antichrists.

At length, after much disputing and wrangling, the Holy Ghost, by the mouths of two hundred and ninety-nine bishops against eighteen, gave the following decision; "Jesus is the only Son of God, begotten of the Father, i. e. of the substance of the Father, God of God, Light of Light, very God of very God, of one substance with the Father; we likewise believe in the Holy Ghost, &c." Such was the form of words in that council, and this instance shews the great superiority of the bishops above mere priests; for, according to two patriarchs of Alexandria, who have written the Chronicle of Alexandria in Arabic, two thousand persons of the second order sided with Arius. He was exiled by Constantine, but soon after the like punishment fell on Athanasius, and Arius was recalled to Constantinople: with such fervour, however, did St. Macarius pray to God that he would deprive Arius of life before he came into the cathedral, that God heard his prayer, and Arius died in 330, in his way to the church. The emperor Constantine departed this life in 337, delivering his will into the hands of an Arian priest, and expiring in the arms of the chief of the Arians,

Eusebius

Eusebius bishop of Nicomedia: he was not baptized till on his death-bed; but he left the church triumphant though divided.

The Athanasians and Eusebians made war on each other with the most implacable animosity; and what is now called Arianism was, for a long time, the established doctrine in all the provinces of the empire.

Julian the Philosopher, nicknamed the Apostate, was for accommodating these divisions, but failed in his good endeavours.

The second general council was held in 381 at Constantinople. In it was explained what the council of Nice had not thought fit to say, concerning the Holy Ghost, adding to the Nicean form, "That the Holy Spirit is the vivifying "Lord, proceeding from the Father, and that "he is worshipped and glorified with the Father "and the Son."

It was not till towards the ninth century, that the Latin Church gradually enacted, "That the Holy "Ghost proceeds from the Father and the Son."

In 1431 the third general council, held at Ephesus, determined that Mary was really the mother of God, and that Jesus had two natures and one person. Nestorius, bishop of Constantinople, for moving that the Blessed Virgin should be called the mother of Christ, was declared by the council a second Judas; and the two natures were farther confirmed by the council of Chalcedonia.

I shall slightly pass over the following ages as pretty well known. Unfortunately every one of these disputes occasioned wars, and the church was obliged to be continually in arms. God farther permitted, to exercise the patience of the faithful, that in the ninth century the Greeks and Latins should come to an irreconcileable rupture; he farther permitted

mitted that the West should be distracted with twenty-nine bloody schisms for the see of Rome.

In the mean time, almost the whole Grecian church, and the whole of the African church, were enslaved by the Arabs, and afterwards fell under the Turks, who erected Mahomedism on the ruins of Christianity. The Roman church subsisted, but always defiled with blood, in the course of above six hundred years of discord between the Western empire and the priesthood: but these very quarrels encreased her power; for the German bishops and abbots made themselves princes, and the popes, by degrees, acquired an absolute dominion in Rome, and a country of a hundred leagues in extent. Thus God tried his church by humiliations, disturbances, and by prosperity and magnificence.

This Latin church, in the sixteenth century, lost half Germany, Denmark, Sweden, England, Scotland, Ireland, Switzerland, and Holland. It has, indeed, by the Spanish conquests, gained more ground in America than it has lost in Europe; but if its territories are enlarged, its subjects are much decreased.

Divine Providence seemed to design that Japan, Siam, India, and China, should be brought to acknowledge the pope's supremacy, as an equivalent for the loss of Asia-minor, Syria, Greece, Egypt, Africa, Russia, and the countries abovementioned. St. Francis Xavier, a Jesuit, who carried the holy gospel to the East Indies and Japan, when the Portuguese went thither for costly merchandize, performed miracles in plenty, all attested by his reverend brethren: some say that he raised nine persons from the dead; but father Ribadeneira, in his Flower of Saints, reduces the number to four, and that's full enough.

enough. Providence so eminently prospered this enterprize, that, in less than an hundred years, there were thousands of Roman Catholics within the Japanese islands. But the devil was not wanting to sow his tares among the good seed. The Christians formed a destructive plot, which being followed by a cruel war, they were all exterminated in the year 1638. Hereupon the natives denied all strangers admittance into their harbours, except the Dutch, accounting them to be mere merchants, and not Christians: they were obliged to tread on the cross before they were allowed to dispose of their goods; and this was done in a prison where they were confined immediately on their arrival at Nangazaki.

The Roman Catholic and Apostolic religion was not proscribed in China till of late, and with less cruelty. The Jesuits, indeed, had not displayed their supernatural power at the court of Pekin, by raising the dead to life; they had humbly limited themselves to the teaching of astronomy, the casting of cannon, and being mandarins. Their unhappy disputes with some Dominicans and others gave such offence to the great emperor Yontchin, that this prince, though all equity and goodness, was so blind as to put a stop to the teaching of our holy religion, because our missionaries did not agree among themselves. He ordered them to depart the empire, but it was with all the tenderness of a father, supplying them with carriages and every conveniency as far as the confines of his dominions.

All Asia, all Africa, half of Europe, the Dutch and English possessions in America, with the several unconquered parts of that vast continent, all the austral countries, which make a fifth part of the globe, are left as a prey to the devil, in verification of that holy saying, " Many are called
" but

"but few are chosen." If, as some learned persons say, the number of all the inhabitants of the several parts of the globe is about sixteen hundred millions, the holy catholic universal Roman church has within its pale near sixty millions, which amounts to more than the twenty-sixth part of the inhabitants of the known world.

CIRCUMCISION.

HERODOTUS, in relating what he had heard from the Barbarians, among whom he travelled, mentions some fooleries, and most of our modern travellers do the like: he, indeed, does not require his readers to believe him, when he is giving an account of Gyges and Candaule; of Arion's being saved by a dolphin; of the consultation of the oracle, to know what Croesus was doing, with its answer that he was then boiling a tortoise in a covered pot; of Darius's horse neighing first, which gave his master the empire; and of a hundred other fables, which children are highly delighted with, and rhetoricians insert in their collections: but when he speaks of what he has seen, of customs which he has inquired into, of antiquities which he has examined, he then speaks to men.

" The inhabitants of Colchis," says he, in the book Euterpe, " appear to come originally from
" Egypt. This opinion I hold more from my
" own observation than from any hear-say; for
" I found that in Colchis the antient Egyptians
" were remembered much more than the antient
" customs of Colchis in Egypt.

" Those people who dwell along the Pontus
" Euxinus said they were a colony settled there by
" Sesostris; this I conjectured of myself, not only
" from

"from their swarthy complexion and frizzled hair,
"but because the people of Colchis, Egypt, and
"Ethiopia are the only people on earth who have
"practised circumcision from time immemorial:
"for the Phœnicians and the inhabitants of Pa-
"lestine own that they adopted circumcision from
"the Egyptians. The Syrians, now seated on
"the banks of the Thermodon and Pathenia, to-
"gether with the Macrons their neighbours, ac-
"knowlege, that it is not long since they con-
"formed to this Egyptian custom. It is chiefly
"by this that they are perceived to be of Egyptian
"original.

"As to Ethiopia and Egypt, this ceremony be-
"ing of a very antient date among both nations,
"I cannot say which was the original; however,
"it is probable that the Ethiopians took it from
"the Egyptians; as, on the other hand, the Phœ-
"nicians, by their traffic and intercourse with the
"Greeks, have abolished the custom of circumcis-
"ing new-born children."

It is clear from this passage of Herodotus (L),
that several nations had taken circumcision from
Egypt,

(L.) Whether the ceremony of circumcision was first introduced into the world by the Jews or by the Egyptians, has
been much contested, and is not very material to the cause of
religion. It is sufficient for us to know that God instituted
circumcision as a covenant to Abraham and his seed, without
giving ourselves the trouble of enquiring whether it had been
ever adopted by other nations. It seems, however, to be certain, that no nation except the Hebrews practised it universally. The priests, indeed, were obliged to be circumcised,
but the rest of the people were left to their liberty. M. Voltaire has adopted the opinion of Le Clerc upon this subject,
which makes the Hebrews to have derived this ceremony
from the Egyptians; and he has also made use of the very

argument

DICTIONARY.

Egypt; but no nation has ever said that they derived it from the Jews. To which then must the origin of this custom be attributed, to that nation from whom five or six others acknowledge they hold it, or to another nation much inferior in power, less commercial, less military, hidden in a nook of Arabia Petrea, and which has never been able to introduce the least of its customs in any nation?

The Jews say that they were first received into Egypt by way of compassion and charity; now is it not very probable, that the little people adopted

---

argument of that learned writer, viz. The improbability that the Egyptians should borrow such a ceremony from so contemptible a nation as the Hebrews. But were the Hebrews so contemptible in the time of Joseph? Or how could they be so contemptible after their departure from Egypt, when the inhabitants of that country beheld the Deity operating miracles in their favour? Besides, our author is mistaken, when he says that the Jews were not circumcised the whole time they resided in Egypt, viz. 205 years. The Scripture tells us, that those "who came out of Egypt had been circumcis-"ed," but were dead; and "those who had been born in the "Desert, were not circumcised," because they were separated from other nations, and had no necessity for any mark to distinguish them, till they entered the Land of Canaan. Then Joshua circumcised all the people, and the Lord said unto him, "This day have I rolled away the reproach of Egypt "from you," "opprobrium Egypti;" the plain sense of which is not, as our author says, I have delivered you from what was a reproach to you among the Egyptians; but I have delivered you from what rendered you like the Egyptians, and redounded to your shame and confusion, by cutting off a little of the foreskin, which was not observed by that unclean and uncircumcised nation. Is not this a more natural construction than that of our author? Besides, what occasion was there for delivering them from what had been a reproach to them among the Egyptians, when they had quitted Egypt, and were gone to reside in another country? They had no need to mind the reproach of the Egyptians in the land of Canaan.

a praca practice of the great people, and that the Jews joined in some of their masters customs?

Clement of Alexandria relates that Pythagoras, when travelling in Egypt, could not gain admittance to the mysteries till he was circumcised; consequently there was no being an Egyptian priest without circumcision. This priestly order subsisted when Joseph came into Egypt; the government was of great antiquity, and the old ceremonies of Egypt were observed with the most scrupulous precisenefs.

The Jews acknowledge that they continued in Egypt two hundred and five years; they say that in all that time they were not circumcised; this shews that, during those two hundred and five years, the Egyptians did not borrow circumcision from the Jews: is it then to be supposed that they borrowed this custom, after the Jews, according to their own testimony, run away with all the vessels which they had so kindly lent them? Will a master adopt the principal mark of his slave's religion, after robbing him, and running away? Human nature is not of such a make.

The book of Joshua says, that the Jews were circumcised in the Desert: " I have delivered you " from what was a reproach to you among the " Egyptians (M)." Now what else could this reproach be to people hemmed in between the Phœnicians, Arabians, and Egyptians, but that for which those three nations despised them? How is this reproach removed? by taking away from them a little of the foreskin. Is not this the natural import of that passage?

(M) Our translation has it: " I have rolled away the reproach of Egypt from off you." Josh. v, 9.

The book of Genesis says that Abraham had been circumcised before; but Abraham having travelled into Egypt, which had, for a long time, been a flourishing monarchy, governed by a powerful king, circumcision may not improbably be supposed to have obtained in a kingdom of such antiquity, before the Jewish nation was formed. Farther, the circumcision of Abraham terminated in himself; it was not till Joshua's time his posterity underwent that ceremony.

Now, before Joshua, the Israelites, by their own confession, came into many of the Egyptian customs; they imitated that nation in several sacrifices and ceremonies, as in fasting on the eve of Isis's feasts, in ablutions, in shaving the priests heads, likewise the burning of incense, the branched chandelier, the sacrifice of the red heifer, the purifying with hysop, the abstaining from pork, the abomination of the kitchen utensils of strangers: all these things bear witness, that the little Hebrew people, whatever aversion they might have to the great Egyptian nation, had retained a vast number of their old masters customs. The driving of the goat Azazel into the desert, as laden with the sins of the people, is a plain imitation of an Egyptian practice; the very rabbins allow, that the word Azazel is not Hebrew. Where, then, is the improbability of the Hebrews having imitated the Egyptians in circumcision; it was no more than the Arabs their neighbours had done?

It is not at all strange that God, having sanctified baptism, which is of such an antient date among the Asiatics, should likewise have sanctified circumcision, of no less antiquity among the Africans. It has already been noticed, that it is in his power to annex his graces to such signs as he shall please to chuse.

Again, the Jews, ever since their circumcision under Joshua, have constantly retained this custom down to the present time. The Arabians have also adhered to it; but the Egyptians, who, at first, circumcised both male and female children, in process of time discontinued this operation on the females, and, at length, limited it to priests, astrologers, and prophets. This we learn from Clement of Alexandria and Origen. None of the Ptolemies appear to have been circumcised.

The Latin authors, who contemptuously call the Jews "Curtus apella; credat Judæus apella, curti Judæi," give no such epithets to the Egyptians. At present the whole people of Egypt are circumcised, but from another reason, because Mahometism borrowed the antient circumcision practised in Arabia.

It is this Arabian circumcision which has been introduced among the Ethiopians, where both females and males are still circumcised.

It must be acknowledged that this ceremony of circumcision seems, at first, something odd; but let it be observed, that the oriental priests consecrated themselves to the deities by particular marks. An ivy leaf was engraved with a bodkin on Bacchus's priests. Lucian tells us, that the votaries of the goddess Isis made certain characters on their wrists and necks; the priests of Cibele emasculated themselves.

It is very likely that the Egyptians, who revered the instrument of generation, and carried the figure of it in pompous processions, took it into their heads to offer up to Isis and Osiris, by whom every thing on earth was engendered, a small part of that member, by which those deities had appointed that the human species should be perpetuated. The eastern customs are so extremely different from ours,

ours, that, to a man of ever so little reading, nothing should appear strange. A Parisian, on being told that the Hottentots cut out one of their male childrens testicles, is quite astonished; and perhaps a Hottentot is equally surprized that the Parisians retain both.

CONVULSION FITS.

ABOUT the year 1724, dancings were seen in St. Medard's church-yard; many were the miracles wrought there; one the duchess Du Maine has immortalized in a song:

" Un décroteur à la royale,
Du talon gauche estropié,
Obtint pour grace speciale
D'être boiteux de l'autre pied."

The substance of which is: that " a tip-top " shoe japanner, lame in his left foot, obtained, as " a special favour, that his right should become as " bad."

The miraculous fits are known to have continued till a guard was placed at the church-yard.

" De par le roi défense à Dieu
De plus frequenter en ce lieu."

" God is hereby forbidden, in the king's name, " ever more to come within this place."

The Jesuits, as is likewise known, being unable to perform any such miracles, since their Xavier had exhausted all the society's gifts by raising nine persons from the dead, by way of counterpoise to the credit of the Janfenifts engraved a print of Chrift in a Jefuit's habit; and it is farther known that a wag of the Janfenift party put under the print,

> " Admirez l'artifice extrème
> De ces moines ingenieux;
> Ils vous ont habillé comme eux,
> Mon Dieu, de peur qu'on ne vous aime."

> " The contrivance of thefe cunning monks!
> " That thou mayft not be loved, O God, they
> " have dreffed thee up in their garb."

The Janfenifts, the better to prove that Jefus Chrift could never have put on the habit of a Jefuit, filled Paris with convulfions, and drew every body to their party. Carré de Montgeron, a counfellor of parliament, went and delivered to the king a collection in quarto of all their miracles, attefted by a thoufand witneffes; for which, with very good reafon, he was put under confinement, and obliged to go thro' a regimen to bring him to his fenfes: but truth is always too ftrong for perfecution; the miracles went on for thirty years fucceffively, without any intermiffion. Sifter Rofe, fifter Illuminated, fifter Promifed, fifter Devout, were perpetually fent for to people's houfes: they ufed to have themfelves whipped, and no marks of it were to be feen the next day. They could bear, without any fhew of pain, to be beaten on the breafts with fticks (no wonder; fince it had been well fenced for the exhibition of fuch a farce); they were laid before a great fire, with their faces copioufly plaiftered over with pomatum, and did not burn. At length, as time improves all arts, the fcenery ended in fticking fwords into their flefhy parts, and crucifying them; even a celebrated divine had likewife

the

the honour of being extended on the cross, and all this to convince the world that a certain bull was absurd and ridiculous, which might have been done at a much cheaper rate. Yet have both Jansenists and Jesuits, one and all, leagued together against the Spirit of Laws, and against ....., and against ....., and against ....., and against .....; and, after such doings, we have the face to laugh at the Laplanders, the Samoyedes, and the Negroes!

COUNTRY.

A Country is composed of several families; and as self-love generally leads us to stand up for, and support our particular families, when a contrary interest does not intervene; so, from the like self-love, a man stands up for his town or village, which he calls his native home.

The more extended this native home is, the less we love it, for division weakens love; it is impossible in nature to have a tender love for a family so numerous as scarce to be known.

The candidate, amidst his ambitious intrigues to be chosen ædile, tribune, prætor, consul, dictator, makes a noise about his love for his country, whereas it is only himself that he loves; every one is for securing to himself the freedom of lying at his own home, and that it shall be in no man's power to turn him out; every one is for being sure of his life and fortune. Thus the whole society coinciding in the like wishes, private interest becomes that of the public; and an individual, in praying only for himself, prays in effect for the whole community.

Every state on the whole earth indisputably has originally been a republic; it is the natural progress of human nature; a number of families at first entered into an alliance to secure one another against bears and wolves; and that which had plenty of grain, bartered with another which had nothing but wood.

On our discovery of America, all the several tribes throughout that vast part of the world were found divided into republics; but there were only two kingdoms. Of a thousand nations, only two were subdued.

It was antiently so on our side of the globe: before the petty kings of Etruria and Rome started up, Europe was full of republics. Africa has still its republics; Tripoli, Tunis, Algiers, which lie so far north as, in some measure, to confine on Europe, are commonwealths of robbers. The Hottentots, a people on the south of Africa, still live, as men are said to have lived in the primitive ages of the world, free, all equal, no masters, no subjects, no money, and few or no wants; their sheep supply them both with food and raiment, and their mansions are huts of wood and earth: they are the very filthiest of men, and with a most rank smell; but this they are not sensible of, and they both live and die more quietly than we.

Europe has eight republics without monarchs; Venice, Holland, Switzerland, Genoa, Lucca, Ragusa, Geneva, St. Marino. Poland, Sweden, and England, may be looked on as republics under a king, but Poland alone calls itself such.

" Now, which would you have your country to be? a monarchy or a republic? This is a question which has been bandied to and fro these four thousand years. Ask the rich which is best, and they

they will unanimoufly vote for an ariftocracy; enquire of the people and they will one and all cry up a democracy: as for royalty, it is only kings who will prefer it. How then comes it to pafs that almoft the whole earth is governed by monarchs? Afk the rats who propofed to hang a bell about the cat's neck. But the true reafon is, that men very rarely deferve to be their own governors.

It is a fad cafe, that often there is no being a good patriot without being an enemy to other men. The elder Cato, that worthy patriot, in giving his vote in the fenate, ufed always to fay, Such is my opinion; and down with Carthage. A great part of patriotifm is thought to confift in wifhing one's native country a flourifhing trade and diftinguifhed fucceffes in war. Now it is manifeft, that for one country to gain, another muft lofe, and its fucceffes in war muft of courfe fpread calamity in other parts. Such, then, is the ftate of human affairs, that to wifh an increafe of grandeur to one's native country is wifhing harm to its neighbours. He who is a citizen of the univerfe would have his country neither greater nor smaller, richer nor poorer.

CRITICISM.

I Do not here intend to speak of the criticism of scholiasts, who pretend to restore a word of an antient author, very well understood before: neither shall I meddle with those real critics, who, as far as is possible, have cleared up antient history and philosophy. The satirical critics are the men I am now to deal with.

A man of letters one day reading Tasso with me, fell on this stanza:

> " Chiama gli habitator dell' ombre eterne
> Il rauco suon della Tartarea tromba,
> Treman le spaziose atre caverne,
> E l'aer cieco a quel rumor rimbomba;
> Né si stridendo mai dalle superne
> Regioni del cielo il fulgor piomba.
> Né si scossa giammai trema la terra,
> Quando i vapori in sen gravida serra."

He afterwards read, as they fell under his eye, several stanzas of the like force and harmony: how, cried he, is this what your Boileau is pleased to call tinsel! Is it thus he strives to depreciate a great man who lived a hundred years before him, the better to exalt another great man who lived sixteen hundred years before him, and who would not have failed to have done justice to Tasso?

Be easy, said I to him, let us look into Quinaut's operas: what we met with at the opening of the book, could not but incense us against the petulancy of criticism; it was the following passage in the admirable opera of Armida.

SIDONIA.

Sidonie.

" La haine est affreuse et barbare,
L'amour contraint les coeurs dont il s'empare,
  A souffrir des maux rigoureux.
 Si votre sort est en vôtre puissance,
  Faites choix de l'indifférence,
 Elle assure un sort plus heureux.

Armide.

Non, non, il ne m'est pas possible
De passer de mon trouble en un état paisible;
 Mon coeur ne se peut plus calmer ;
Renaud m'offense trop, il n'est que trop aimable,
C'est pour moi désormais un choix indispensable
 De le haïr ou de l'aimer."

We went through the whole piece, and it must be owned that the beauty of Tasso's genius is enhanced by Quinaut : Well, said I to my friend, after this could you think that Boileau should continually make it his business to expose Quinaut as a wretched poetaster ? He even brought Lewis XIV. to believe, that this beautiful, soft, pathetic, elegant writer owed all his merit to Lully's music. That I can very easily account for, answered my friend ; it was not the musician Boileau was jealous of, but the poet : however, what signifies the saying of a man who, to tag a rhime to a line ending in AUT, sometimes fell foul of Boursaut, sometimes of Henaut, sometimes of Quinaut, according to the terms on which he stood with those gentlemen ? But, that your warmth against injustice may not cool, only go to the window, and view that grand front of the Louvre, by which Perraut has gained immortal reputation :

this ingenious artift happened to be brother to a very learned member of the academy, between whom and Boileau there had been fome literary wrangling, and for this, truly, Mr. Boileau tranfmits this man to pofterity with the character of a paltry architect.

My friend, after a paufe, replied with a figh, this is the temper of man. The duke de Sully, in his Memoirs, fpeaks of the cardinal d'Offat and fecretary Villeroy as bad minifters. Louvois ftrove to fupprefs in himfelf any efteem for the great Colbert: they, faid I, did not print any thing againft each other whilft living, that is a folly fcarce feen in any but divines, fcholars, and lawyers.

We had a man of merit, Lamotte, who has written very fine ftanzas.

> " Quelquefois au feu qui la charme,
> Refifte une jeune beauté,
> Et contre elle meme elle s'arme,
> D'une pénible fermeté.
> Helas cette contrainte extrême
> La prive du vice qu'elle aime,
> Pour fuir la honte qu'elle hàit :
> Sa feverité n'eft que fafte,
> Et l'honneur de paffer pour chafte
> La réfout à l'étre en effet."

" A blooming beauty fometimes withftands
" a pleafing paffion, and to prompting nature op-
" pofes a painful firmnefs. This violent conftraint,
" to avoid dreaded'fhame, preferves her from the
" vice to which her heart is attached; her purity
" was pride and fhow; and the reputation of chaf-
" tity determined her againft the violation of it."

" En vain ce févere ftoique
Sous mille defauts abattu,
Se vante d'une ame héroique,
Toute vouée a la vertu ;
Ce n'eft point la vertu qu'il aime,
Mais fon coeur yvre de lui meme
Voudroit ufurper les autels ;
Et par fa fageffe frivole
Il ne veut que parer l'idole
Qu'il offre au culte des mortels."

" This auftere Stoic, the flave of a multitude of
" vices, boafts of heroifm, of a foul abfolutely con-
" fecrated to virtue. Abfurd conceit ! Virtue has
" none of his love; but his inflated heart claims
" altars ; and the fole fcope of his varnifhed wif-
" dom is to deck the idol for univerfal worfhip."

" Les champs de Pharfale & d'Arbelle
Ont vû triompher deux vainqueurs,
L'un et l'autre digne modele
Que fe propofent les grands coeurs,
Mais le fucces a fait leur gloire ;
Et fi le fceau de la victoire
N'eût confacré ces demi-dieux,
Alexandre aux yeux du vulgaire
N'aurait été qu'un Téméraire,
Et Cefar qu'un feditieux."

" Pharfalia and Arbella's plains beheld the tri-
" umph of two victors, the model and admiration
" of all martial fpirits ; but to fuccefs they owe
" their whole glory ; for had not victory confe-
" crated thefe demi-gods, Alexander would have
" been accounted a Hotfpur, and Cæfar an incen-
" diary."

This

This amiable author, says he, more than once arrayed philosophy in the graceful attire of poesy. Had he always written such stanzas, he would have been the chief lyric poet among us; yet whilst such beautiful pieces came from him, a cotemporary of his could call him a Green Goose, and in another place say, "the tiresome beauty of his "propositions;" and in another, "they have but "one fault, they should have been been written in "prose; one sees with half an eye they came from "Quinaut."

He pursues him every where, every where charges him with driness and want of harmony.

Perhaps you would be glad to see the odes written some years after by this same censor, who tried La Motte in so arbitrary a manner, and decried him with such contempt. Here are some specimens.

"Cette influence souveraine
N'est pour lui qu'une illustre chaine,
Qui l'attache au bonheur d'autrui;
Tous les brillans qui l'embellissent,
Tous les talents qui l'annoblissent,
Sont en lui, mais non pas à lui."

"This sovereign power is but a glittering chain,
"binding him to the happiness of others; all the
"brilliant qualities which adorn him, all the ta-
"lents which ennoble him, though in him, are not
"his."

"Il n'est rien que le temps n'absorbe ne devore,
 Et les faits qu'on ignore,
Sont bien peu differents des faits non avenus."

"Nothing escapes the devouring jaws of time;
"and what is unknown differs very little from
"what never happened."

"La

"La bonté qui brille en elle
De ses charmes les plus doux,
Est une image de celle,
Qu'elle voit briller en vous.
Et par vous seule enrichie,
Sa politesse affranchie
Des moindres obscurités,
Est la lueur refléchie,
Des vos sublimes clartés."

"That goodness which in her displays its most
"engaging charms, is the image of that which,
"admiring, she beholds in you; and by you alone
"enriched: her politeness, freed from the least
"darkening spot, is a light reflected from your
"resplendency."

"Ils ont vû par ta bonne foi
De leurs peuples troublés d'effroi
La crainte heureusement déçue.
Et déracinée à jamais
La haine si souvent reçue,
En survivance de la paix."

"Through thy probity they have seen the ter-
"rors of their appaled people happily mistaken;
"and hatred, often received in reversion for peace,
"for ever extirpated."

"Dévoile à ma vüe empressée
Ces deités d'adoption,
Synonimes de la pensée,
Symboles de l'abstraction."

"Unveil to my eager sight those adopted dei-
"ties, synonimous with cogitation, emblems of
"abstractedness."

"N'est

"N'eſt ce pas une fortune,
Quand d'une charge commune,
Deux moitiés portent le faix ?
Que le moindre le réclame,
Et que du bonheur de l'ame
Le corps ſeul faſſe les fraix."

"Is it not a rare happineſs, where, in a burthen common to two, the leaſt inſiſts on bearing the whole load ? Thus the body lays itſelf out for the gratifications of the ſoul."

To be ſure, ſaid my judicious philologiſt, this is wretched traſh to be publiſhed as models, after criticiſing a writer with ſo much ſcurrility. The author had done much better to have left his adverſary in the quiet enjoyment of his merit, and have retained his own ſhare of it ; but alas ! the " genus irritabile vatum," is ſtill as ſick as ever with the overflowings of an acrid bile. The public, its views extending no farther than amuſement, overlooks theſe trifles in men of talents. It ſees, in an allegory called Pluto, ſome judges condemned to be flead, and ſitting in hell, on a ſeat covered with their ſkins, inſtead of the lillies (N): the reader never troubles himſelf whether the judges deſerved it or not, or whether the plaintiff who had ſummoned them before Pluto be in the right or wrong ; he reads thoſe verſes purely for his pleaſure, and if they give him pleaſure that is all he deſires : if the allegory diſguſts him, he ſhuts the book, and would not ſtir a foot to have the ſentence confirmed or annulled.

(N) The arms of France embroidered on the covering of the benches in courts of juſtice.

Racine's

Racine's inimitable tragedies have been all criticised, and very badly, becaufe the critics were rivals. The competent judges of an art are the artifts; true, but when is it the artifts are not corrupted?

An artift very fkilful, and, withal, a man of tafte, without either prejudice or envy, would make an excellent critic; but a hard matter it is to find fuch a man.

DELUGE.

THAT ever the whole globe was at one time totally overflowed with water, is phyfically impoffible. The fea may have covered all parts fucceffively, one after the other; and this could be only in a gradation fo very flow, as to take up a prodigious number of ages. The fea, in the fpace of five hundred years, has withdrawn from Aiguesmortes, from Frejus, and from Ravenna, once large ports, leaving about two leagues of land quite dry. This progreffion fhews, that, to make the circuit of the globe it would require two millions two hundred and fifty thoufand years. A very remarkable circumftance is, that this period comes very near to that which the earth's axis would take up in raifing itfelf again, and coinciding with the equator; a motion fo far from improbable, that, for thefe fifty years paft, fome apprehenfion has been entertained of it, but it cannot be accomplifhed under two millions three hundred thoufand years.

The ftrata, or beds of fhells, every where found, fixty, eighty, and even a hundred leagues from the fea, prove, beyond all difpute, that it has infenfibly depofited thofe maritime products on grounds
which

128 A PHILOSOPHICAL

which were once its shores: but that the water, at one and the same time, covered the whole earth, is a physical absurdity, which the laws of gravitation, as well as those of fluids, and the deficiency of the quantity of water, demonstrate to be impossible. Not that any thing here is meant in the least to affect the great truth of the universal deluge as related in the Pentateuch ; on the contrary, this is a miracle, and therefore to be believed ; it is a miracle, therefore could not be effected by physical causes.

The whole history of the deluge is miraculous. It is a miracle that forty days rain should have submerged the four parts of the world ; that the waters rose fifteen cubits above all the highest mountains : it is a miracle that there should have been cataracts, doors, and apertures in heaven ; it is a miracle that all animals should have repaired to the ark, from the several parts of the world ; it is a miracle that Noah should have found fodder for them during ten months ; it is a miracle that all the creatures, with the provisions, could be contained in the ark ; it is a miracle that most of them did not die there ; it is a miracle that, at going out of the ark, sustenance could be found for man and beast; it is likewise a miracle, that one Pelletier should have conceited that he had explained how all the several kinds of creatures might very naturally be contained and fed in the ark.

Now, the history of the deluge being the most miraculous thing ever heard of, it is idle (O) to go about

---

(O) Our author is mistaken, when he says it is idle to go about elucidating the history of the deluge, and that the whole must be resolved into a miracle. That the divine assistance must be called in on this occasion may be allowed ;
but

DICTIONARY. 129

about elucidating it; there are mysteries which we believe through faith; and faith consists in believing what reason does not believe: which again is another miracle.

---

but that every part of the history is miraculous we cannot assent to. The difficulty of finding out such a prodigious quantity of water as was requisite for covering all the globe to fifteen cubits above the highest mountains, has made some modern writers imagine, that this deluge overwhelmed only one part of the earth. But all antiquity believed that the deluge was universal, and the Scripture expresses it in the strongest terms. Had not all the earth been covered with the waters of the deluge, the building of the ark would have been needless. It would have been sufficient for God to have warned Noah to go to some other country, which was not to have been overwhelmed with water. Besides, it would have required no less a miracle to keep up the waters in one part of the earth, than to drown the whole. As to the difficulty of finding out waters sufficient to overflow the world, without having recourse to a miracle, is it not very rational to make answer, that as, in the beginning, the whole mass of the earth was covered with waters, which retired into the cavities of the earth, or were drawn up in clouds; so those cavities having thrown out those waters by the motion of the earth, and the clouds being dissolved into water, the same quantity of water meeting, might again cover the globe of the earth. This is what Moses meant, when he said, "That the fountains of the deep and the cataracts of heaven were opened." It must be owned, indeed, that to draw this quantity of water out of the abyss on the surface of the earth required the exertion of the Divine Power. The other difficulties about Noah's ark may be easily solved. That the space in such a vessel was abundantly sufficient to contain both Noah and his family, as well as the animals, and all necessary provisions for them, appears most evidently, whatever our author may pretend, from the geometrical calculations of learned men, as Bishop Wilkins and others. See the Univ. Hist. vol. i. p. 220. as also Wilkins's Essay towards a real Character, and Pelelier Differt. sur l'Arche de Noé.

K   Thus

Thus the story of the universal deluge is like that of the tower of Babel, of Balaam's ass, of the fall of Jericho at the blowing of the trumpets, of the waters turned into blood, the passage of the Red Sea, and all the miracles which God was pleased to perform in behalf of his chosen people. These are depths unfathomable by the line of human reason.

DESTINY.

OF all the books which have reached our times, the most antient is (P) Homer: here we become acquainted with the manners of profane antiquity, with heroes and gods, as rude and unpolished as if made in the likeness of man; but there, on the other hand, we meet with the elements of philosophy, and especially the notion of Destiny, no less lord of the gods, than the gods are lords of the world.

Jupiter would fain save Hector; he consults the destinies; he weighs the fates of Hector and Achilles in scales, and finding that the Trojan must absolutely be slain by the Greek, he is sensible all opposition to it would be fruitless: and from that moment Apollo, Hector's guardian genius, is obliged to forsake him (Iliad, lib. xxii.) and though Homer, according to the privilege of

---

(P) This is a mistake, the history of Moses is the most antient book in the world: for whether Moses was cotemporary with Inachus, the first king of Argos, who lived 600 years before the Trojan war; or whether he did not live till the days of Cecrops, king of Athens, who reigned 300 years before that war, it is certain he is much more ancient than Homer or Hesiod.

antiquity, often interlards his poem with quite opposite ideas, yet is he the first in whom the notion of destiny occurs; so that it must be supposed to have been current in his time.

This notion of destiny was not received by the Jewish Pharisees till several ages after; for the Pharisees themselves, who, among that insignificant people, were the principal literati, were but of a modern date. At Alexandria they adulterated the ancient Jewish opinions with many Stoic tenets. St. Jerom even says, that their sect is but little prior to our vulgar æra.

Philosophers never stood in need of Homer, or the Pharisees, to be convinced that every thing is done by immutable laws, that every thing is settled, and that every thing is a necessary effect.

Either the world subsists by its own nature, by its physical laws, or a Supreme Being has formed it by his primitive laws; in either case, these laws are immutable; in either case every thing is necessary: heavy bodies gravitate towards the center of the earth, and cannot tend to remain in the air; pear-trees can never bear pine-apples; the instinct of a spaniel can never be the instinct of an ostrich; every thing is arranged, set in motion, and limited.

Man can have but a certain number of teeth, hairs, and ideas; and a time comes when he necessarily loses them: it is a contradiction that what was yesterday has not been, and what is to-day should not be; no less a contradiction is it that a thing which is to be should not come to pass.

If thou couldst give a turn to the destiny of a fly, I see no reason why thou mightest not as well determine the destiny of all other flies, of all other animals, of all men, and of all nature; so that, at last, thou wouldst be more powerful than God himself.

It is common for weak people to say, such a physician has cured my aunt of a most dangerous illness; he has made her live ten years longer than she would. Others as weak, but, in their own opinion, very wise, say, the prudent man owes his fortune to himself.

"Nullum numen abest, si sit prudentia, sed nos
Te facimus fortuna Deam cœloque locamus."

But the prudent man oftentimes is crushed by his destiny, instead of making it; it is their destiny that renders men prudent.

Some profound politicians affirm, that, had Cromwell, Ludlow, Ireton, and about a dozen more parliamentarians, been made away with a week before the cutting off Charles the First's head, that king might have lived longer, and have died in his bed. They are in the right, and may farther add, that, had all England been swallowed up by the sea, that monarch would not have ended his days on a scaffold at Whitehall, near the Banqueting-house; but by the arrangement of occurrences Charles was to have his head cut off.

Cardinal d'Ossat was unquestionably a man of more prudence than yon lunatic in Bedlam; but is it not manifest that the wise d'Ossat's organs were of another texture than that madman's? So a fox's organs differ from those of a crane or a lark.

The physician has saved thy aunt. Allowed; but herein he certainly did not reverse the order of nature; he conformed to it. It is evident that thy aunt could not hinder her being born in such a town, and having a certain illness at such a time; that the physician could be no-where but in the town where he was; that thine aunt was to send for him; and that he was to prescribe for her those medicaments which have effected her cure.

A pea-

A peasant imagines that the hail which has fallen in his ground is purely matter of chance; but the philosopher knows that there is no such thing as chance; and that by the constitution of the world, it must necessarily have hailed that day, in that very place.

Some, alarmed at this truth, are for halving it, as straitened debtors offer half to their creditors, desiring some forbearance for the remainder. There are, say they, necessary events (Q), and others which are not so: but it would be odd, indeed, that one part of this world were fixed and not the other; that some things which happen were to happen, and that others which happen were not necessarily to happen. On a close examination, the doctrine which opposes that of destiny, must appear loaded with absurdities, and contrary to the idea of an eternal providence: but many are destined to reason wrongly, others not to reason at all, and others to persecute those who do reason.

You ask me what, then, becomes of liberty? I understand you not. I know nothing of that liberty you speak of, nor yourself, indeed; else you would not be so long controverting about its nature. If you will, or, rather, if you can, calmly examine with me what it is, turn to the letter L.

(Q) The physical world is subject to invariable laws; man, therefore, as a physical being, is, like other bodies, governed by those invariable laws: but as an intelligent being, his nature requires him to be a free agent. Our author has taken his notions on this article, and on that of Liberty, from Mr. Locke, who denies that there is such a power in man as a Liberty of Will; which you may see refuted by the ingenious Dr. Clarke, on the Being and Attributes, p. 86.

DREAMS.

DREAMS.

" Somnia quæ ludunt animos volitantibus umbris,
Non delubra deum, nec ab æthere numina mittunt,
Sed sua quisque facit."

BUT how so, when all the senses are deadened in sleep, is there one within still alive and active (R)? What! when your eyes have lost their sight, and your ears their hearing, do you still see

---

(R) M. Voltaire does not seem to be sufficiently acquainted with the cause of dreams, or to have rightly examined that part of natural philosophy. In order to clear up this matter, we should previously inquire into the nature of waking and sleeping. Waking consists in this, that the animal spirits being at that time in great plenty in the brain, and capable of being easily determined to run from thence through all the nerves, they fill them in such a manner as to keep all the capillaments of them stretched and distinct from each other. Sleeping, on the contrary, is caused by a scarcity, or failure, of spirits; so that the pores of the brain, through which the spirits usually run into the nerves, not being kept open by the continual flowing of the spirits, shut up of themselves. The spirits being dissipated, and no new ones flowing in, the capillaments of the nerves will become soft, and cleave to each other; and if, at that time, any object makes an impression on any part of the body, those nerves cannot transmit it to the brain. And hence it follows, that there can be no sensation. But, it may happen that, while we are asleep, some of the animal spirits which are in the brain may shake some of the parts of the brain, in the same manner as they would be shaken by an external object affecting the corporeal senses; then there will be a sensation raised in the soul, and such a sort of perception, is called a dream.

and

and hear in your dreams? The dog hunts in his dreams, barks, chafes his prey, and feafts on his reward. That the poet verfifies in his fleep, the mathematician views figures, the metaphyfician reafons right or wrong, we have many ftriking inftances.

Is this the action only of the body's organs, or is it merely the foul, which, now freed from the power of the fenfes, acts in the full enjoyment of its properties.

If the organs alone produce our dreams by night, why not our ideas by day? If it be merely the foul, acting of itfelf, and quiet by the fufpenfion of the fenfes, which is the only caufe and fubject of all your fleeping ideas, whence is it, that they are almoft ever irrational, irregular, and incoherent? Can it be, that, in the time of the foul's moft abftract quietude, its imagination fhould be the moft confufed? Is it fantaftical when free? Were it born with metaphyfical ideas, as fome writers, who were troubled with waking dreams, have affirmed, its pure and luminous ideas of being, of infinitude, and of all primary principles, naturally fhould awake in her with the greateft energy when the body is fleeping, and men fhould philofophife beft in their dreams.

Whatever fyftem you efpoufe, however you may labour to prove that memory ftirs the brain, and your brain your foul, you muft allow that, in all your ideas in fleep, you are intirely paffive; your will has no fhare in thofe images. Thus it is clear, that you can think feven or eight hours on a ftretch, without having the leaft inclination to think, and even without being certain that you do think. Confider this, and tell me what is man's compound?

Superftition has always dealt much in dreams; nothing, indeed, was more natural. A man deeply concerned about his miftrefs who lies ill, dreams that he fees her dying; and the next day fhe actually dies: then, to be fure, God had given him previous knowledge of his beloved's death.

A commander of an army dreams of gaining a battle; gains it; then the gods had intimated to him that he fhould be conqueror.

It is only fuch dreams as meet with fome accomplifhment that are taken notice of, the others we think not worth remembrance. Dreams make full as great a part of antient hiftory as oracles.

The end of ver. 26. cap. xix. of Leviticus, the Vulgate renders thus: "Thou fhalt not obferve "dreams (S)." But the word DREAM is not in the Hebrew; and it would be fomething odd, that the obfervance of dreams fhould be forbidden in the fame book, which tells us that Jofeph faved Egypt, and brought his family to great profperity by interpreting three dreams.

The interpretation of dreams and vifions was fo common, that fomething beyond this knowledge was required; the magician was fometimes even to guefs what another had dreamed. Nebuchadnezzar forgetting a dream, ordered the magicians, on pain of death, to find it out; Daniel the Jew, who was of the fame fchool as the magicians, faved their lives, both finding out and interpreting the king's dream. This and many other accounts prove, that oneiromancy, or the intrepretation of dreams, was not prohibited by the Jewifh inftitutes.

(S) Moft tranflations have TIMES.

END.

END, FINAL CAUSES.

A MAN, it seems, must be stark mad to deny that the stomach is made for digestion, the eye to see, and the ear to hear.

On the other hand, he must be strangely attached to final causes, to affirm, that stone was made to build houses, and that China breeds silk-worms to furnish Europe with sattin.

But it is said, if God has manifestly made one thing with design, he had a design in every thing. To allow a Providence in one case, and deny it in another, is ridiculous. Whatever is made was foreseen and arranged; now every arrangement has its object, every effect its cause; therefore every thing is equally the result, or the product, of a final cause; therefore it is equally true to say that noses were made to wear spectacles, and fingers to be decorated with diamonds, as it is true to say, that the ears have been made to hear sounds, and the eyes to receive light.

This difficulty, I apprehend, may be easily cleared up, when the effects are invariably the same in all times and places; when such uniform effects are independent of the beings they appertain to, there is then evidently a final cause.

All animals have eyes and they see; all have ears and they hear; all a mouth with which they eat; a stomach, or something similar, by which they digest; all an orifice which voids the excrements; all an instrument of generation, and these natural gifts operate in them without the intervention of any art. Here are clear demonstrations of final causes, and to gainsay so universal a truth, would be to pervert our faculty of thinking.

But

But it is not in all places, nor at all times, that stones form edifices; all noses do not wear spectacles; all fingers have not a ring, nor are all legs covered with silk stockings: therefore a silk worm is not made to cover my legs, as your mouth is made to eat, and your backside for evacuation. Thus there are effects produced by final causes, but withal many which cannot come within that appellation.

But both the one and the other are equally agreeable to the plan of general Providence; for certainly nothing comes to pass in opposition to it, or so much as without it. Every particular within the compass of nature is uniform, immutable, and the immediate work of their Author. From him are derived the laws by which the moon is three-fourths of the cause of tides, and the sun the other fourth; it is he who has given a rotary motion to the sun, by which in five minutes and a half it emits rays of light into the eyes of men, crocodiles, and cats.

But if, after many centuries, we have hit on the invention of shears and spits, with the former shearing the sheep of their wool, and with the latter roasting them for food, what can be inferred from thence, but that God has so made us, that, one day we should necessarily grow ingenious and carnivorous?

Sheep, doubtless, were not absolutely made to be dressed and eaten; since several nations abstain from that sanguinary practice. Men were not essentially created to butcher one another, for the Bramins and Quakers never kill any body; but the composition we are made of is frequently productive of massacres, as it produces calumnies, vanities, persecutions, and impertinencies: not that the formation of man is precisely the final cause of our follies and brutalities, a final cause being universal and invariable

riable in all places and at all times. The crimes and absurdities of the human mind are, nevertheless, in the eternal order of things. In threshing corn, the flail is the final cause of the grain's separation; but if the flail, in threshing the corn, destroys a thousand insects, this is not from any determinate will of mine, neither is it mere chance: these insects were at that time under my flail, and it was determined they were to be there.

It is consequential to the nature of things, that a man is ambitious, forms other men into military bodies, that he is beaten or gains a victory; but never can it be said that man was created by God to be knocked on the head in battle.

The instruments given to us by nature cannot always be final causes, ever in motion, and infallible in their effect. The eyes, given us for sight, are not always open; every sense has its its intervals of rest: there are even some senses we make no use of; for instance, in the case of a poor girl of fourteen, immured in a convent, that door, from which was to proceed a new generation, is for ever shut up; still the final cause subsists, and as soon as it is free will act.

EQUALITY.

WHAT does one dog owe to another, and one horse to another horse? Nothing. No animal depends on its fellow; but man, partaking of that spark of divinity called reason, what advantage accrues to him from this? To be a slave almost every-where throughout the earth.

Were this earth what it apparently should be, that is, did man every-where meet with an easy, certain,

certain, and safe subsistence, and a climate suitable to his nature, it is manifestly impossible that one man could have enslaved another. When this earth shall every-where produce salubrious fruits; when the air, which should contribute to our life, shall not bring us sicknesses and death: when man shall stand in need of no other lodging and bed than that of the deer and roebuck; then the Gengis-Khans and the Tamerlanes will have no other domestics than their children, and these will have so much natural affection as to assist them in their old age.

In this so natural state, which all quadrupeds, birds, and reptiles enjoy, man would be as happy as they; dominion would then be a chimera, an absurdity, which no one would think of; for who would make a bustle to get servants without any want of their service?

Should any individual, of a tyrannical disposition, and extraordinary strength, take it into his head to make a slave of his weaker neighbour, the thing would be impracticable; the party oppressed would be an hundred leagues out of the oppressor's reach before he had taken his measures.

Thus a freedom from wants would necessarily make all men equal. It is the distress annexed to our species which subjects one man to another: not that inequality is a real misfortune; the grievance lies in dependance. What signifies one man being stiled his highness, another his holiness? but to serve either is disagreeable.

A numerous family has successfully cultivated a good soil, whilst two small neighbouring families cannot bring their stubborn grounds to produce any thing; the two poor families must either become servants to the opulent family, or extirpate it; this is self-evident: one of the two indigent families,

families, for a subsistence, goes and offers its labour to the rich; the other goes to dispossess it by force of arms, and is beaten. The former is the origin of domestics and labourers, and from the latter slavery is derived.

In our calamitous globe, it is impossible that men living together in society, should not be divided into two classes, one the rich who command, the other the poor who serve or obey: these two are subdivided into a thousand, and these thousands have their farther subdivisions and gradations.

All the oppressed are not absolutely unhappy. Most of them being born in a servile state, continual labour preserves them from too sensible a feeling of their situation; but whenever they feel it, wars are the consequence, as at Rome between the plebeian and patrician parties; likewise those of the peasants in Germany, England, and France. All these wars terminate, soon or late, in the subjection of the people, because the great have money, and money does every thing within a state; I say within a state; for between nation and nation it is otherwise. A nation which handles iron best, will ever be too strong for that which, with its abundance of gold, is deficient in skill and courage.

Every man is born with no small propensity to power, riches, and pleasure, and has naturally a delight in indolence; consequently every man is for having the money, wives, or daughters of others; would subject them to all his humours, and do no work, at or least what only pleased himself. You see that, for men with such fine dispositions to be equal, is as impossible as that two preachers, or two professors of divinity, should not be jealous of one another.

Mankind, in the present state, cannot subsist, unless an infinity of useful men have the misfortune of being without any possession whatever: for, to be sure, no man in easy circumstances will plough your grounds; and, if you are in want of a pair of shoes, you must find some other hand than a serjeant at law to make them for you. Thus, inequality is, at the same time, both the most natural and the most chimerical thing in the world.

Men being excessive in every thing where they can be so, this inequality has been carried too far; in several governments it is a standing maxim, that a citizen is not allowed to quit the country where he happened to be born: the import of this law is visibly this: "The country is so bad and ill go-"verned, that we forbid any person whatever to "go out, left every body should leave it." Now act more wisely, create in your subjects a delight to stay in your country, and in foreigners a desire of coming thither.

Every man has a right to believe himself naturally equal to other men: but it does not from hence follow that a cardinal's cook may order his eminence to dress his dinner; the cook indeed may say, I am as much a man as my master; like him I cried at my birth, and he will die in the same agonies, and amidst the same ceremonies as I; the animal functions are alike in both; if the Turks make themselves masters of Rome, and I should then come to be a cardinal, and my master reduced to turn cook, I will take him into my service. There is nothing in this soliloquy but what is rational and just; yet till the grand seignor makes himself master of Rome, the cook is to do his duty, else there's an end of human society.

As to him who is neither cook to a cardinal nor holds any state employment, and who has no connection or dependence, but who is chagrined at being every where received either with an air of protection

DICTIONARY.   143

tection or contempt; who plainly sees, that many Monsignors have neither more learning, more genius, nor more virtue than himself, and to whom it is a torment to be sometimes in their anti-chamber—What would you have him do? Take himself away.

EZEKIEL.

Of some singular Passages in that **Prophet***, and some antient Customs.*

IT is at present very well known, that we are not to judge of antient customs by modern times. He who would go about to reform the court of Alcinoüs in the Odyssey, by that of the grand seignor or of Lewis XIV. would be little applauded by the learned; and to find fault with Virgil for having represented king Evander receiving ambassadors with a bear skin for his mantle, and a dog on each side of him, would be very bad criticism.

The manners of the antient Egyptians and Jews vary from ours still more than those of king Alcinoüs, of Nausicae his daughter, and the good man Evander.—Ezekiel, when a slave among the Chaldeans, had a vision near the little river of Chebar, which runs into the Euphrates.

It is not to be thought strange that he should have seen animals with four faces, and four wings, and their feet like those of calves; nor that he saw wheels self-moving, and having in them the spirit of life. These symbols are pleasing to the very imagination; but several critics cannot be reconciled (T) to the order given him by the Lord that, during

―――――――――――――――――――――――――――――

(T) Our author acknowledges that the descriptions which he has extracted from this prophet, how shocking soever they may

during three hundred and ninety days he should eat barley, wheat, and millet bread, besmeared with man's

---

may appear at first sight, only denote the iniquities of Jerusalem and Samaria; yet as weak minds may be offended at his picking out these passages, without explaining them, we shall make a few remarks on that head.

The prophet Ezekiel is very obscure, particularly towards the beginning and end, for which reason the Jews would not permit their people to read him till the age of thirty. He foretels the captivity and destruction of Jerusalem, the restoration of the Jewish people, and the rebuilding of the temple.

In the fourth chapter, under the type of a siege, he shews the time from Jeroboam's defection to the captivity. Here he enumerates the hardships of the besieged, for want of provisions. Their bread, he says, is to be given them by weight, because of the scarcity of grain. They shall also drink their water by measure; and there will be so great a scarcity of fuel, that they will be obliged to bake their bread with dung that cometh out of man; that is, they will be obliged to make fire of man's dung instead of cow-dung, because of the scarcity of cattle. This is very different from ordering the prophet to besmear the bread with man's dung, as M. Voltaire understands it, according to the vulgar acceptation. The prophet is still uneasy, and tells the Lord, he hath hitherto abstained from every thing that the law deems polluted, and therefore begs he may not be obliged to make use of what is naturally polluted; viz. man's dung for the purpose of baking. The Lord is moved with his prayer, mitigates his sentence, and says he shall have cow's dung for man's dung, to prepare his bread therewith; that is, to bake it, not, according to our author's comment, to knead it. The conclusion is, that, as cow's dung was also unclean, the Israelites should, in punishment for their iniquities be certainly polluted.

With regard to the contradiction mentioned by our author, between the passage in this prophet, chap. xviii. viz. That the son shall not bear the iniquity of the father, and that in Numbers chap. xxviii. we are to observe in the first place, that our author mistakes the book of Numbers for that of Exodus, where, chap. xx. ver. 5. the passage referred to is to be found.

Secondly,

man's dung. Then said the prophet, "Ah, Lord God, behold, my soul hath not hitherto been polluted. And the Lord answered, Well, instead of man's excrements, I allow thee cow dung, and thou shalt prepare thy bread therewith."

As it is not customary with us to eat bread with such marmalade, these orders, to the generality of men, appear unworthy of the Divine Majesty. It must, however, be owned, that cow dung and all the diamonds of the mogul, are entirely alike, not only in the eyes of a Divine Being, but in those of a ge-

---

Secondly, the contradiction is removed by a right consideration of the whole passage in Ezekiel: the Jews complained that they underwent great hardships in punishment for the sins of Manasseh, "The fathers have eaten sour grapes, and the "children's teeth are set on edge." This has been the case in all times, for people labouring under calamities to exculpate themselves, and to blame their forefathers; hence Horace, "Delicta majorum immeritus lues, Romane." The prophet makes answer, that they are punished for their own guilt, and not for that of their ancestors. See other explications in Pool's Synopsis.

The objection against the 25th verse of the 20th chapter of Ezekiel is easily answered; "God gave the Jews statutes that were not good," that is, unpleasant on account of the multiplicity of ceremonial laws, which were troublesome in practice, yet necessary to that stiff-necked people, because of their proneness to idolatry.

With respect to the other passages from chap. xvi. and xxiii. they are certainly allegorical, and denote the wickedness and corruption of Jerusalem, which was grown worse than Sodom. And as the communication with the Deity is represented frequently in the Scriptures under the emblem or figure of nuptials, so the estrangement or wandering from the Deity is described as a spiritual prostitution, or whoredom. But we refer the reader to the different commentators for an application of the allegory, and agree with our author, that the expressions which to us may appear indelicate, were not so in regard to the Jews.

L ruine

nuine philosopher; and as to the reasons God might have for ordering such repasts to his prophet, it is not for us to be examiners.

It is sufficient to shew, that these orders, however odd and disgustful to us, did not seem so to the Jews. True it is, that in St. Jerom's time, the synagogue did not allow the reading of Ezekiel under thirty years of age; but this was because, in chap. xviii. it is said that " the son shall no longer bear the iniquity " of the father," and it shall be no more said " the fathers have eaten sour grapes " and the children's teeth have been set on edge."

This was expresly contradicting Moses, who, in the xxviii. chapter of Numbers, declares that the children shall bear the iniquity of their fathers to the third and fourth generation.

Farther, Ezekiel in chap. xx. makes the Lord to say, that he gave to the Jews " precepts which " were not good." This was the principal reason of the synagogue's prohibiting young persons from reading Ezekiel, as it might bring them to doubt of the irrefragability of the Mosaic laws.

The cavillers of our times are still more astonished at the manner of the prophet's describing the wickedness of Jerusalem, in chapter xvi. where he introduces the Lord speaking to a girl: and the Lord said to the girl, " In the day thou wast born, thy navel-string was not cut, thou wast neither salted nor swaddled; I pitied thee; thou art grown up, thy breasts are fashioned, and thine hair is grown; I passed by thee, and looked upon thee, behold thy time was the time of love. I spread my skirt over thee, and covered thy nakedness: thou becamest mine, I washed thee with water, and anointed thee with oil, I cloathed thee and shod thee; I girded thee about with fine linen, and covered thee with silks; I decked thee also with ornaments, and put bracelets

bracelets on thy hands, and a chain on thy neck; I put a jewel on thy forehead, and ear rings in thy ears, and a crown on thy head, &c. But thou didst trust in thy beauty, and playedst the harlot because of thy renown, and pouredst out thy fornications on every one that passed by: thou hast built an eminent place, thou hast proftituted thyself in public places, thou hast spread thy legs to every one that passed by.... and thou hast lain with Egyptians.... and, lastly, thou hast paid thy lovers, and hast made presents to them to lie with thee, ... and in paying instead of being paid, thou hast done the reverse of other girls .... there is a proverb, Like mother like daughter, and the like is said of thee."

Still greater clamour is raised against chap. xxiii. A mother had two daughters, who parted with their virginity very early in life; the name of the elder was Aholah, and of the younger Aholibah: ..... " Aholah doated on young lords, and cap-
" tains, and rulers; she committed whoredom
" with the Egyptians in her youth .... Aholibah
" her sister was more corrupt in her whoredoms
" 'than she, with captains and rulers cloathed most
" gorgeously, horsemen riding upon horses, all of
" them desirable young men; she has discovered
" her nakedness; she has increased her whoredoms,
" she has eagerly sought the embraces of those (U)
" whose flesh is as the flesh of asses, and whose issue
" is like the issue of horses."

These descriptions, which scandalize so many weak minds, signify no more than the sins of Je-

---

* (U) M. Voltaire translates the above passage thus: " Whose
" member is like that of an ass, and who cast their seed like
" horses." Whether that be more agreeable to the original than ours, is not of great consequence; the idea is the same.

rusalem and Samaria. Expressions to us indelicate and obscure, were not so at that time. The like plainness openly shews itself in other passages of Scripture. It often speaks of "opening the womb." The terms in which are expressed the junction of Boaz with Ruth, and of Judah with his daughter in-law, in Hebrew, have nothing unseemly in them; but would be very much so in our language.

He who is not ashamed of being naked does not cover himself: where was the shame of naming the genitals in those times, when it was customary, on any important promise, to touch the genitals of him to whom the promise was made? It was a mark of respect, a symbol of fidelity; as formerly among us, the feudal tenants put their hands between those of their paramounts.

We have thought fit to render the genitals by thigh; Eliezer puts his hand under Abraham's thigh; the like Joseph does to Jacob. This had been a custom of very great antiquity in Egypt, and so far were that people from annexing shame and turpitude to what we dare neither expose nor name, that they carried in procession a large figure of the virile member called PHALLUM, in thanksgiving to the gods for their goodness in making that member the instrument of human propagation.

All this sufficiently proves, that our ideas of decency and purity do not correspond with those of other nations. At what period of time did politeness prevail among the Romans more than in the Augustan age? Yet Horace, the ornament of that age, and in a moral piece, roundly says,

"Nec metuo, ne dum futuo vir rure recurrat."

Augustus makes use of the same expression in an epigram against Fulvia.

He

He who, among us, should openly pronounce the word answering to FUTUO, would be looked on with as much contempt as a drunken porter: this word, and several others made use of by Horace and other elegant authors, to us appear still more indecent than Ezekiel's expressions. Whether we read antient authors, or travel in distant countries, let us lay aside all our prejudices. Nature is every-where the same, and customs every-where different.

FABLES.

ARE not the most antient fables manifestly allegorical? The first we know of, according to our chronology, is it not that related in the 9th chapter of the book of Judges? The trees were about chusing a king; the olive would not quit the care of its oil, nor the fig-tree of its figs, nor the vine-tree of its rich juice; and all the other trees had their fruit no less at heart; so that the thistle being good for nothing, and having prickles which could do hurt, made itself king.

The pagan fable of Venus, as we have it in Hesiod, is it not an allegory of all nature? The generative parts fell from the sky on the sea-shore; Venus receives her being from this precious spume: her first name signifies "Lover of generation:" can there be a more sensible image? This Venus is the goddess of beauty; beauty is no longer amiable than when accompanied by the graces; beauty gives rise to love, love has shafts which every heart has felt; he is hoodwinked, to conceal the faults of the object beloved.

Wisdom is conceived in the brain of the sovereign of the gods, under the name of Minerva; the soul of man is a divine fire, which Minerva shews to

Prometheus, and he made use of this divine fire to animate man.

Every body must perceive in these fables a lively portraiture of nature. Most of the other fables are either corruptions of antient histories, or the chimeras of imagination. It is with ancient fables as with modern tales; some are of the moral kind and quite charming, and there are others as insipid.

FALSITY of HUMAN VIRTUES.

WHEN the duke de Rochefoucault had published his Thoughts on Self-love, one M. Esprit of the Oratory wrote a captious book, intitled, The Falsity of Human Virtues. This genius says there is no such thing as virtue; but, at the close of every chapter, kindly refers his readers to Christian charity: so that, according to M. Esprit, neither Cato, nor Aristides, nor Marcus Aurelius, nor Epictetus, were good men; and a good reason why, these are only to be found among Christians. Again, among Christians the catholics are the only virtuous; and among the catholics the Jesuits, enemies to the Oratorians, should have been excepted; therefore there is scarce any virtue on earth but among the enemies of the Jesuits.

This Sieur Esprit sets out with saying that prudence is not a virtue; and his reason is, because it is often mistaken: which is as much as to say, Cæsar was nothing of a soldier because he had the worst of it at Dyrachium.

Had this reverend gentleman been a philosopher, he would not have treated of prudence as a virtue, but as a talent, a happy and useful quality; for a villain may be very prudent, and I have known

known such. The madness of pretending that virtue is the portion only of us and our partisans!

What is virtue, my friend? It is doing good. Do me some, and that is enough; as for your motive, that you may keep to yourself. How! According to you, there is no difference between the president de Thou and Ravaillac? between Cicero and that wretch Popilius, whose life he had saved, and who yet hired himself to cut off his head? You will pronounce Epictetus and Porphyry to be rascals, because they did not hold with our doctrines? Such insolence is quite shocking; but I have done, lest I grow warm.

FANATICISM.

FANATICISM is to superstition what a delirium is to a fever, and fury to anger: he who has extasies and visions, who takes dreams for realities, and his imaginations for prophecies, is an enthusiast; and he who sticks not at supporting his folly by murder, is a fanatic. Bartholomew Diaz, a fugitive at Nuremberg, who was firmly convinced that the pope is the Anti Christ in the Revelations, and that he has the mark of the beast, was only an enthusiast; whereas his brother, who set out from Rome with the godly intention of murdering him, and who actually did murder him for God's sake, was one of the most execrable fanatics that superstition could form.

Polieuctes, who, on a pagan festival, went into the temple, pulling down and breaking the images and other ornaments, shewed himself a fanatic, less horrible, indeed, than Diaz, but equally rash and imprudent. The murderers of Francis duke of Guise,

Guise, of William prince of Orange, of the kings Henry III. and Henry IV. and of so many others, were demoniacs, agitated by the same evil spirit as Diaz.

The most detestable instance of fanaticism is that of the citizens of Paris, who, on the feast of St. Bartholomew, could massacre their fellow-citizens, for not going to mass.

Some are fanatics in cool blood: these are the judges who can sentence people to death without any other guilt than for not being in their way of thinking: these judges are the more guilty, and the more deserving of universal execration, as not being under a fit of rage like the Clements, the Chatels, the Ravaillacs, the Gerards, the Damiens, one would think they might listen to reason.

When once fanaticism has touched the brain, the distemper is desperate. I have seen convulsionists, who, in speaking of the miracles of St. Paris, grew hot involuntarily; their eyes glared, they trembled in all their limbs, their countenance was quite disfigured with rancour, and they unquestionably would have killed any one who had contradicted them.

The only remedy to this infectious disease is a philosophical temper, which spreading through society, at length softens manners, and obviates the accesses of the distemper; for whenever it gets ground, the best way is to fly from it, and stay till the air be purified. The laws and religion are no preservative against this mental pestilence. Religion, so far from being a salutary aliment in these cases, in infected brains becomes poison. These unhappy creatures dwell continually on the example of Ehud, who assassinated king Eglon; of Judith, who cut off Holophernes's head when lying with him; and of Samuel hewing king Agag in pieces,

pieces. They are not aware that these instances, however respectable in antiquity, are abominable in our times: they foment their phrensy with religion, which absolutely condemns it.

The laws, likewise, have proved very ineffectual against this spiritual rage; it is, indeed, like reading an order of council to a lunatic. These creatures are firmly persuaded that the spirit by which they are actuated is above all laws, and that their enthusiasm is the only law they are to regard.

What can be answered to a person who tells you that he had rather obey God than men, and who, in consequence of that choice, is certain of gaining heaven by cutting your throat?

The leaders of fanatics, and who put the dagger into their hands, are usually designing knaves; they are like the old man of the mountain, who, according to history, gave weak persons a foretaste of the joys of paradise, promising them an eternity of such enjoyments, provided they would go and murder all those whom he should name to them. In the whole world, there has been but one religion clear of fanaticism, which is that of the Chinese literati. As to the sects of philosophers, instead of being infected with this pestilence, they were a ready and preservative against it: for the effect of philosophy is to compose the soul, and fanaticism is incompatible with tranquility. As to our holy religion having been so often corrupted by these infernal impulses, it is the folly of men that is to be blamed.

A PHILOSOPHICAL FRAUD.

Whether pious Frauds are allowable?

BAMBABEF, the Fakir, one day met a difciple of Confutſee, whom we call Confucius; and this diſciple's name was Ouang: Bambabef maintained that it is proper ſometimes to deceive the people, and Ouang inſiſted that we are never to deceive any one. The ſubſtance of their diſpute was as follows.

BAM. We are to imitate the Supreme Being, who does not ſhew us things as they are; he ſhews us the ſun in a diameter of only two or three feet, though that body be a million of times larger than the earth; he ſhews us the moon and the ſtars as fixed on one and the ſame blue ground, though they are at different and immenſe diſtances; he would have a ſquare tower appear round to us afar off; he would have the fire ſeem hot to us, though it be neither hot nor cold; in a word, he encompaſſes us with errors ſuitable to our nature.

Ou. What you call error is no ſuch thing. That ſun, which is placed millions of millions of *lis** from our globe, is not that ſun we ſee; we cannot have any real ſight but of the ſun which reflects itſelf on our retina in a determinate angle. Our eyes were not given us for the knowledge of dimenſions and diſtances; this requires other inſtruments and operations.

Bambabef ſtared at ſuch language; but Ouang, being endued with an uncommon patience, explained to him the theory of optics; and Bambabef,

---

* A *lis* ſignifies 124 paces.

having a clear head, acquiefced in the demonftrations produced by Confutfee's difciple, and then returned to the difpute in thefe terms.

BAM. If God does not deceive us by the medium of our fenfes, as I thought; you muft own, however; that phyficians always cheat children for their good; they will tell them they are giving them fugar, when, at the fame time, it is rhubarb, fo that I, as a Fakir, may deceive the people, they having no more knowledge or underftanding than children.

Ou. I have two fons, and never have I deceived them. When they are fick, I fay to them this phyfic is very bitter, but you muft pluck up a good heart and take it, the more bitter the more good will it do you; were it fweet it would hurt you: I never allowed their governeffes or preceptors to frighten them with ghofts and apparitions, with hobgoblins and wizards: and thus they are grown up to be brave and fenfible young men.

BAM. The common people are not born with the like happy talents and difpofitions as your family.

Ou. All men are alike, they are born with the fame propenfities; it is the Fakirs who vitiate human nature.

BAM. We do teach them errors, I own, but it is for their good; we make them believe that, if they do not buy of our confecrated nails, or expiate their fins by giving us money, they will, in the next world, be poft-horfes, dogs, or lizards. This terrifies them into goodnefs.

Ou. Are you not aware that this is perverting the poor people? Reafoning is not fo fcarce among them as is imagined; there are great numbers who reflect; who laugh at your nails, your miracles, your fuperftitions; and who know better than their being changed into lizards or poft-horfes. What is the confequence? They have fenfe to fee

that

that you preach up a sophisticated religion, but not enough to raise themselves to a pure religion, free from superstition and folly such as ours. Their passions lead them to believe there is nothing in religion; the only religion taught them being manifestly ridiculous; and thus you share in all the guilt into which they plunge themselves.

BAM. Not in the least; for we only teach them a good morality.

OU. You would get yourself stoned to death were you to preach a false morality; men are of such a make that amidst all their iniquity they will not bear the preaching of it to them: but absurd fables should not be intermixed with good morality; for thus, by your impostures, which might as well be suppressed, you weaken that morality, which, for self-preservation, you are obliged to teach.

BAM. How! do you imagine there is any such thing as teaching truth to the people without calling in fables?

OU. To be sure I do. Our literati are of the same texture as our taylors, weavers and farmers. They worship one God, the creator of all things, who rewards and punishes; their religion is not darkened with absurd systems, nor disfigured with fantastical ceremonies; and much less wickedness is there among the literati than among the common people. Wherefore then do you not condescend to instruct our artificers as we instruct our literati?

BAM. That would be idle indeed, as if they were to have all the good breeding and knowledge of a counsellor; that is neither possible nor proper. White bread for masters; and brown bread will go down with servants.

OU. All men, I own, should not have an equal stock of knowledge; but some points there are necessary

cessary to all: it is necessary that all men should be just; and the surest method to make men so, is to teach them pure religion, without any superstitions.

BAM. A specious scheme, only impracticable. Think you that for men to believe a rewarding and punishing God, will do the business? You say that the sensible part of the people are offended at my fables; and as little will they digest your bare truths; they will say, how am I certain that God punishes and rewards? Your proofs? Where is your mission? What miracles have you done for me to believe you? It is you they will flout at, and not me.

Ov. There lies your mistake. Because they reject dangerous absurdities, and fictions shocking to common sense, you fancy they will not admit a doctrine highly probable, conducive to virtue, productive of the greatest benefit to all mankind, and perfectly consonant with human reason?

The people are thoroughly inclined to refer to their magistrates: when the belief recommended by these is rational, they readily close with it. Miracles are not necessary to inforce a belief of a just God, to whom all hearts are open; the idea is too natural to be long opposed. To tell precisely how, and in what manner, God will punish and reward is out of the question. Believe him just, and that's enough; I assure you I have seen whole cities with scarce any other tenet, and no where have I observed so much virtue.

BAM. Fair and softly: those same cities swarm with philosophers, who deny both rewards and punishments.

Ov. You must withal own that those philosophers will much more peremptorily deny your inventions, so that makes but little on your side. As for philosophers differing from my principles,
they

they may still be good men, still as sedulous in the cultivation of virtue, which is to be embraced from love, and not out of fear. But I aver that no philosopher can ever be assured that Providence has not in store punishments for the wicked, and recompences for the good: for should they ask me; who told me that God punishes? my answer is, who told them that God does not punish? In short, the philosopher, I dare say, instead of opposing me would second me. Are you inclined to be a philosopher?

BAM. Very much so; but not a word of it to the Faquirs.

FRIENDSHIP.

FRIENDSHIP is a tacit contract between two sensible and virtuous persons, I say SENSIBLE; for a monk, a hermit, may not be wicked, yet live a stranger to friendship. I add VIRTUOUS, for the wicked have only accomplices, the voluptuous have companions, the designing have associates, the men of business have partners, the politicians form a factious band; the bulk of idle men have connections, princes have courtiers: but virtuous men alone have friends. Cethegus was Cataline's accomplice, and Mecenas was Octavius's courtier; but Cicero was Atticus's friend.

What is implied in this contract between two tender and ingenuous souls? Its obligations are stronger and weaker, according to their degree of sensibility, and the number of good offices performed, &c.

The enthusiasm of friendship was stronger among the Greeks and Arabs than among us. The tales on friendship composed by those people are admirable:

ble: we have nothing like them; in every thing we are somewhat dry and jejune.

Among the Greeks friendship was a point of religion, and an object of the legislation. The Thebans had a regiment called the regiment of lovers, and a fine regiment I dare say it was; some have mistaken it for a regiment of SODOMITES, but this is a gross error, taking an accessory for the principal. Among the Greeks friendship was recommended both by the law and religion. Unhappily their manners allowed of pederasty; but the law is not to be charged with any shameful abuses.

GLORY. (X)

BEN-AL-BETIF that worthy superior of the Dervises, one day said to them: Brethren, it is very fit, that you should often use that sacred form in our Koran, "in the name of the most merciful God," for God sheweth mercy, and you learn to practise it by the frequent repetition of words, recommending a virtue, without which there would be few people remaining on earth: but, brethren, far be it from you to imitate the presumption of those, who are continually boasting, that what they do is for the glory of God. When a raw scholar

---

(X) There is a good deal of quibble in this article. If by GLORY our author means addition of real power or greatness, it is certain, that the creature can make no such addition to the Creator. But this should not hinder us from expressing our gratitude for the favours received of the Supreme. This we are taught to do in sundry parts of scripture: thus the multitude of the heavenly host praised God, saying, Glory to God in the highest. To deny the propriety of giving glory to God in this sense betrays an ingratitude in man, and strikes at all external worship.

main-

maintains a thesis on the Categories before some furred ignoramus of a president, he is sure to write in large characters at the head of his thesis: Ek allha abron doxa, " Ad majorem Dei gloriam." So a devout mussulman, having caused his saloon to be white-washed, must have the like folly engraved over his door; a Saka likewise carries water to promote God's glory. This is a devout practice of a profane custom. What would you say of a pitiful Chiaoux, who, when emptying our Sultan's close-stool should bawl out, To the greater glory of our invincible monarch? Now certainly the difference is greater between the Sultan and God, than between the pitiful Chiaoux and the sublime Sultan.

Ye poor earth-worms, called men, what have you in common with the glory of the infinite essence? can he desire glory, can he receive any from you? Can he enjoy it? How long, ye two-legged featherless animals, will you make God in your likeness! being your selves vain and fond of glory, God must needs be so too! Were there several Gods, each of them would be desirous of the applause of his equals, and in that would consist the glory of a God. If infinite grandeur might be brought into a comparison with the extremity of meanness, such a God would be like king Alexander or Scander, who would enter the list against kings only: but you, poor creatures, what glory can you give to God? Forbear any longer to profane his sacred name. An emperor, named Octavius Augustus, ordered no panegyrics to be made on him in the schools of Rome, that his name might not be debased. But you can neither debase, nor exalt the Supreme Being. Prostrate yourselves, and worship in silence.

Thus spoke Ben-al-bétif, and the Dervises shouted. Glory to God! well has Ben-al-bétif spoken.

GOD.

GOD.

IN the reign of Arcadius, **Logomacos**, a theologue of Constantinople, went into Scythia, and stopped at the foot of mount Caucasus in the fertile plains of Zephirim, bordering on Colchis. The good old man Dondindac was, after a light repast, kneeling in his large hall between his vast sheepfold and his ample barn, with his wife, his five sons and five daughters, some of his kindred and his domestics, all chanting the praises of the bounteous giver of all good things. Ho! what art thou about, idolater, said Logomacos to him? I am no idolater, said Dondindac. An idolater thou must be, said **Logomacos**, as being a Scythian, or at least no Greek. Well, and what wast thou gabbling in thy Scythian jargon? All languages are alike in God's ear, answered the Scythian; we were singing his praises. Very extraordinary indeed, replied the theologue, a Scythian family worshipping God without any previous instruction from us! He soon entered into a conversation with Dondindac, for the theologue had a smattering of the Scythian, and the other understood a little Greek. This conversation is lately come to light in a manuscript kept in the Imperial library at Constantinople.

Log. I will see whether thou knowest thy catechism; why prayest thou to God?

Don. Because it is just and proper to worship the Supreme Being, as of him we hold all we have.

Log. Pretty well for a barbarian: and what askest thou of him?

Don. I thank God for the good things he gives me, and even for the crosses with which he tries me.

me. But as for asking him any thing, that's what I never presume to do; he knows what we stand in need of better than ourselves; besides, I should be afraid to ask for sun-shine, when rain would better suit my neighbour.

Log. Ah! I apprehended we should soon have some nonsense or other from him. Let us take a retrospect of things: who told thee there is a God?

Don. All nature.

Log. That's nothing; what idea hast thou of God?

Don. That he is my creator, my master, who will reward me if I do well, and punish me if I do amiss.

Log. That is but trivial and low; let us come to the essential. Is God infinite " secundum quid," or in his essence?

Don. I don't understand you.

Log. Stupid dolt! is God in a place, or out of all place, or is he every where?

Don. I know nothing of that; it may be just as you please.

Log. Ignorant wretch! Well; can he make what has been not to have been, or that a stick shall not have two ends? Is futurity to him as future or as present? How does he do to bring nothing into existence, and to annihilate existence?

Don. I never bestow a thought on those things.

Log. What an oaf is this! well, I must let myself down, I must suit myself to the meanness of his intellects. Tell me, friend, believest thou that matter can be eternal?

Don. What is it to me whether it exists from eternity or not? I did not exist from eternity. God is always my master and instructor. He has given me the knowledge of justice, and it is my duty to

act

act accordingly. I do not defire to be a philofo-pher, let me be a man.

Log. What a plague it is to have to do with fuch thick-headed creatures. I muft proceed gradually with him? What is God?

Don. My fovereign, my judge, my father.

Log. That's not what I afk you; what is his nature?

Don. To be powerful and good.

Log. But whether is he corporeal or fpiritual?

Don. How fhould I know.

Log. What! not know what a fpirit is!

Don. Not I in the leaft, and what fhould I be the better for fuch knowledge? Will it mend my morals, make me a better hufband, a better father, better mafter, or better member of fociety?

Log. A man muft be abfolutely taught what a fpirit is, fince it is, it is, it is —— well, we will let that alone till another time.

Don. I fancy, inftead of being able to tell me what it is, you will rather tell me what it is not. But after fo much queftioning, may I take the freedom to afk you a queftion? I was formerly in one of your temples, and why do you paint God with a long beard?

Log. That is a very abftrufe queftion, and the folution of which would be above your comprehenfion, without fome preliminary inftructions.

Don. Before you enter on your inftructions, I muft tell you a circumftance, which I hope never to forget. I had juft built a fummer-houfe at the end of my garden; and one day fitting in it, heard a mole and a chafer defcanting on it: A fuperb edifice it certainly is, faid the mole, and of very great parts muft that mole have been who built it. A mole forfooth! I fay a mole too! quoth the chafer; the architect of that pretty building could be no other than some chafer of an extraordinary genius This colloquy put me on a resolution never to dispute.

GOVERNMENTS,
Which the best?

I Never yet knew any man who had not governed some state or other. I do not speak of their High Mightinesses the ministers, who govern in reality, some two or three years, others six months, and others as many weeks; I mean all other men, who over a bottle, or in their closet, display their system of government, and reform navy, army, law, finances, and church.

Abbé Bourzeis took upon himself to govern France about the year 1645 under the name of cardinal Richelieu, and composed that Political Will, in which he is for having the nobility enrolled in the cavalry for three years, the land tax to be paid to the chambers of accounts and the parliament, and taking away from the king the produce of the salt-tax: in order to take the field with 50,000 men, he makes it a point of œconomy to raise 100,000. He affirms, that " Provence alone has many more " fine sea-ports than Spain and Italy put together."

This ecclesiastical schemer had not travelled. Besides, his work swarms with anachronisms and errors. As he makes cardinal Richelieu speak what he never did speak, so his signature is no less different from that of the cardinal. Farther, he fills a whole chapter with saying, that " reason is to be the rule " of a state;" and in labouring to prove such a notable discovery. This work of darkness, this bantling of the abbé Bourzeis passed a long time for cardinal Richelieu's legitimate offspring, and all the academicians in their inauguration speeches never failed to pour forth the most excessive elogiums on this master-piece of policy.

One St. Gratien de Courtils, seeing the great success of cardinal Richelieu's Political Legacy, fell to writing Colbert's Legacy, with a fine letter to the king: whereas had that minister drawn up such will, he ought to have been declared NON COMPOS; yet have some authors thought fit to quote this composition. Another starveling, too mean to be known, published Louvois's Will, which, if such a thing could be, was still worse than Colbert's; and by the fertile brain of one abbé de Chevremont, duke Charles of Lorrain likewise had his Will. We have also had the political testaments of cardinal Alberoni, marshal Belleisle, and lastly, that of Mandrin.

M. de Boisguilbert, author of *le Detail de la France*, printed in 1695, troubled the public with the impracticable project of the regal tenths, under the name of marshal Vauban.

One Jonchere, a crazy fellow who had not bread to eat, met with a bookseller who published a scheme of his on the finances in four volumes; and some blockheads have quoted this production as a work of the treasurer-general, on a notion that a book of finances, written by a treasurer, must be a choice piece.

It must, however, be owned that very wise men, and men perhaps every way qualified for government, have in France, in Spain, and in England, written on political administration. And great good have their books done; not that they have amended the ministers who were in place when those books came out; for a minister never amends, there is no changing him; he has taken his bent; and for informations and counsels, the stream of business carries him away so as not leave leisure to listen to them:

them: but young persons designed for employments, and princes themselves are instructed by these good books; and thus the second generation reaps the benefit of them.

The advantages and disadvantages of all governments have of late been closely canvassed. Now you who have travelled, and read, and seen a great deal, pray, in which state, and under what form of government would you chuse to be born? I fancy a French nobleman with a large landed estate would not be sorry to have been born in Germany, as there, instead of being a subject, he would be a sovereign. A peer of France doubtless would be very glad to have the privileges of the English peerage, as raising him to a share in the legislature.

For the lawyer and the financier, France is the country which of all others brings the most grist to their mill.

But what country would a wise man, of a free turn of mind, unprejudiced, and of a middling fortune, make choice of?

A member of the council of Pondicherry, a gentleman of some learning, was returning into Europe over land, in company with a Bramin, who knew more than most of his brethren. How do you like the Grand Mogul's government, said the counsellor? Nothing more abominable, answered the Bramin; but how can a state be well governed by Tartars? If our Rayas, our Omrahs, our Nabobs, are entirely satisfied and easy; it is otherwise with the people, and millions of people are something.

The counsellor and the Bramin traversed all Upper Asia, amidst political conversations. An observation occurs to me, said the Bramin, that all this vast part of the world does not afford one republic. Here was, antiently, that of Tyre, said the

the counsellor, but it did not continue long: then there was another towards Arabia Petrea, in a small nook called Palestine, if the honourable appellation of republic may be given to a tribe of robbers and usurers, sometimes governed by judges, sometimes by a sort of kings, sometimes by high-priests, subdued and enslaved seven or eight times, and, at last, driven out of the country which it had usurped.

I apprehend, said the Bramin, that republics are very scarce in all parts; it is but seldom that men deserve to govern themselves. This happiness must belong only to small nations, concealing themselves in islands, or amidst mountains, like rabbits shunning carnivorous beasts, but at length discovered and devoured.

The two travellers being come into Asia Minor, the counsellor said to the Bramin, Could you think there had ever been a republic in a corner of Italy, which subsisted above five hundred years, and made itself mistress of this Asia Minor, Asia, Africa, Greece, the Gauls, Spain, and all Italy? I dare say, it soon became changed to a monarchy, said the Bramin. Very right, said the other; but that monarchy is long since come to nothing, and every day fine dissertations are composed to find out the causes of its declension and catastrophe. You give yourselves a deal of needless trouble, said the Indian; that empire fell because it existed: every thing will fall; I hope in God the empire of the great mogul will one day have its fall.

Now we are upon this head, said the European, do you think honour is most necessary in a monarchy, and virtue in a republic? The Indian, after the meaning of the word honour had, at his desire, been explained to him, answered that honour was of greater necessity in a republic and virtue in a monarchy: For, says he, a man who sets up to be chosen by the people will not be chosen, if he be reputed a man of no honour; whereas at court he may easily insinuate himself into a post, according to the maxim of a great prince, that a courtier to make his fortune should be without honour or pride. As to virtue, an immense deal of it is requisite to dare speak truth at court; a virtuous man is much more at ease in a republic; there's nobody to flatter.

Is it your opinion, said the native of Europe, that the laws and religions are made for the climates, as furs suit Moscow, and gauze stuffs Delly? To be sure, said the Bramin, all laws relative to the human constitution are calculated for the climate where one lives; one wife will do for a German, a Persian must have three or four.

It is the same with religious rites. Were I a Christian, how could I say mass in my province, which affords neither bread nor wine? As to articles of faith, that's another case; in these the climate is out of the question. Did not your religion commence in Asia, from whence it has been expelled? and again, is it not established about the Baltic Sea, where it was once unknown?

In what state, under what government should you like best to live? said the counsellor. Any where but in my own country, said his companion; and many Siamese, Tunquinese, Persians, and Turks have I met with, who said the very same thing. But tell me, in what particular state you would preferably like to spend your days. The Bramin answered, In that where obedience is paid only to the laws. That's an old answer, said the counsellor. And never the worse for that, said the Bramin. But where is that country, said the Pondicherrian? It must be sought for, said the Bramin.

GRACE.

GRACE.

YE sacred counsellors of modern Rome, ye illustrious and infallible theologists, no person has more respect for your decisions than myself; but were Paulus Emilius, Scipio, Cato, Cicero, Cæsar, Titus, Trajan, and Marcus Aurelius to revisit that Rome which they formerly raised to some consideration, you must own they would be a little staggered at your determinations concerning grace. What would they say to your debates on St. Thomas's grace of health, on Cajetan's medicinal grace, on external and internal grace, on gratuitous, sanctifying, actual, habitual, co-operating grace, on effectual grace which is sometimes ineffectual, on sufficient grace often insufficient, on versatile and congruous grace; sincerely, would they understand it more than yourselves or I?

Those illustrious personages would be quite at a loss without your sublime instructions: I think I hear them say,

Reverend fathers, you are stupendous geniuses; we foolishly conceived the eternal Being never to be guided by particular laws like mean mortals, but by his own general laws, eternal like himself. It never came into any of our heads that God was like a brain-sick master, giving a comfortable farm to one slave, and denying necessary food to another; ordering one slave without a hand to knead dough, a dumb slave to read to him, and a cripple to be his courier.

Every thing from God is grace: by his grace the globe which we dwell in was formed; by his grace the trees grow, and animals are nourished: but if a wolf finds a lamb in his way to make a good meal

meal of, and another wolf is famishing, will any one say that God has shewn particular grace to the former wolf? has he by a preventing grace been busied in causing one oak to grow preferably to another oak, which has withered for want of sap? If all beings throughout all nature are subject to general laws, how can any single species of creatures be exempt from those laws?

Why should the absolute master of all have been more intent on disposing the inside of one man alone (Y), than in conducting all the other parts of nature? From what humour or fickleness

---

(Y) Our author may be right in ridiculing the opinions of schoolmen concerning grace, as they abound in fantastical niceties altogether unintelligible. But whatever Marcus Aurelius may say, a Christian is bound to believe that without the grace of God by Christ, we have no power to do good works, pleasant and acceptable to the Deity. As to the above question, Why should the absolute master of all have been more intent on disposing the inside of one man alone, than in conducting all the other parts of nature? it shews our author to be ignorant of the doctrine of continual providence, as he indeed is of many other sound doctrines. The infinitely wise Being cannot but know every thing that is done in every part of the universe, and with equal ease take notice of the minutest things as of the greatest: but it is a mistake to believe him more intent upon one thing than upon another; and it is only according to our weak conceptions that we say, God takes more particular notice of the moral actions of his rational creatures. M. Voltaire labours very hard on all occasions to represent man as a vile worm unworthy of the care of the Deity, not reflecting that such a care is attended with no difficulty in the supreme creator of all things. Besides, how inconsiderable soever man may be, yet he is the chief, and indeed, the only inhabitant, for whose sake our earthly globe was formed into a habitable world; and this earth of ours, as Dr. Clarke observes, for aught we know, is as considerable, and worthy of the divine care, as any other part of the system, and this system as considerable as any other system in the universe.

should

should he make any alteration in the heart of a Courlander or a Biscayan, when he is seen not to make the least alteration in the laws, which he has impressed on all the heavenly bodies?

How weak is it to suppose that he is continually making, unmaking, and remaking sentiments in us! and what presumption is it to think ourselves privileged above all other beings! farther, it is only for those who observe confession that all these mutations are invented. A Savoyard or native of Bergamo shall, on Monday, have the grace to bestow twelve sous to have a mass said; on Tuesday grace will fail him, and he will go to the tavern; on Wednesday he shall have co-operating grace, which will send him away to confession, but without the efficacious grace of perfect contrition; Thursday it will be a sufficient grace, which will prove insufficient. God shall be continually at work in the head of this Savoyard, sometimes forcibly, other times weakly, without minding any other thing upon earth, without caring what becomes of the inside of the Indians and Chinese. Really, my reverend fathers, if you have a spark of reason left, does not this system appear to you prodigiously ridiculous?

Wretches, behold that oak towering to the clouds, look down on that rush bending at its feet; you will not say that efficacious grace has been given to the oak, and denied to the rush. Lift up your eyes to the heavens, see the eternal Demiurgus creating millions of worlds, all gravitating towards each other by general and eternal laws. Behold the same light reflected from the sun to Saturn, and from Saturn to us; and amidst this harmony of so many luminous bodies in a course amazingly rapid, amidst this general obedience of all nature, I defy you to believe that God minds giving a verſatile grace to ſiſter Thereſa, and a concomitant grace to ſiſter Agnes.

Thou atom, to whom a ſtupid atom has ſaid that the Eternal has particular laws for ſome atoms in thy neighbourhood; that he gives his grace to this, and refuſes it to that; and that which has not grace to day ſhall have it to morrow; never let ſuch impious folly come from thy lips. God has created the univerſe, and does not concern himſelf about making new winds to ſhake ſome bits of ſtraw in a corner of that univerſe. Theologiſts are like Homer's warriors, who thought that the gods ſometimes fought on their ſide, and ſometimes againſt them. Homer is to be conſidered as a poet, otherwiſe we make him a blaſphemer.

Theſe are Marcus Aurelius's words, not mine; for God, who inſpires you, has given me grace to believe all you ſay, all you have ſaid, and all you ſhall ſay.

The HEAVENS (Z),

Or Sky, according to the Antients.

A Silk worm might as well give the name of heaven to the little down which ſurrounds its ſhell, as the antients gave that appellation to the

---

(Z) In this article our author diſplays ſome erudition, but he is very reprehenſible, when he ſays, "There is properly no heaven." By heaven we mean not the air, nor the ſtars nor planets, nor the vaſt expanſe in which thoſe great orbs perform their motions, but the ſeat or manſion of the bleſſed. Where that is we cannot pretend to determine, but we are bound to believe there is ſuch a place. In this ſenſe we ſay,

the atmosphere, which, as M. Fontenelle in his Plurality of Worlds, prettily says, is the down of our shell.

The vapours which exhale from our seas and land, and form clouds, meteors, and thunder, were at first taken for the residence of the gods. Homer always brings down the deities in golden clouds; and thence it is that our painters still represent them seated on a cloud: but it being very proper that the master of the gods should live in greater state than the others, he was provided with an eagle to carry him, the eagle flying higher than any other bird.

The antient Greeks seeing that princes lived in citadels built on the top of some mountain, conceived that the gods might likewise have their citadel, and placed it in Thessalia on mount Olympus, the summit of which is sometimes hid in the clouds, so that their palace was even with their heaven.

Afterwards the stars and planets which seemed fixed to the azure arch of our atmosphere, became the mansion of deities; seven of whom had their respective planet, the others taking up with what quarter they could find; the general council of the gods was held in a large saloon, to which they went by the milky way; for men having council-chambers on earth, the gods, to be sure, should have one in the heavens.

---

say, "Our father, who art in heaven." To say absolutely there is no heaven, subverts the notion of a future state, and the consolation of the just from the expectation of eternal happiness. This our author cannot intend, as in more places than one he acknowledges a place of future rewards and punishments.

When the Titans, a kind of creatures between the gods and men, declared war, and not without some grounds against those deities, to recover part of their inheritance, (being on the father's side the sons of Cœlum and Terra,) they only heaped two or three mountains one on the other, concluding, that would be full enough for them to reduce the citadel of Olympus, together with the heavens,

> Neve foret terris fecurior arduus æther,
> Affectâffe ferunt regnum cœlefte gigantes,
> Altaque congeftos ftruxiffe ad fidera montes.

This abfurd fyftem of phyfics was of prodigious antiquity; yet certain it is, that the Chaldeans had as juft ideas of what is called the heavens as we ourfelves. They placed the fun in the centre of our planetary world, and nearly at the fame diftance we have found it to be; and they held the revolution of the earth, and of all the planets round that body: this we are informed of by Ariftarchus of Samos; and it is the true fyftem of the world, fince revived by Copernicus. But the philofophers, to be the more refpected by fovereigns and people, or rather to avoid being perfecuted, kept the fecret to themfelves.

The language of error is fo familiar to men, that we ftill give the name of heavens to our vapours, and to the fpace between the earth and moon: we fay to go up to heaven, as we fay the fun turns round, though we know it does not; probably we are the heaven to the moon, and every planet makes the neighbouring planet its heaven. Had Homer been afked to which heaven the foul of Sarpedo went, and where that of Hercules was, the poet would have been a little puzzled, and eluded the queftion by fome harmonious verfes.

What

What certainty was there that the aerial foul of Hercules would have had a better time of it in Venus, or Saturn, than on our globe? it is not to be fuppofed that its refidence was appointed in the fun; the place would have been too hot. After all, what did the antients mean by the heavens? They knew nothing of the matter; they were perpetually bawling HEAVEN and EARTH, which is juft as much as to cry infinitude and an atom. Properly fpeaking, there is no fuch thing as the heavens; there is a prodigious number of vaft globes rolling in the void expanfe, and our globe rolls like the others.

The antients thought that the way to the heavens was by afcent: no fuch thing; the celeftial globes are fometimes above our horizon, and fometimes below: thus, fuppofing Venus was returning from Paphos to her planet after its fetting, the goddefs, relatively to our horizon, inftead of going up went down; and in fuch a cafe we ought to fay to go down to heaven. But the antients were not fo nice; their notions in every thing relating to natural philofophy were vague, uncertain, and contradictory. Immenfe volumes have been written to know what their opinion was on many fuch queftions; whereas five words would have done, "they never thought of it."

Here, however, we muft except a few wife men; but they came late: few opened their minds freely, and thofe who did, the empyrics on earth took care to difpatch them to heaven the fhorteft way.

A writer, I think his name is Pluche, has pretended to make Mofes a great natural philofopher; another before him, in a piece called Cartefius Mozaizans had reconciled Mofes with Defcartes. According to him, Mofes firft found out the vortices and the fubtile matter; but it is well known that

that God meant Moses for a great legislator and a great prophet, and not for a professor of physics; he instructed the Jews in their duty, and not a word in philosophy. Calmet, who has compiled a vast 'deal, and never once reflected, talks of the system of the Hebrews; but so far was that rude people from having a system, that they had not so much as a geometry-school; the bare name was unknown to them, all they understood was brokerage and usury.

In their books we meet with some vague incoherent ideas on the structure of the heavens, and such as shew them to have been a dull illiterate people. Their first heaven was the air, the second the firmament, to which the stars were fastened. This firmament was solid and of ice, and supported the upper waters, which, at the time of the deluge, made their way out of this reservoir, thro' gates, sluices, and cataracts.

Over this firmament, or these upper waters, was the third heaven or the EMPYREUM, to which St. Paul was caught up. The firmament was a kind of demi-arch round the earth. They little thought of the sun moving round a globe, whose form they were ignorant of. When it got to the west, it had some unknown path for returning to the east; and as to its not being seen, baron Feneste accounts for that, by saying it came back in the night.

Farther, these whimsical ideas the Hebrews had borrowed from other nations, of whom, except the Chaldean school, the greater part looked on the heavens as solid; the earth was fixed and immoveable, and by a third longer from east to west than from south to north, whence are derived our geographical terms longitude and latitude. This opinion, it is evident, admitted no antipodes;

accord-

accordingly, St. Auftin calls the notion of antipodes an abfurdity; and Lactantius flatly fays, "Are there any fo foolifh as to believe there are men whofe head is lower than their feet?"

St. Chryfoftom, in his fourteenth homily, calls out, "Where are they who fay the heavens are moveable, and their form round?"

Lactantius again fays, b. iii. of his Inftitutions, "I could prove to you by a multitude of arguments, that it is impoffible the heavens fhould encompafs the earth."

The author of Spectacle de la Nature is welcome to tell the chevalier over and over, that Lactantius and Chryfoftom were eminent philofophers; ftill it will be anfwered that they were great faints, which they may be without any acquaintance with aftronomy. We believe them to be in heaven, but own that in what part of the heavens they are we know not.

HELL.

WHEN men came to live in fociety, they could not but perceive, that many evil doers efcaped the feverity of the laws: thefe could affect only open crimes; fo that a curb was wanting againft clandeftine guilt, and religion alone could be fuch a curb. The Perfians, the Chaldeans, the Egyptians, and the Greeks, introduced a belief of punifhments after this life; and of all antient nations we are acquainted with, the Jews alone admitted only temporal punifhments. It is ridiculous to believe, or to pretend to believe from fome very obfcure paffages, that the antient Jewifh laws, their Leviticus, and their Decalogues correfpond with the doctrine of future punifhments; when the author

author of those laws says not a single word which bears any relation to that doctrine. One might justly say to the compiler of the Pentateuch: you are inconsistent with yourself; you have no more judgment than probity; you a legislator, as you stile yourself! How! you conscious of a tenet so coercive, so powerful, so necessary to people as that of hell, and yet not make it known explicitly, nor urge it? and though received among all the nations round about you, you leave so momentous a doctrine to be guessed at by some commentators, who are not to come into existence till four thousand years after your time, and will wrest and distort some of your words to find in them what you never said? Either you are an ignoramus, who don't know that this was the universal belief in Egypt, in Chaldea, and Persia; or a very weak man, if being acquainted with this doctrine you did not make it the basis of your religion.

The very best answer the authors of the Jewish laws could make, is this: we own ourselves extremely ignorant; it was very late before we learned to write; our people, a savage and barbarous tribe, which, by our own accounts, wandered for near half a century amidst deserts, at length by the most heinous violences, and the most detestable cruelties ever mentioned in history, seized on a small territory: we had no intercourse with policed nations; then how could we (the most earthly minded of all men) invent a system entirely spiritual?

We used the word answering to SOUL only to signify LIFE; we thought God and his angels to be corporeal beings: the distinction of soul and body, the idea of a life after death, can be only the result of long meditation, and refined philosophy. Ask the Hottentots and Negroes, whose country is a hundred times larger than ours, whether they

know

know any thing of a future life? We thought we had done wonders in perfuading our people that God punifhed evil-doers to the fourth generation, either by the leprofy, a fudden death, or the lofs of what little fubftance a perfon might have poffeffed.

To this apology, it may be replied: you have invented a fyftem palpably ridiculous; for the evildoer, who was in health, and whofe family profpered, muft neceffarily laugh at you.

The apologift of the Jewifh law would then rejoin: that is your miftake; for among us where one delinquent reafoned rightly, a hundred did not reafon at all. He who on the commiffion of a crime, found no punifhment declaring itfelf againft him nor his fon, ftill feared for his grandfon. Farther, though to-day he had no putrid ulcer on him, to which by the by we were very fubject, it was odds within fome years it happened not to be his cafe; no family is without misfortunes and afflictions, and we brought the people to believe that thefe misfortunes were fent by a divine hand, punifhing fecret tranfgreffions.

This anfwer admits of an eafy reply: your excufe will not hold water; for every day we fee very good people feized with ficknefs, and by one misfortune or other deprived of their fubftance; now if there be no family totally free from all misfortunes, and if thefe misfortunes are divine chaftifements, all the individuals of your families were then knaves and profligates.

The Jewifh prieft might farther reply, that there are misfortunes annexed to human nature, and others fent exprefsly by God. But this reafoner's mouth might foon be ftopped, by fhewing the extreme abfurdity of thinking, that ficknefs and hail are fometimes a divine punifhment, and fometimes a natural effect.

At length the Pharisees and the Essenes among the Jews admitted the belief of a hell in their way: This dogma the Greeks had already disseminated among the Romans, and the Christians made it a capital article of faith.

Several fathers of the church did not hold the eternity of hell torments; they thought it very hard that a poor man should be burning for ever and ever only for stealing a goat. Virgil might as well have held his tongue as to say in his sixth canto in the Eneid (A),

> Sedet æternumque sedebit infelix Theseus.

His IPSE DIXIT, that Theseus is seated in a chair, where he must sit world without end, and that this posture is his punishment, is protested against by many; who farther think the poet to have wronged him greatly, as rather deserving a place in the Elysian fields, than in Tartarus.

Not long since an honest well meaning huguenot minister advanced in his sermons, and even in print, that there would be a day of grace to the damned; that there must be a proportion between the trespass and the penalty; and that a momentary fault could not deserve an everlasting punishment. This clement judge was deposed by a body of mi-

---

(A) The wisest of the heathen philosophers, without the help of revelation, did believe it agreeable to right reason, that the punishment of the incorrigible should be αἰώνιος, without any determinate or known end. See Plato in Phæd. This however, we may be certain of, says the learned Dr. Clarke, that the degrees or intenseness of the punishment which shall be inflicted on the impenitent, will be exactly proportionate to their sins, as a recompence of their demerit, so that no man shall suffer more than he has deserved.

nisters,

nisters, of whom one said to him: Brother, I as little believe the eternity of hell torments as yourself; but let me tell you it is very proper that your servant-maid, your taylor, and even your attorney should believe so.

HISTORY

Of the Kings of Judah and the Chronicles.

(B) ALL nations have written their history, as soon as they ever knew what writing was; the Jews have also written theirs. Before they had kings they lived under a theocracy, and were reputed to be governed by God himself.

When the Jews clamoured to have a king, like the other neighbouring nations, the prophet Sa-

---

(B) Under this article our author advances a very bold assertion, though with great appearance of diffidence, viz. that the books of Kings and the Chronicles, are not a part of Holy Writ. He is certainly mistaken; they were always reckoned both by Jews and Christians among the canonical books, and therefore are of the same weight as the other parts of Scripture, of whose divine authority the church never entertained any doubt. As for any contradictions between the books of Kings and Chronicles, it is a bare assertion, unsupported by proof. There may be difficulties in regard to chronology, the solution of which the reader will find in the writings of our learned expositors. His arguments are so weak as to deserve no serious refutation; for surely the divine authority of a history does not suppose it to be a relation of divine actions, otherwise no historical part of scripture whatever would be divine; the actions of bad as well as good princes are recorded in Holy Writ, to the end that we make the former an object of our abhorrence, the latter of our imitation. It is, therefore, a most insolent conclusion to say, that if the holy spirit dictated this history, he did not chuse a very edifying subject.

muel, whose iuterest it was to exclude a regal government, declared to them, in the name of God, that it was God himself whom they were rejecting. Thus the beginning of monarchy among the Jews was the period of their theocracy.

It may be therefore said without blasphemy, that the history of the Jewish kings was written like that of other nations; and that God did not trouble himself to dictate the history of a people whom he no longer governed.

This opinion, however, is advanced with all possible mistrust and deference. What may be thought a confirmation of it is, that the Paralipomena or Chronicles, very often contradict the book of Kings both in the chronology and the events, as profane histories are known to disagree. Farther, if God continued to write the history of the Jews, we are of course to believe, that he still writes it; the Jews being still his favourite people. They are one day to be converted, and, apparently they may as justly look upon the history of their dispersion to be of divine composition, as to say that God wrote the history of their kings.

Another remark likewise offers itself: if God, after having been their sole king for a very long time, condescended to be their historian, it becomes us to entertain the most profound respect for all Jews universally; the very meanest Jewish pedlar is infinitely above Cæsar and Alexander. Shall we not prostrate ourselves before an old cloath's man, who proves to you that his history was written by the deity himself, whilst all the Greek and Roman histories are but the productions of profane pagans?

If the stile of the history of the book of Kings and Chronicles be divine, it does not necessarily follow that the actions related in those histories are also divine. David murders Uriah; Isbosheth and
Me-

Mephibosheth are murdered; Absalom murders Ammon; Joab murders Absalom; Solomon murders Adonijah, his brother; Baza murders Nabab; Zimri murders Ela; Hamri murders Zimri; Ahab murders Naboth; Jehu murders Ahab and Joram; the inhabitants of Jerusalem murder Amaziah, Joash's son; Selom the son of Jabes murders Zachariah the son of Jeroboam; Manahaim murders Selom the son of Jabes; Phaceus the son of Romeli murders Phaceia the son of Manahaim; Hoshea the son of Ela murders Phaceus the son of Romeli; with a multitude of other murders of less note. Thus it must be owned, if the holy spirit did write this history, he has not chosen a very edifying subject.

IDOL, IDOLATER, IDOLATRY (C).

IDOL comes from the Greek εἶδος, a figure, EIDOLOS, the representation of a figure, LATREUEIN, to serve, to revere, to adore. The word adore

---

(C) This article of idols is a strong attack against the Roman Catholic worship of images; and the author seems to justify Dr. Middleton's treatise upon the Romish ceremonies. He displays his erudition in treating this subject; but surely he is fond of paradox, when he maintains that neither the Greeks nor Romans, nor indeed no other nation, were idolaters. The point is not to know what might be the private opinion of a few philosophers, but what was the practice of those nations in their external forms of religious worship. Now it must be running counter to all antiquity, to affirm that the honours paid by those people to the statues and images of their god, were not rank idolatry. To say that the Roman Catholics do the same is not answering the question: he may represent those of his own religion (if he can be said

adore is originally Latin, and has various meanings; as to put the hand to the mouth in token of respect, to bend the body, to kneel, to salute, and more commonly to pay a supreme worship.

It is proper to observe here, that the Trevoux dictionary begins this article with saying that all the Pagans were idolaters, and that the Indians are still so. First, no body was called Pagan before the time of Theodosius the younger, when that appellation was given to the inhabitants of the country-towns of Italy, " Pagorum incolæ Pagani," who retained their antient religion. Secondly, Indostan is entirely Mahometan, and the Mahometans are implacable enemies to images and idolatry. Thirdly, many people of India, who are of the antient religion of the Parsis, a certain tribe which admit of no idols, cannot, with any propriety, be termed idolaters.

Whether IDOLATRY was ever the Professed Religion of any Nation.

It appears that there never was any people on the earth, who took to themselves the name of idolaters. It is rather an abusive word, a term of detestation; as the Spaniards formerly used to call the French GAVACHOS, which the French returned by calling the Spaniards MARANAS. Had the senate of Rome, the Areopagus of Athens, the court of the kings of Persia, been asked, " Are you idolaters? They would hardly have known what the question meant; at least not one of them would have answered, " We worship " idols or images." The word idolater or idolatry do not occur either in Homer, Hesiod, He-

---

said to have any) as guilty of idolatry; but this does not prove that the others were not also idolaters,

rodotus,

rodotus, or any gentile author. Never was there any edict or law, ordering idols to be worshipped, to be accounted as deities, or to be considered as such.

The Roman and Carthaginian generals, at the making of a treaty, called all their gods to witness; it is in their presence, say they, that we swear to this peace. Now the statues of all these gods, their number being none of the smallest, were not in the general's tent; but they held the gods to be, as it were, present at the actions of men as witnesses and as judges; and certainly it was not the image which made the deity.

In what light did they then look on the statues of their false deities, which stood in the temples? In the same light, if I may be allowed the expression, as we view the images of the objects of our veneration. Their error was not the worshipping a piece of wood or marble, but the worshipping a false deity, represented by the wood and marble. The difference between them and us is not that they had images and we have none; but that their images represented imaginary beings, and in a false religion; whereas ours represent real beings, and in a true religion. The Greeks had the statue of Hercules; and we that of St. Christopher; they had Esculapius and his goat, and we St. Roch and his dog; they had Jupiter with his thunder-bolts, and we St. Anthony of Padua, and St. James of Compostella.

When the consul Pliny in the exordium of his Panegyric on Trajan, addresses his petitions to the IMMORTAL GODS, he cannot be thought to mean the images, which were far from being immortal.

Neither in the later nor the most remote times of paganism, one single fact occurs to conclude that they worshipped idols. Homer mentions only gods dwelling in lofty Olympus. The palladium, tho' it fell from heaven, was no more than a sacred pledge of Pallas's protection; it was the goddess herself who was reverenced in the palladium.

But the Romans and Greeks kneeled down before statues, put crowns on them, decked them with flowers, burnt incense to them, and carried them in solemn state through public places. These usages we have consecrated in our religion, and yet we are not idolaters.

In times of drought the women, after keeping a fast, carried forth the statues of the gods in public, walking barefooted, with their hair loose; and immediately, according to Petronius, the rain would pour down by pales full, " statim urceatim " pluebat." Have we not adopted this rite which, though an abomination among the Gentiles, is doubtless genuine devotion with Catholics? How common is it among us to carry barefooted the shrines of saints, in order to obtain a blessing from heaven by their intercession? A Turk, a lettered Chinese, at seeing those ceremonies, might, from his ignorance, accuse us of placing our confidence in the images which we thus carry about in procession; but a word or two would undeceive him.

We are surprised at the prodigious number of declamations thundered out in all ages against the idolatry of the Romans and Greeks; and afterwards, our surprize is still greater, at finding that they were not idolaters.

Some temples were more privileged than others. The great Diana of Ephesus stood in higher fame than a village Diana; more miracles were performed in the temple of Esculapius at Epidaurus than in any other of his temples. More offerings were made to the statue of Jupiter the Olympian, than to that of the Paphlagonian Jupiter: but since it is proper always to contrast the usages of a

true

true religion to those of a false worship; have not some of our altars, for ages past, been more frequented than others? what are the offerings to our lady DES NEIGES in comparison of those made to our lady of Loretto? It is our business to examine whether this affords a just pretence for charging us with idolatry.

The original invention was only one Diana, one Apollo, and one Esculapius, not as many Dianas, Apollos, and Esculapius's, as they had temples and statues. Thus it is evidenced, as far as a point of history can be, that the ancients did not hold a statue to be a deity; that the worship could not relate to the statue or idol; and consequently that the antients were not idolaters.

A rude superstitious populace incapable of reflection, either to doubt, to deny, or believe, who flocked to the temples, as having nothing else to do, and because the little are there on a level with the great, who carried their offerings merely out of custom, who were continually talking of miracles without having ever examined any one, and who were very little above the victims they brought, such a populace, I say, might, at the sight of the great Diana, and the thundering Jupiter, be struck with a religious horror, and, without knowing it, worship the statue itself. This is no more than what has been the case of our ignorant peasants; and care is accordingly taken to give them to understand, that it is the blessed in heaven they are to invoke for their intercession, and not figures of wood and stone, and that their worship is due to God only.

The Greeks and the Romans increased the number of their deities by apotheoses; the Greeks deified illustrious conquerors, as Bacchus, Hercules, and Perseus; Rome raised altars to its emperors. Of a very different kind are our apotheoses; if we
have

have faints anfwerable to their demi-gods and feconḍary gods, it is without any regard to rank or conquefts. We have erected temples to men, merely for their exemplary virtues, and moft of whom would not have been known on earth, had they not been placed in heaven. The apotheofes of the antients were acts of adulation, ours of refpect to virtue. But thefe antient apotheofes are another convincing proof that the Greeks and Romans cannot properly be called idolaters. It is manifeft that they no more held a divine virtue refiding in the ftatues of Auguftus and Claudius than in their medals.

Cicero, in his philofophical works, does not leave fo much as the leaft fufpicion, that any miftake could be committed with regard to the ftatues of the gods, fo as to confound them with the deities themfelves. His fpeakers inveigh with great acrimony againft the eftablifhed religion, but not one of them dreams of charging the Romans with miftaking marble and brafs for deities. Lucretius, who never gives any quarter to the fuperftitious, reproaches no body with this folly ; I muft, therefore, again fay it, this opinion never exifted, never was thought of; and never was there any fuch thing as idolaters.

Horace introduces a ftatue of Priapus, faying:

> Olim truncus eram ficulnus, inutile lignum,
> Cum faber incertus fcamnum, faceretne Priapum,
> Maluit effe Deum.

What is to be inferred from this paffage? Priapus was one of thofe petty deities which were given up to the farcafms of the jocular ; and this very joke is as ftrong a proof as can be, that the figure of Priapus was not greatly revered, being made a fcarecrow.

Dacier,

Dacier, commentator like, has taken care to observe that Baruch had foretold this business; saying, they shall be whatever the artist pleases. But he might withal have remarked, that the like might be said of all the statues that ever existed.

A tub may be made out of a block of marble, as well as the statue of Alexander or Jupiter, or something still more respectable. The matter of which were formed the cherubims of the holy of holies, might have equally served for the meanest purposes. A throne, or an altar, lose nothing of the reverence due to them, because the artist might have formed them into a kitchen table.

Dacier instead of inferring that the Romans worshipped Priapus's image, and that Baruch had predicted it, ought rather to have concluded that the Romans made a jest of it. Look into all the authors who speak of the statues of their gods, not one shall you find mentioning idolatry; but quite the contrary. You read in Martial,

" Qui finxit sacros auro vel marmore vultus,
Non facit ille Deos."

In Ovid,
" Colitur pro Jove forma Jovis."

In Statius,
" Nulla autem effigies nulli commissa matello,
Forma Dei mentes habitare ac numina gaudet."

In Lucan,
" Est ne Dei sedes, nisi terra et pontus et aer."

To enumerate all the passages in confirmation that images were accounted images would take up a volume.

The

The only case which could favour an opinion that images had any thing divine in them, was the oracular images. But certainly the current opinion was, that the gods had chosen some particular altars, and particular statues, where they sometimes condescended to reside, giving audience to men, and answering them. In Homer, and the choruses of Greek tragedies, we only meet with prayers addressed to Apollo himself, as delivering his oracles on such a mount, in such a temple, or such a city. All antiquity throughout has left no vestige of supplications made to a statue.

They who professed magic, who believed it to be a science, or who feigned to believe it, pretended to be possessed of the secret of bringing down the gods into statues; but not the great gods, only the secondary, the genii. This Mercurius Trismegistus used to term MAKING DEITIES, and it is refuted by St. Austin in his City of God. But this very thing evidently shews the images to have had nothing divine in them, as not animated without the art of a magician. And I fancy few magicians were found so dexterous as to animate a statue so as to make it speak.

In a word, the images of the gods were not gods; it was Jupiter, and not his image which hurled the thunderbolt; it was not the statue of Neptune which agitated the sea, nor that of Apollo which diffused light. The Greek and Romans were gentiles, politheists, but by no means idolaters.

Whether the Persians, the Sabeans, the Egyptians, the Tartars, and Turks, have been idolaters? Æra of the origin of figures called idols. History of their worship.

To call those nations, who worshipped the sun and stars idolaters, is wronging them. For a long time

time neither images nor temples were known among them: if they were miftaken, it was in paying to the heavenly bodies the homage due only to the Creator. Befides, the doctrine of Zoroafter or Zerduft, as preferved in the Sadder, teaches the exiftence of a Supreme Being, who punifheth and rewardeth. Now this is very far from idolatry. The Chinefe government never admitted idols, conftantly adhering to the fimple worfhip of Kingtien, the mafter of heaven. Gengiskan among the Tartars cannot be charged with idolatry, never having had any fuch thing as an image. The Muffulmen of Greece, Afia-minor, Syria, Perfia, India, and Africa, call the Chriftians idolaters, GIAOURS, imagining that the Chriftians worfhip images. Several images which they found at Conftantinople in St. Sophia, and in the church of the holy apoftles, and others, they broke to pieces, converting the churches into mofques. Appearance, as ufual, deceived them, and led them to believe that the dedicating of temples to faints, who had formerly been men, the worfhipping of their images with genuflection, and the performing of miracles in thofe temples, were undeniable proofs of the moft arrant idolatry: yet, the fartheft from it in the world. The Chriftians, in reality, worfhip only one God, and in the blefled themfelves revere only the virtue of God acting in his faints. The Iconoclafts and the proteftants have brought the fame charge of idolatry againft the church of Rome, and the fame anfwer has been given them.

Men having very feldom precife ideas, and ftill more feldom expreffing their ideas in precife words, clear of all ambiguity, the name of idolaters was given to the Gentiles, and efpecially the Politheifts. Immenfe volumes have been written, according to the multitude of varying fentiments on the origin of

of worshipping God, or several gods, and under sensible representations: now this multitude of books and opinions only proves the ignorance of the authors.

We know not who invented any part of our clothing, and yet we would fain know who was the first inventor of idols. What signifies a passage of Sanchoniathon, who lived before the Trojan war? What information does he give us, in saying, that the cahos, the mind, that is, the breath, being enamoured with its principles, extracted the mud from them; that he made the air luminous; that the wind Colp and his wife Baü, begot Eon, and he begot Genos; that Cronos, their descendant, had two eyes behind as before; that he came to be god, and gave Egypt to his son Jaut? This is one of the most respectable monuments of antiquity.

Orpheus, who was prior to Sanchoniathon, gives us just as much light in his Theogonia, which Damascius has preserved. He represents the mundane principle in the form of a dragon, with two heads, one of a bull, and the other of a lion, with a face in the middle, which he terms GOD FACE, and gilded wings to the shoulders.

Yet these ideas, fantastical as they are, give us an insight into two important truths, one that sensible images and hieroglyphics are derived from the most remote antiquity; the other that all ancient philosophers acknowledged a primordial principle.

As to politheism common sense will tell you, that, at the commencement of mankind, that is, of weak creatures susceptible of reason and folly, subject to every accident, to sickness and death, they soon came to a sense of their weakness and dependence: they easily conceived that there was something superior to themselves; they felt a power in the

the earth, which produced their food, another in the air which often destroyed them, and another in the consuming fire and the submerging water. What could be more natural in men, absolutely ignorant, than to fancy that there were beings which presided over these elements? What could be more natural than to revere the invisible power which made the sun and the stars to shine? And on proceeding to form an idea of these superior powers, what was again more natural than to represent them in a sensitive way? Or I may even say, how could they go about it otherwise? Judaism, anterior to our religion, and prescribed by God himself, was full of those images, under which the deity is represented. He condescends to speak the language of men in a bush; he makes his appearance on a mountain; the heavenly spirits sent by him all come in a human shape; in a word, the sanctuary itself is filled with cherubims, human bodies, and the wings and heads of beasts. This led Plutarch, Tacitus, Appian, and so many others, into the ridiculous mistake of upbraiding the Jews with worshipping an ass's head. Thus God, who had forbidden the painting and carving of any figure, has been pleased nevertheless to accommodate himself to human weakness, which require the senses to be spoken to by images.

Isaiah, chap vi. sees the Lord seated on a throne, and his train fill the temple: in chap. i. of Jeremiah, the Lord stretches out his hand, and touches the prophet's mouth. Ezekiel, chap. iii. sees a throne of saphire, and God appears to him like a man seated on that throne. This imagery does not in the least defile the purity of the Jewish religion, which never made use of pictures, statues, and idols as public representations of the deity.

The

The lettered Chinese, the Parsis, the antient Egyptians, had no idols; but Isis and Osiris were soon represented in figures; Bel at Babylon was as soon exhibited in a huge colossus; Brama was in the Indian peninsula an hideous kind of monster. The Greeks above all multiplied the names of the deities, and of course the statues and temples; but ever attributing the supreme power to their Zeus, by the Latins named Jupiter, the sovereign of gods and men. The Romans imitated the Greeks; both always placed their gods in heaven, without knowing what they meant by heaven and their olympus: these superior beings could not be supposed to reside in the clouds, which are only water. At first seven of them were placed in the seven planets, among which was reckoned the sun; but afterwards the residence of all the gods was extended to the whole heavenly expanse.

The Romans had twelve great deities, six male and six female, whom they distinguished by the appellation of " Dii majorum gentium," Jupiter, Neptune, Apollo, Vulcan, Mars, Mercury; Juno, Vesta, Minerva, Ceres, Venus, Diana. Pluto was then omitted, and Vesta took his place.

Next were the gods " minorum gentium," the indigetes, or heroes, as Bacchus, Hercules, Esculapius; the infernal deities, Pluto, Proserpine; the sea gods, as Thetis, Amphitrite, the Nereïdes and Glaucus; afterwards the Dryades, the Naïades; the gods of gardens; the pastoral deities; every profession, every action of life, children, maidens, wives, women in childbed, all had their deity: there was even the god FART; lastly, emperors were deified: not that these emperors, nor the god FART, nor the goddess Pertunda, nor Priapus, nor Rumilia the goddess of bubbies, nor Stercutius the god of privies, were accounted the lords of heaven and earth.

Some

Some of the emperors indeed had temples; the petty houshold gods went without them, but all had their image, or their idol.

These were little grotesque figures, set up in a closet by way of ornament; old women and children were highly delighted with them; but never were these figures authorized by any public worship; every one was left to follow his own private superstition. These little idols are still found in the ruins of antient cities.

Though we cannot fix the precise time when men began to make idols, they are, however, known to belong to the most remote antiquity. Thara, Abraham's father, used to make them at Ur in Chaldea. Rachael purloined and carried off Laban's idols. There is no going higher.

But what did the antient nations think of all these images? what virtue, what power did they attribute to them? Was it thought that the Gods quitted heaven to come down, and hide themselves in these statues? or that they imparted to them a portion of the divine spirit, or did not impart any thing at all to them? a great deal of useless erudition has been thrown away on this point, it being evident that every one's notions of them were proportioned to his reason, his credulity, or his fanaticism. The priests, we may be sure, would not be wanting to annex to their statues all the divinity they possibly could, in order to draw the more offerings. The philosophers, it is well known, censured these superstitions; the military people made a jest of them; and the commonalty, ever ignorant and silly, knew not what it was doing. This is, in a few words, the history of all the nations to which God has not made himself known.

The premises are applicable to the worship universally paid in Egypt to an ox, and in several cities

cities to a dog, a monkey, a cat, and onions. In all appearance they were at first only emblems. Afterwards a certain ox called Apis, a certain dog named Anubis, were worshipped; still the people went on eating beef and onions; but what the Egyptian old women thought of sacred onions and oxen, is not cleared up.

It was not uncommon for idols to speak. On the anniversary of Cybele's festival, the city of Rome commemorated the beautiful distich uttered by the statue on it's removal from king Attalus's palace:

" Ipsa pati volui, ne sit mora, mitte volentem,
Dignus Roma locus, quó Deus omnis eat."

" I allowed myself to be carried off; away with
" me quickly; Rome is worthy to be the residence
" of every deity."

The statue of Fortune had spoke: the Scipios, the Ciceros, the Cæsars, indeed believed nothing of the matter; but the old women, to whom Encolpus gave a crown to buy geese and gods, might very well believe it.

The idols likewise pronounced oracles, the priests concealed within the statues speaking in the name of the deity.

Amidst so many gods, so many different theogonies and separate worships, whence is it, that no such thing as a religious war was ever known among the people called idolaters? This tranquility was a good springing from an evil, from error itself; for every nation owning several inferior gods, peaceably allowed its neigbours to have theirs likewise. Except Cambyses's killing the ox Apis, not one instance is to be found, in all prophane history, of a conqueror offering any insult to the gods of a
vanquish-

vanquished nation. The Gentiles had no exclusive religion; and all the priests minded was to multiply offerings and sacrifices.

The first offerings were the fruits of the earth. But the priests soon came to want animal food for their table: with their own hands they slew the victims; and as they made themselves butchers, they became sanguinary. At length they introduced the horrible practice of offering human victims, and especially comely boys and girls, abominations never known among the Chinese, the Parsis, or the Indians; but at Hieropolis in Egypt, Porphyry tells us, it was nothing extraordinary to sacrifice men.

In Tauris strangers were sacrificed; but this savage custom being known, the priests of Tauris, it is to be supposed, did not much business. This execrable superstition prevailed among the most ancient Greeks, the Cypriots, the Phenicians, the Tyrians and the Carthaginians. The Romans themselves gave into this religious guilt; and, according to Plutarch, sacrificed two Greeks and two Gauls, to expiate the incontinency of three vestals. Procopius, who was cotemporary with Theodobert, king of the Francs, says, that the Francs sacrificed men on their entrance into Italy under that prince. These horrid sacrifices were common among the Gauls and Germans. There is no reading history, without being very much displeased with one's own species.

What if, among the Jews, Jephthah sacrificed his daughter, and Saul was going to slay his son; what if they, who were devoted to the lord by anathema, could not be redeemed, as beasts were redeemed, but were indispensably put to death; what though Samuel, a Jewish priest, cut to pieces with a consecrated cleaver king Agag, prisoner of war, whom Saul had spared, and sharply reproved Saul for having treated that king according to the laws of nations;

tions; what of all this? God is the sovereign of mankind, and may take away their lives when he will, as he will, and by whom he will; but men are not to put themselves on a footing with the lord of life and death, and usurp the prerogatives of the Supreme Being.

Amidst such detestable proceedings, it is some relief to the feeling heart, to know that in almost all those nations called idolatrous, there was the sacred theology and popular error, private worship and public ceremonies, the religion of the wise and that of the vulgar. To those who were initiated in the mysteries, the existence of one only God was preached. Of this a sufficient testimony is the hymn attributed to the elder Orpheus, which was sung in the celebrated mysteries of Ceres Eleusina: "Contemplate the di-
" vine nature, illume thy mind, govern thy heart,
" walk in the path of justice, take care that the
" God of heaven be before thine eyes; there is
" none but him, he alone is self-existent; all be-
" ings derive their existence from him; he up-
" holds them all; never has he been seen by mor-
" tals, and he sees all things."

The following passage of the philosopher Maximus of Madaura, in his letter to St. Augustine, is likewise worth attention, "What man is so dull, so
" stupid, as to question the existence of an eternal,
" a supreme, infinite deity, who has created no-
" thing like himself, and is the common father of
" all things?"

A thousand monuments might be produced, that wise men in all times abhorred both idolatry and polytheism.

Epictetus, that pattern of resignation and patience, so great in so mean a condition, never speaks but of one only God. One of his maxims is this,
" God

"God has created me, God is within me, I carry him about every where. Shall I defile him with obscene thoughts, unjust actions, or infamous desires? My duty is to thank God for every thing, to praise him for every thing; and to thank, praise, and serve him continually, whilst I have life." All Epictetus's ideas turn on this principle.

Marcus Aurelius, who perhaps was on the throne of the Roman empire not less great than Epictetus in servitude, does indeed often mention gods, in conformity to the current phraseology, or to express intermediate beings, between the Supreme Essence and men; but in how many passages does he shew, that in reality he acknowledges only one eternal infinite God? "Our souls, says he, are an emanation of the Deity; my body, my spirits, proceed from God."

The Stoics, the Platonics, held one divine and universal nature; the Epicureans denied it. The priests in their mysteries spoke only of one God: where then were the idolaters?

Besides, it is one of the great mistakes in Morery's Dictionary to say, that in the time of Theodosius the Younger, no idolaters remained but in the remote parts of Asia and Africa. There was still, and even down to the seventh century, many Gentile nations in Italy. All Germany north of the Weser were strangers to Christianity in Charlemain's time; and, long after him, Poland and the whole North continued in what is called idolatry. Half Africa, all the realms beyond the Ganges, Japan, the innumerable commonalty of China, a hundred Tartarian hords, retain their antient worship; whereas in Europe, this religion is to be found only among some Laplanders, Samoiedes, and Tartars. To conclude, in the time which we distinguish by the appellapellation of the middle age, the Mahometans were called Pagans: a people who execrate images were branded as idolaters and image-worshippers; and it must be frankly owned, that the Turks, seeing our churches crowded with images and statues, are more excusable in calling us idolaters.

JEPHTHAH.
Or, Human Sacrifices.

IT is clear from the book of Judges, that Jephthah did promise to sacrifice the first person who came out of his house, in order to congratulate him on his victory against the Ammonites: and who should this prove to be but his only daughter? Hereupon he rent his garments for grief; and after permitting her to go and lament among the hills her misfortune in dying a maid, he actually sacrificed her. The Jewish maidens for a long time commemorated this event, lamenting Jephthah's daughter four days in a year. (See Judges, ch. xi.)

In whatever time this history was written, whether it be an imitation or the original of the Grecian story of Agamemnon and Iphigenia, be it prior or posterior to some similar Assyrian tale, is what I do not examine; I abide by the text: Jephthah vowed his daughter for a burnt-offering, and performed his vow.

It was expresly enjoined in the Jewish law to sacrifice all who had been devoted to the Lord. No man shall be redeemed, but shall be put to death, without remission: (D) the Vulgate has it, "Non

---

(D) Our translation is, "None devoted, which shall be devoted of men, shall be redeemed, but shall surely be put to death."

redi-

redimetur, sed morte morietur." Lev. chap. xxvii. ver. 29.

In consequence of this law it was, that Samuel hewed king Agag in pieces, though Saul had spared him; and for his improper clemency, Saul was reproved by the Lord, and forfeited his kingdom.

Here is an evident proof of human sacrifices; no point of history can be more authentically verified; certainly a nation cannot be better known than by records, and what it relates of its self.

JOSEPH.

THE history of Joseph, considered only as an object of curiosity and literature, is one of the most valuable monuments of antiquity which have reached our times. It appears to have been the model of all the oriental writers; it is more pathetic than Homer's Odyssy, as a forgiving hero is more moving than he that gluts his vengeance.

We account the Arabs to have been the first authors of those ingenious fictions, which have been adopted in all other languages; but for my part, I meet with no tale among them comparable to that of Joseph: in almost every part it is of admirable beauty; and the conclusion draws forth tears of tenderness. It exhibits a youth in his sixteenth year, of whom his brothers are jealous. He is sold by them to a caravan of Ishmaelite merchants, carried into Egypt, and bought by one of the king's eunuchs. This eunuch had a wife, at which we are not to be startled, for the Kislar-aga of Constantinople, who is an arch-eunuch, the whole of his genital parts being abscinded, has a seraglio: his eyes and hands are left, and nature is still nature

ture in him. The other eunuchs, having been deprived only of the two appendages of the generative organ, often make use of it; and Potiphar, to whom Joseph was sold, might very well be of the latter class of eunuchs.

Potiphar's wife becomes enamoured with young Joseph, who, faithful to his master as a most gracious benefactor, rejects her sollicitations. Such behaviour turns her love into rancour, and she charges Joseph with an attempt to seduce her. This is the history of Hippolitus and Phædra, of Bellerophon and Stenobæa, of Hebrus and Damasippe, of Tanis and Peribea, of Marsillus and Hipodamia, of Peleus and Demenetta.

Which is the original of all these histories is not easily known; but the ancient Arabian authors have a passage relating to the transaction between Joseph and Potiphar's wife, which is very ingenious. The author supposes that Potiphar, hesitating between his wife and Joseph, did not look upon his wife's having torn a piece of Joseph's robe, as any weighty proof of the young man's crime. There was at that time, in the wife's chamber, a child in a cradle. Joseph said that she had forcibly taken hold of his robe, and torn it in the child's presence; Potiphar asked the child, who it seems was of a very pregnant wit for his age. The child said to Potiphar, see whether the robe be torn before or behind; if before, it shews that Joseph was for laying hands on your wife, and that she stood on her defence; if behind, it is plain your wife run after him. Thus did this child's genius clear up Joseph's innocence. This is the account given in the Alcoran from an ancient Arabian author, without informing us to whom this witty child belonged. If it was a son of dame Potiphar's, phar's, Joseph was not the first with whom this woman had desired an intimacy.

However it be, Joseph, according to the book of Genesis, is clapped up in prison, and happens to be with the king's cup-bearer and butler: both these state prisoners had a dream the same night, which Joseph explained to them; he foretold that within three days the cup-bearer should be restored to favour, and the butler hanged, which fell out accordingly.

Two years after the king of Egypt had a very perplexing dream, on which his cup-bearer acquaints him, that there is in prison a Jewish young man who had not his equal for explaining dreams; he is sent for, and predicts the seven years of plenty and the seven barren years.

Here we must make a small interruption in the thread of the story, to observe the prodigious antiquity of the interpretation of dreams. Jacob had seen in a dream the mysterious ladder, at the top of which was God himself: in a dream he learned the method of multiplying his flocks, a method which has never succeeded but with him. Joseph himself had been informed by a dream, that he should one day be superior to his brothers. Abimelech, long before, had notice given him in a dream, that Sarah was Abraham's wife. See the article DREAM. We shall now return to Joseph.

On his having explained Pharaoh's dream, he was immediately created prime minister. It is a question whether now a-days any king, even in Asia, would bestow a post of that importance for having explained a dream; Pharaoh made up a match between Joseph and a daughter of Potiphar's. This Potiphar is said to have been high priest of Heliopolis, so that it could not be the eunuch his first master; or if it was, he must certainly

tainly have had another title than that of high prieſt; and his wife had been a mother more than once.

In the mean time the famine came on, according to Joſeph's prediction; and this miniſter, to rivet himſelf into the royal favour, ſo managed matters, that all the people were under a neceſſity of ſelling their lands to Pharaoh; and the whole nation, to procure corn, became ſlaves to the crown. This may probably be the origin of deſpotiſm. It muſt be owned that never king made a better bargain; but, on the other hand, the people owed little gratitude and applauſe to the prime miniſter.

At length Joſeph's father and brothers likewiſe came to want corn, for the famine was ſore in all the land: as for Joſeph's reception of his brethren, his forgiving them, and loading them with kindneſs, we ſhall take the liberty to omit thoſe particulars, obſerving only, that this hiſtory has every intereſting part of an epic poem; the ſublime, the marvellous, the expoſition, connection, diſcovery, and reverſe of fortune. I know nothing more ſtrongly marked with oriental genius.

The anſwer of good Jacob, Joſeph's hoary father, to Pharaoh, ought deeply to impreſs every one who can read. What may your age be, ſaid the king to him? A hundred and thirty years, anſwered the old man; and in this ſhort pilgrimage, I have not ſeen one happy day.

LAWS.

IN the time of Veſpaſian and Titus, when the Romans uſed to rip up and draw the Jews, a very wealthy Iſraelite, to avoid that diſagreeable treatment,

treatment, moved off with all the fruits of his ufury, carrying with him to Eziongaber all his family, which confifted of his aged wife, a fon, and a daughter; for retinue, he had two eunuchs, one a cook, the other a kind of gardener and vine-dreffer: an honeft Effene, who knew the Pentateuch by heart, officiated as his chaplain. All thefe going aboard a veffel at Eziongaber, croffed the Red Sea, as it is called, though it has nothing of that colour, and entered the gulph of Perfia, in queft of the country of Ophir, without knowing where it lay: a dreadful ftorm drove this Hebrew family towards India, where the veffel was ftranded on one of the Maldivia iflands, then defert, but now called Padrabranca.

The old hunks and his joan were drowned; but the fon and daughter, with the two eunuchs and chaplain, got fafe to land. They made fhift to fave fome of the provifions; and, having built huts in the ifland, began to be fomething reconciled to their difafter. The ifland of Padrabranca, you know, is five degrees from the line, and produces the largeft cocoa-nuts and the beft pine-apples in the whole world: it was not uncomfortable living there at a time when every where elfe, the favoured people were flaughtered as faft as they could be found; but the good Effene frequently wept at thinking, that they might be the only Jews on earth, and that the feed of Abraham was drawing to an end.

What fignify your tears, faid the young Jew: it is in your power to prevent it's ending; marry my fifter. Very willingly, anfwered the chaplain; but it is againft the law. I am an Effene, and have made a vow againft marriage; and, by the laws, vows are to be obferved: come of the Jewifh race what will, never will I marry your fifter, sister, though she were ten times handsomer than she is.

My two eunuchs, answered the Jew, cannot raise seed from her; so, with your leave, I will do the business, and you shall marry us.

Let me be ripped up and drawn over and over, said the chaplain, rather than have any hand in making you commit incest: were she your sister only by the father's side, I would not hesitate so much about it, as not being directly against law; but she is your sister by the mother's side, so that it would be quite abominable.

I am very well aware that it would be a crime at Jerusalem, where I might have other young women; but on the island of Padrabranca, where I see only cocoa-nuts, ananas, and oysters, I hold it very allowable. Thus the Jew married his sister, and, notwithstanding all the Essene's protestations, had by her a daughter, who was the sole fruit of a marriage, by one held legal, and by the other abominable.

Fourteen years after the mother departed this life: Well, said the father to the chaplain, have you got over your former prejudices? Will you marry my daughter? God forbid! said the Essene. If you will not, I will, said the father; the seed of Abraham shall not come to an end, if I can help it. The Essene, quite frightened at such horrible words, would not live any longer with one who made so light of the law, and fled. The bridegroom called after him, Stop, honest Ananeel, I observe the law of nature, I am preserving the chosen race, do not leave your friends; but the Essene, full of the Mosaic law, without so much as looking back, swam over to the nearest island.

This was Attola, a large island, both populous and thoroughly civilized; at his landing he was made

made a slave. When he had got a little of the Attola tongue, he complained very bitterly of his being used so inhospitably; but he was given to understand, that such was their law, and that since the island had narrowly escaped being surprized by the inhabitants of Shot Ada, it had been wisely provided, that all strangers coming to Attola should be made slaves. A law it cannot be, said the Essene, for no such thing is in the Pentateuch: to which he had for answer, that it was in the country code, and a slave he remained; but with the good fortune of having an excellent master, who was very rich, and ruled him in a manner which much endeared him to the Essene.

Some ruffians came one day to rob and kill the master: they asked the slaves whether he was at home and had a great deal of money by him? By all the gods, said the slaves, he has little or no money at all, neither is he at home. But the Essenian said, the law does not allow of lying; and I swear to you that he is at home, and has a great deal of money; so the master was robbed and murdered: on this, the slaves had the Essene before the judges for betraying his master. The Essene own'd his words, saying, that he would not tell a lye on any account; and he was hanged.

This story, and many such, were told me in my last journey from the Indies to France. On my arrival, some business calling me to Versailles, here I saw a very fine woman followed by several other fine women: Who is that fine woman, said I to my lawyer, who was come with me; for having a process in the parliament at Paris, on account of cloaths made for me in the Indies, I had my counsellor always with me: It is the king's daughter, said he; and, besides her beauty, she is of a most excellent temper; it is a

pity

pity that she can never be queen of France. How! said I, if, which God forbid, all her royal relations and the princes of the blood were to die, could not she inherit her father's kingdom? No, said the counsellor, the Salic law is expresly against it. And who made that Salic law, said I. That I know nothing of, answered he; but the tradition is, that an ancient people called the Salians, who could neither read nor write, had a law, by which in the Salic country no female was to inherit an hereditary fief; and this law has been admitted in a country which is not Salic. Has it so, said I, and I annul it: You assure me that, besides this princess's beauty, she is of an excellent temper; she has therefore an indisputable right to the crown, if unfortunately she should survive all the rest of the royal family: my mother was heiress to her father, and this princess shall be heiress to hers.

The next day my cause came on in one of the courts of parliament, and they all gave it against me: my counsellor told me, that in another court I should have gained it unanimously. Very odd, indeed, said I; then so many courts so many laws. Yes, said he, there are no less than twenty-five commentaries on the common law at Paris; that is, the Paris common law has been twenty-five times proved to be ambiguous; and were there twenty-five courts, there would be twenty-five different bodies of laws. We have, continued he, a province called Normandy, about fifteen leagues from Paris; and there your cause would have been decided quite otherwise than here. This made me desirous of seeing Normandy, and I went thither with one of my brothers. At the first inn we came to, was a young man storming most furiously. I asked him what was the matter? Matter enough answered he; I have an elder brother. Where is the

the mighty misfortune of having a brother, said I to him? my brother is my elder, and yet we live very easy together. But here, Sir, said he, the damned law gives every thing to the elder, and the younger may shift for themselves. If that be the case, said I, well may you be angry; with us, things are equally divided, yet sometimes brothers do not love one another the better for it.

These little adventures led me to some very profound reflections on the laws, and I found them to be like our garments; at Constantinople it is proper to wear a doliman, and at Paris a coat. If all human laws are by compact, said I, the only point is to make good bargains. The citizens of Deli and Agra say, that they made a very bad agreement with Tamerlane: the citizens of London again value themselves for the good bargain they made with king William III. One of that opulent body was saying to me, it is necessity which makes laws, and force causes them to be observed. I asked him whether force did not likewise make laws, and whether William the conqueror, had not prescribed to England laws, without any previous convention? Yes, said he, we were then oxen, and William put a yoke upon us, and goaded us along. Since those times we are become men; but with our horns still remaining, we are sure to gore any one that will make us plough for him, and not for ourselves.

Full of these reflections, I was pleased to find that there is a natural law independant of all human conventions; that the fruit of my labour should be my property; that it is my duty to honour my parents; that I have no right to my neighbour's life, nor my neighbour to mine, &c. But when it came into my mind that, from Cordolaomer down to Mentzel, colonel of hussars, it has been customary,

mary, to shew one's loyalty by effusion of human blood, and to pillage one's neighbour by patent, I was touched to the heart.

I am told that robbers had their laws, and that war had also its laws. On my asking what were those laws of war, I was answered: It is to hang up a brave officer for maintaining, against a royal army, a bad post and without cannon; it is to hang up a prisoner if one of your men has been hanged; it is to burn and destroy those villages which have not brought in their whole subsistence at the day appointed by the gracious sovereign of the neighbourhood. So that is the spirit of laws, said I.

By farther information I heard of some very wise laws, condemning a shepherd to the galleys for nine years, for giving a little foreign salt to his sheep. A neighbour of mine has been ruined by an indictment for cutting down two oaks in his own wood, not observing a formality which he had not been able to know any thing of: his wife died of grief in extreme distress, and his son lives, if it may be so called, very wretchedly. I own that these laws are just, tho' the execution of them is a little hard; but I cannot bear with those laws which authorize a hundred thousand men to go, under the pretence of loyalty, and massacre as many peaceable neighbours. The generality of mankind appear to be naturally endued with sense enough to make laws; but then it is not every one who has virtue sufficient to enact good laws.

Call together from all the ends of the earth, the husbandmen, a simple quiet class, they will, at once, agree that the surplus of one's corn should be allowed to be sold to our neighbours; and that a law to the contrary is both absurd and inhuman; that coin, as representing provisions, should be no more
adulte-

adulterated than the products of the earth; that a father of a family should be master within his own walls; that religion should promote friendship and benevolence among men living in society, and not make them fanatics and persecutors; that the labouring and busy part of the world should not deprive themselves of the fruits of their industry, to bestow them on superstition and sloth: this plain assembly would in an hour make thirty such laws, all beneficial to mankind.

But should Tamerlane come and subdue India; then you will see nothing but arbitrary laws. One shall squeeze a province to enrich a publican of Tamerlane's; another shall make it high-treason only for having dropped a free word concerning the mistress of the raja's first valet de chambre; a third shall take away from the farmer half his harvest, and dispute the remainder with him; and, what is worse than all this, there will be laws, by which a Tartar messenger shall come and take away your children in the cradle, making them sodiers or eunuchs according to their constitutions, and leave the father and mother to wipe away each other's tears.

Now, whether is it best to be Tamerlane's dog or his subject? Doubtless, his dog has by much the best of it.

CIVIL and ECCLESIASTICAL LAWS.

THE following minutes were found among the papers of an eminent lawyer, and peraps deserve a little consideration.

No ecclesiastical law should ever be in force till has formally received the express sanction of the government; by this it was that Athens and Rome never had any religious quarrels.

Those quarrels appertain only to barbarous nations.

To permit or prohibit working on holidays, should only be in the magistrates power; it is not the fit concern of priests to hinder men from cultivating their grounds.

Every thing relating to marriages should depend solely on the magistrate; and let the priests be limited to the august function of the solemnization.

Lending at interest to be intirely within the cognizance of the civil law, as by it, commercial affairs are regulated.

All ecclesiastics whatever should, as the state's subjects in all cases, be under the control and animadversion of the government.

Away with that disgraceful absurdity of paying to a foreign priest the first year's produce of an estate, given to a priest of our own country.

No priest should have it in his power to deprive a member of society of the least privilege, on pretence of his sins; for a priest being himself a sinner, is to pray for sinners: he has no business to try and condemn them.

Magistrates, farmers, and priests, are alike to contribute to the expences of the state, as alike belonging to the state.

One weight, one measure, one custom.

The punishments of criminals should be of use; when a man is hanged he is good for nothing, whereas a man condemned to the public works still benefits his country, and is a living admonition.

Every law should be clear, uniform, and precise; explanations are for the most part corruptions.

The

The only infamy should be vice.
Taxes to be proportionate.
A law should never clash with custom, for if the custom be good, the law must be faulty.

LIBERTY.

A. A Battery of cannon is playing close by your ears; are you at liberty to hear or not to hear it?

B. Unquestionably I cannot but hear it.

A. Would you have those cannon carry off your head, and your wife's and daughter's, who are walking with you?

B. What a question is that? in my sober senses it is impossible, that I should will any such thing. It cannot be.

A. Well, you necessarily hear the explosion of those cannon, and you necessarily are against you and your family being cut off by a cannon shot as you are taking the air; you have not the power not to hear, nor the power of willing to remain here.

B. Nothing more evident.

A. Accordingly you have come thirty paces to be out of the cannons way: thus you have had the power of walking that little space with me.

B. That again is clear.

A. And if you had been paralytic you could not have avoided being exposed to this battery; you would not have had the power of being where you are; you would, necessarily, not only have heard the explosion, but received a cannon shot; and thus you would necessarily have been killed.

B. Very true.

A. In what then consists your liberty? if not in the power which your body has made use of to do,

what

what your volition, by an absolute necessity, required.

B. You put me to a stand. Liberty then is nothing but the power of doing what I will.

A. Think of it, and see whether liberty can have any other meaning.

B. At this rate my grey hound is as free as I am: he has necessarily a will to run at the sight of a hare, and likewise the power of running, if not lame; so that in nothing am I superior to my dog; this is levelling me with the beasts.

A. Such are the wretched sophisms of the wretched sophists who have tutored you. Wretched thing indeed, to be in the same state of liberty as your dog! And are not you like your dog in a thousand things? in hunger, thirst, waking, sleeping; and your five senses, are they not common to him? are you for smelling otherwise than through the nose? why then are you for having liberty in a manner different from him.

B. But I have a soul continually reasoning, which my dog knows little of: simple ideas are very nearly all his portion, whereas I have a thousand metaphysical ideas.

A. Well, you are a thousand times more free than he; that is, you have a thousand times more power of thinking than he: still you are not free in a manner different from him.

B. How! am I not at liberty to will what I will?

A. Your meaning?

B. I mean what all the world means; is it not a common saying, Will is free?

A. A proverb is no reason: please to explain yourself more clearly.

B. I mean that I have the liberty of willing as I please.

A. By

A. By your leave, there is no sense in that; don't you perceive that it is ridiculous to say, I will will; you will necessarily, in consequence of the ideas occurring to you: Would you marry, yes, or no?

B. But were I to say, I neither will the one nor the other?

A. That would be answering like him who said, some think cardinal Mazarine dead, others believe him still living, and I believe neither one nor the other.

B. Well, I have a mind to marry.

A. Good! that is something of an answer; and why have you a mind to marry?

B. Because I am in love with a young gentlewoman, who is handsome, of a sweet temper, well bred, with a tolerable fortune, sings charmingly, and her parents are perhaps of good credit: besides, I flatter myself, that my addresses are very acceptable both to her family and herself.

A. Why, there is a reason: you see you cannot will without a reason, and I declare you have the liberty of marrying; that is, you have the power of signing the contract.

B. How! not will without a reason! What then becomes of another proverb? "Sit pro ratione voluntas;" my will is my reason. I will because I will.

A. My dear friend, under favour, that is an absurdity; there would then be in you an effect without a cause.

B. What! when I am playing at even or odd, is there a reason for my choosing even rather than odd?

A. Yes, to be sure.

B. And pray let us hear that reason?

A. Becaufe the idea of odd prefented itfelf to your mind before the contrary notion. It would be ftrange, indeed, that in fome cafes you will be-caufe there is a caufe of volition; and that in fome cafes you will without any caufe. In your willing to be married, you evidently perceive the determining reafon; and in playing at even or odd, you do not perceive it; and yet one there muft be.

B. But again, am I not then free?

A. Your will is not free, but your actions are; you are free to act when you have the power of acting.

B. But all the books I have read on the liberty of indifference ——

A. Are nonfenfe: there is no fuch thing as liberty of indifference; (E) it is a word void of fenfe, and coined by thofe who were not overloaded with it.

LIMITS of the human UNDERSTANDING.

POOR doctor, thefe limits are every where. Art thou for knowing how it comes to pafs, that thine arm and thy leg obey thy will, and thy liver does not? Wouldft thou inveftigate how thought is formed in thy minute underftanding, and the child in that woman's womb? I give thee what

---

(E.) Here our author has followed Mr. Locke, who fays, " that liberty belongs not to the will; and that it is as in-" fignificant to afk, whether a man's will be free, as to afk, " whether his fleep be fwift, or his virtue fquare. For li-" berty being but a power belongs only to agents, and can-" not be an attribute of the will, which is alfo but a power." See this notion refuted by Dr. Clarke in his Demonftration of the Being and Attributes of a God.

time thou wilt. Tell me alfo what is matter. Thy equals have written ten thoufand volumes on this article: fome qualities of this fubftance they have found, and children know them as well as thyfelf; but what is that fubftance effentially? and what is that to which thou haft given the appellation of fpirit, from a Latin word fignifying breath, in the want of a better, becaufe thou haft no' idea of it?

See this grain of corn which I throw into the ground, and tell me how it rifes again to fhoot forth a ftem with an ear? Inform me how the fame ground produces an apple on this tree, and a chefnut in that next to it: I could fill a folio with fuch queftions, to which thy anfwer ought to be, I know not.

And yet thou haft taken thy degrees, and weareft a furred gown and cap, and art called mafter; and there is another fool, who, priding himfelf upon a petty employment in fome paltry town, conceits that he has likewife purchafed the privilege of judging, and condemning what he does not underftand.

Montaigne's motto was, "What do I know?" (Que fai-je?) and thine is, "What do I not know?" (Que ne fai-je pas?)

LOVE.

AMOR omnibus idem. Here we muft call in the conftitution; the ground is natural, and embroidered by imagination. Shall I give you an idea of love? View the fparrows in thy garden; view thy pidgeons; behold the bull led to thy heifer; look on that fpirited horfe, which two of thy fervants are bringing to thy mare, who quietly waits his coming, and turns afide her tail to admit him;

him; how his eyes glare, how he neighs; observe how he prances; his erect ears, his convulsed mouth, his snorting, his turgid nostrils, his fiery breath issuing from them; the flutterings of his mane; the impetuosity with which he rushes on the object that nature has appointed for him: but forbear all jealousy, and consider the advantages of the human species; in matters of love they make up for those which nature has given to beasts, strength, beauty, activity, and velocity.

There are even creatures strangers to fruition. It is a delight of which shell-fish are deprived; the female ejects millions of eggs on the slime and mud; the male, in passing by fecundates them by his sperm, without troubling himself what female they belong to.

Most creatures in copulation receive pleasure only from one sense, and that appetite satisfied, sink into insensibility. Thou alone of all animals art acquainted with the warm endearments of embraces; thy whole body glows with ecstatic sensations; thy lips especially enjoy a most sweet delight, without satiety or weariness, and this delight is peculiar to thy species. Lastly, thou canst at all times give thy self to love; whereas other creatures have only a stated season. Reflect on these pre-eminences, and thou wilt say with the earl of Rochester, " Love would cause the deity to be worshipped in a land of atheists."

As it has been imparted to mankind to improve the several gifts of nature, they have made improvements in love. Cleanliness, or the care of one's person, rendering the skin softer, increases the pleasure of touch; and attention to health adds a more exquisite sensibility to the organs of voluptuousness.

All other sentiments combine with that of love, as metals amalgamate with gold: friendship and esteem

esteem join to support it; and the talents, both of the body and mind, are additional ties.

" Nam facit ipsa suis interdum fæmina factis,
Morigerisque modis et mundo corpori cultu,
Ut facile insuescat secum vir degere vitam."

Self-love especially adds, force to the several ties. We are enraptured with our choice, and a crowd of illusions decorate that work, of which the foundation is laid in nature.

Such is thy pre-eminence above other animals; but if thou enjoyest so many pleasures withheld from them; how many vexations are thy portion of which beasts have no idea! One dreadful circumstance to thee is, that, in three-fourths of the earth, nature has infected the delights of love and the source of life with a horrible distemper, to which man alone is subject, and in him affecting only the organs of generation.

This contagion is not like many other distempers, the consequence of excesses; neither was it debauchery which brought it into the world. Phryne, Laïs, Flora, and Messalina, knew nothing of it. It received its birth in islands, where mankind lived in innocence; and thence it has spread itself into the old world.

If ever nature could be arraigned of neglecting its work, of thwarting its own plan, and counteracting its own views, it is here. Is this the best of the possible worlds? What! has Cæsar, Antony, Octavius never had this distemper; and was it not possible that it should not prove the death of Francis I.? No, it is said, things were so ordered for the best; I will believe so, but that's very melancholy for those to whom Rabelais dedicated his book.

SOCRA.

A PHILOSOPHICAL

SOCRATIC LOVE;
As it is called (F).

HOW could it be, that a vice, which if general, would extinguish the human species, an infamous crime against nature, should become so natural? It appears to be the last degree

---

(F) The very ingenious and learned critics, known by the vulgar name of the Monthly Reviewers, have passed a most severe censure upon this whole article. "We conceive, say they, it could only come from the pen of one of the most inconsiderate, dissolute, and abandoned of mankind. Nothing can be more infamous than what is there advanced, in palliation of the most detestable of all crimes." But nothing can be more false, than that our author attempts to palliate this crime. Does not he set out with affirming it to be destructive of the human race, a debasement and violation of nature, and the highest degree of corruption? Is this a palliation? or is it not rather a representation of that infamous vice in the light it deserves. Whether he be mistaken in tracing its source, we cannot pretend to affirm, not being so well acquainted as those learned critics with the practices of the courts of justice, nor with the arts of those hypocritical monsters, hackneyed in the ways of iniquity. But after all, this is a mere point of speculation, not at all tending to immorality. He may be mistaken again, when he says, that the Greeks never authorized this vice, and that the Socratic Love was not infamous. But these are historical matters, concerning which men of very great learning have differed in opinion. Our author, however, thinks the crime so horrid and unnatural, that it could never be authorized by any government; so that, instead of looking on this article of Socratic Love with the same horror as the scrupulous Reviewers, we rather apprehend it to be one of the least exceptionable parts of the whole work. But as Mr. Dryden well observes, much of ill nature and a very little judgment, go far in finding the mistakes of writers.

of

of reflective corruption; and yet it is ufually found in thofe who have not had time to be corrupted. It makes its way into novice hearts, who are ftrangers to ambition, fraud and a thirft after wealth; it is blind youth, which at the end of childhood, by an unaccountable inftinct, plunges itfelf into this enormity.

The inclination of the two fexes for each other declares itfelf very early; but after all that has been faid of the African women, and thofe of the fouthern part of Afia, this propenfity is much ftronger in man than in woman. Agreeably to the univerfal law of nature in all creatures, it is ever the male who makes the firft advances. The young males of our fpecies brought up together, coming to feel that play which nature begins to unfold to them, in the want of the natural object of their inftinct, betake themfelves to a refemblance of fuch objects.

It is nothing uncommon for a boy by the beauty of his complexion, and the mild fparkle of his eyes for two or three years, to have the look of a pretty girl: now the love of fuch a boy arifes from a miftake in nature; the female fex is honoured in our fondnefs for what partakes of her beauties, and when fuch refemblance is withered by age, the miftake is at an end.

citraque juventam
Ætatis breve ver et primos carpere flores,

This miftake in nature is known to be much more common in mild climates than amjdft the northern frofts, the blood being there more fervid and the occafion more frequent: accordingly, what feems only a weaknefs in young Alcibiades, is in a Dutch failor or a Ruffian futler, a loathfome abomination.

I can-

I cannot bear that the Greeks should be charged with having authorized this licentiousness. The legislator Solon is brought in because he has said,

"Thou shalt caress a beauteous boy,
Whilst no beard his smooth chin deforms."

But who will say that Solon was a legislator at the time of his making those two ridiculous lines? He was then young, and when the rake was grown virtuous, it cannot be thought that he inserted such an infamy among the laws of his republic: it is like accusing Theodore de Beza of having preached up pederasty in his church, because, in his youth, he had made verses on young Candidus, and says:

"Amplector hunc et illam."

Plutarch likewise is misunderstood, who, among his rants in the dialogue on love, makes one of the speakers say, that women are not worthy of a genuine love; but another speaker keenly takes the women's part.

It is as certain, as the knowledge of antiquity can be, that Socratic love was not an infamous passion. It is the word love has occasioned the mistake. The lovers of a youth were exactly what among us are the minions of our princes, or, formerly the pages of honour; young gentlemen who had partaken of the education of a child of rank, and accompanied him in his studies or in the field: this was a martial and holy institution, but it was soon abused, as were the nocturnal feasts and orgies.

The troop of lovers instituted by Laïus, was an invincible corps of young warriors engaged by oath, mutually to lay down their lives for one another;

ther; and, perhaps, never had antient difcipline any thing more grand and ufeful.

Sextus Empiricus and others may talk as long as they pleafe of pederafty being recommended by the laws of Perfia. Let them quote the text of the law, and even fhew the Perfian code, yet will I not believe it; I will fay it is not true, by reafon of its being impoffible. I do aver that it is not in human nature to make a law contradictory and injurious to nature; a law which, if literally kept to, would put an end to the human fpecies. The thing is, fcandalous cuftoms being connived at, are often miftaken for the laws of a country. Sextus Empiricus, doubting of every thing, might as well doubt of this jurifprudence. If living in our days he had feen two or three young jefuits fondling fome fcholars, could he from thence fay that this fport was permitted them by the conftitutions of Ignatius Loyola?

The love of boys was fo common at Rome, that no punifhment was thought of for a foolery into which every body run headlong. Octavius Auguftus, that fenfualift, that cowardly murderer, dared to banifh Ovid, at the fame time that he was very well pleafed with Virgil's finging the beauty and flights of Alexis, and Horace's making little odes for Ligurinus. Still the old Scantinian law againft pederafty was in force: the emperor Philip revived it, and caufed the boys who followed that trade to be driven out of Rome. In a word, I cannot think that ever there was a policed nation, where the laws were contrary to morality.

SELF-

SELF-LOVE.

A BEGGAR, about the skirts of Madrid, used to ask alms with great dignity: one passing by said to him, Are not you ashamed to follow this scandalous trade, you who are able to work? Sir, answered the beggar, I ask you for money and not for advice; then turned his back upon him with all the stateliness of a Castilian. Don was a lofty beggar indeed, his vanity soon took pet. He could ask alms out of self-love; and from another kind of self-love, would not bare reproof.

A missionary in India met a facquier loaded with chains, as bare as an ape, lying on his belly, while his countryman, at his request, was whipping him for his sins, and at the same time dropping him some farthings. What self-denial is this, what abasement, said one of the spectators. Self-denial, abasement! answered the facquier; I would have you to know, that I consent to be flogged in this world, only to give it you home in the other, when you shall be horses and I the rider.

Thus they who have affirmed self-love to be the basis of all our sentiments and all our actions, are much in the right, in India, Spain, and all the habitable parts of the earth; and as there is no occasion to demonstrate that men have a face, as little need there is of proving to them that they are actuated by self-love. This self love is the means of our preservation; and like the instrument of the perpetuation of the species, it is necessary, it is dear to us, it gives us pleasure, but still is to be concealed.

LUXURY.

LUXURY.

FOR these two thousand years past luxury has been declaimed against, both in verse and prose, and still mankind has always delighted in it.

What encomiums have been bestowed on the primitive Romans, when those banditti ravaged their neighbours fields! when, to increase their poor village, they destroyed the poor villages of the Volsci and Samnites. They were, to be sure, men of a glorious disinterestedness, and elevated virtue! gold, silver, and jewels they never had stolen, because there were no such things in the towns which they pillaged; their woods and fens afforded no partridges nor pheasants; and their temperance is cried up.

When having gradually plundered people after people, from the Adriatic to the Euphrates, they had sense enough to sit down in the quiet enjoyment of their rapine for seven or eight hundred years; when they cultivated every art and lived in every pleasure, and even introduced them among those whom they had conquered; then they are said to have lost both their prudence and virtue.

The substance of all these declamations is to prove, that a robber ought never to eat the dinner he has taken away, nor wear the cloaths or ring which he has stolen. Those things, say the declaimers, to keep themselves honest, they should have thrown into the river. Rather say, gentlemen that they ought not to have robbed; execrate robbers as much as you please, but do not call them madmen, for quietly enjoying what they have got. Are those English to be blamed, who, after filling their purses at the taking of Pondicherry and the Havanna, made them something

Q lighter

lighter amidst the diversions of London, in amends for the hardships they had undergone in Asia and America?

Would those declaimers have a man bury the riches which he may have acquired by war or agriculture, by trade and ingenuity? They quote Lacedemon, and why do they not also quote the republic of St. Marino? What good did Sparta ever do to Greece? Did it ever produce a Demosthenes, a Sophocles, an Apelles, or a Phidias? whereas the luxury of Athens gave rise to great men of every kind. Sparta had some good commanders, and yet not so many as the other cities. But we will allow so petty a republic as Lacedemon to retain its poverty. Whether we live in scarcity, or in the affluent fruition of whatever makes life pleasant, we shall one day come to our journey's end. The Canadian lives, and lives to old age, as well as the Englishman who has fifty thousand pounds a year; but who will compare the country of the Iroquois to England?

That the republic of Ragusa and the Canton of Zug, make sumptuary laws, is right; the poor man is not to spend beyond his ability; and I have read somewhere,

> " Luxury enriches the ample state,
> Whilst the less prosp'rous sinks beneath its weight."

If by luxury you mean excess, excess in every thing is certainly pernicious: in abstinence as in gluttony, in parsimony as in liberality. I don't know how it comes to pass that, in my villages, where the soil is very indifferent, the taxes heavy, the prohibition against the exportation of grain intolerably rigid; yet is there scarce a farmer, who is
not

not well cloathed and fed. But should this farmer follow his rural occupations in his best cloaths, clean linnen, and his hair curl'd and powdered; a greater piece of luxury there could not be, besides the ridiculousness of it: but for a citizen of Paris or London, to go to the play apparell'd like this farmer, is a most clownish and indecent piece of stinginess.

"Est modus in rebus, sunt certi denique fines, Quos ultra citraque nequit consistere rectum."

On the invention of Scissors, which certainly does not belong to the most remote antiquity, doubtless severe were the declamations against the first who pared their nails, and cropped off part of their hair, which hung down to their nose. To be sure they were called fops and spendthrifts, laying out their money for an instrument of vanity, to mar the creator's work. What an enormity, to cut off the horn which God has caused to grow at our fingers ends! it is an insult to the Deity. But much worse was it on the first appearance of shirts and socks: it is still well known, with what heat the old counsellors, who had never worn any, exclaimed against the younger, who came into this destructive piece of luxury.

MADNESS.

I AM not going about to revive Erasmus's treatise, which in our times would be but a common place-book, and that none of the most entertaining.

By madness is meant that distemper of the organs of the brain, which necessarily hinders a man from thinking and acting like others; if unable to manage his substance, a commission is issued out against him; if incapable of ideas suitable to society, he is excluded; if he be dangerous, he is shut up; and, if frantic, he is bound.

An important observation here is, that this man is not without ideas; he has them, whilst waking, like all other men, and often in his sleep. It may be asked how his soul, being spiritual and immortal, and residing in his brain, whither all the ideas are conveyed to it by the senses very plain and distinct, yet never forms a right judgment of them. It sees objects equally as the souls of Aristotle, Plato, Locke, and Newton; it hears the same sounds, it has the same sense of the touch; how happens it then, that with the same perceptions as the wisest men, it makes a wild incoherent jumble, without being able to help it self? If this simple and eternal substance has the same instruments for acting as the souls of the wisest brains, it should reason like them; what can hinder it? If this madman sees red and the sensible man blue; if when this hears music, the madman hears the braying of an ass; if when they are at church, the madman thinks himself at the play; if when they hear yes, he hears no, I must of necessity conclude that his soul must think differently from the others. But this madman has the like perceptions as they; and there is no apparent reason why his soul, having through the senses received all its tools, cannot make use of them. It is said to be pure, to be, of itself, subject to no infirmity, to be provided with all necessary helps; and whatever happens in the body, its essence remains unalterable; yet it is carried in its case to Bedlam.

This reflection may give rise to an apprehension, that the faculty of thinking, with which man is endued, is liable to be disordered like the other senses. A madman is a patient, whose brain suffers; as a gouty man is a patient whose feet and hands suffer; he thought by means of the brain, as he walked with his feet, without knowing any thing of his incomprehensible power to walk, nor of his no less incomprehensible power to think. The brain may have the gout as well as the feet: after all, let us argue ever so long, perhaps it is faith, alone, which can convince us, that a simple and immaterial substance can be sick (G).

Some Doctors will say to the madman, Friend, Tho' thou hast no longer common sense, thy soul is no less pure, spiritual, and immortal than ours; but our soul is in good quarters, and thine otherwise. The windows of its apartment are stopped up; and it is stifled for want of air. The madman, in his calm intervals, would give them this answer: This is always your way, you are begging the question; my windows are as much open as yours, I see the same objects and hear the same words: so that my soul must necessarily either make a bad use of its senses, or itself be but a vitiated sense, a depraved quality. In a word, either my soul is naturally mad, or I have no soul.

(G) Our author is all of a sudden a great stickler for faith; but we are afraid it proceeds from his ignorance in philosophy. The soul has its perceptions, it is true, by means of the senses. But these perceptions may be impeded by bodily indisposition, or by an irregular construction of the internal or external organs. In that case it does not see the objects in the same manner as the soul of Plato and Aristotle; that is, it does not receive the same perceptions; and therefore it may be said to be sick and disordered as to the exercise of its faculties. See the article SOUL, where the reader will find the proofs of its being an immaterial substance.

One of the doctors will answer, Brother, God may perhaps have created mad as well as wise souls. The madman will reply, To believe what you say, I must be madder than I am. For God's sake, you who are so very knowing, tell me wherefore is it that I am mad?

If the doctors have any sense remaining, their answer will be: We know not. Why a brain has incoherent ideas is above their comprehension; and they as little comprehend why, in another brain, the ideas are regular and connected. They will fancy themselves wise, and they are no less mad than he.

MATTER (H).

WISE men, on being asked what the soul is, answer, they are entirely ignorant of it; and if asked what matter is, they give the like answer.

(H) M. Voltaire pretends to give under this article the opinions of the ancient philosophers in regard to matter, which he does not however attempt to refute. It is sufficient for him to know by faith that God drew matter out of nothing. He therefore supposes that the non-eternity of matter, or the creation of the world in time, is not to be demonstrated strictly by bare reasoning; but the proof of it can be taken only from revelation. And herein perhaps he is right. But he is grossly mistaken in several other points, as that, according to the light of reason only, motion must be essential to matter, and matter itself necessarily existing. Were motion essential to matter, it would imply a contradiction in terms to suppose matter at rest, which is highly absurd. Then that matter is not necessarily self-existing, evidently appears from the doctrine of a vacuum. It has been demonstrated that all space was not filled with matter; consequently there must be a vacuum. If so, it is evidently
more

fwer. Professors indeed, and especially schoolmen, are perfectly versed in those things; and when they say as they have been taught, that matter is extended and divisible, they fancy that is all; but when desired to tell what this extended thing is, then they are hard put to it. It is composed of parts, say they. And these parts, of what are they composed? Are the elements of those parts divisible? Then they are struck dumb or talk without end, which is equally suspicious. This almost unknown being called matter, is it eternal? So all antiquity believed. Has it, of it self, an active force? This is the opinion of several philosophers. Have they who deny it, any superior reason for their opinion? You do not conceive that matter can, intrinsically, have any property; but how can you affirm that it has not intrinsically such properties as are necessary to it? You know nothing of its nature, and yet deny it to have modes, which reside in its nature: for, after all, as matter exists, it must have a form and figure; and being necessarily figured, is it impossible that there are other modes annexed to its configuration? Matter exists, this you know; but you know it no farther than by your sensations. Alas! what avail all subtilties and sophisms, since reasoning has been in vogue? Geometry has taught us many truths, and metaphysics very few. We weigh, we

---

more than possible for matter not to be; therefore it is not a necessary being. And some may answer, that matter may be necessary, though not necessary to be every where; but this is infinitely absurd; for if it be no impossibility for matter to be absent from one place, it is no absolute impossibility, in the nature of the thing, that matter should be absent from any other place, or from every place. See Dr. Clarke on the Being and Attributes of God, and Wollaston's Religion of Nature Delineated.

measure,

measure, we analyse, we decompound matter; but on offering to go a step beyond these rude operations, we find ourselves bewildered, and an abyss opens before us

Forgive, I intreat you, the mistake of the whole universe, in believing matter self-existent. How could they do otherwise? how could they conceive that, what is without succession has not always been? were the existence of matter not necessary, why exists it? and if it was to exist, why should it not always have existed? never was axiom more universally received than this: nothing produces nothing. The contrary indeed is incomprehensible: all nations have held their chaos anterior to the divine disposition of the world. The eternity of matter never was known to do any hurt to the worship of the Deity. Religion never took offence at an eternal God's being owned as the master of an eternal matter; it is the happiness of our times to know by faith, that God drew matter from nothing; an article, which no nation had been informed of: the very Jews know nothing of it. The first verse of Genesis says, that the gods Eloïm, and not Eloi, made heaven and earth; it does not say that heaven and earth were created out of nothing.

Philo, who came at the only time when the Jews had any erudition, says, in his chapter of the creation, "God being naturally good, did not "envy substance or matter, which of itself had "nothing good, which naturally is nothing but "inertness, confusion, and disorder; but from bad "as it was, he condescended to make it good."

The opinion of the chaos being arranged by a deity is to be met with in all the ancient theogonies. Hesiod, in saying, "the chaos was first in existence," delivered the thoughts of the whole east; and Ovid declared

declared the sentiments of the Roman empire in the following verse:

" Sic ubi dispositam quisquis fuit ille deorum Congeriem secuit."

Matter therefore was looked on in the hands of God as clay under the potter's wheel; if such faint images may be used to express the divine power. Matter being eternal should have eternal properties, as configuration, the inert power, motion, and divisibility. But this divisibility is no more than the consequence of motion, as without motion there can be no division, separation, nor arrangement; therefore motion was looked on as essential to matter. The chaos had been a confused motion; and the arrangement of the universe was a regular motion, impressed on all bodies by the Sovereign of the world. But how should matter of itself have motion; as, according to all the antients, it has extension and impenetrability?

It cannot, however, be conceived without extension, and it may without motion. To this the answer was, It is impossible but matter must be permeable; and if permeable, something must be continually passing into its pores; where is the use of passages, if nothing passes through them?

There would be no end of replying: the system of the eternity of matter has, like all other systems, very great difficulties. That of matter formed out of nothing is not less incomprehensible. It must be admitted, without flattering ourselves to account for it; philosophy does not account for every thing. How many incomprehensible things are admitted, even in geometry itself! can you conceive two lines ever approaching to each other, and never meeting?

Geome-

Geometricians, indeed, will tell us, the properties of the asymptotes are demonstrated to you, so that you cannot but admit them; the creation is not, wherefore then do you admit it? what difficulty do you find to believe, with all antiquity, the eternity of matter? On the other hand, the divine pushes you, and says, that in believing the eternity of matter, you make two principles, God and matter, and fall into the error of Zoroaster and Manes.

The Geometricians shall go without an answer, for they pay no regard to any thing but their lines, their surfaces, and their solids; but to the divine it may be said, how am I a manichee? There is an heap of stones which no architect has made, but with them he has built a vast edifice. Here I do not admit of two architects; only the rough stones have submitted to the operations of power and genius.

Happily, which ever system be espoused, morality is hurt by neither; for what signifies it, whether matter be made or only arranged? God is equally our absolute master. Whether the chaos was only put in order, or whether it was created of nothing, still it behoves us to be virtuous: scarce any of these metaphysical questions have a relation to the conduct of life; disputes are like table-talk, every one forgets after dinner what he has said, and goes away where his interest and inclination lead him.

MESSIAH.

MESSIAH or Meshiah in Hebrew, Christos or Celomenos in Greek, Unctus in Latin, signifies anointed.

We

We see in the Old Testament that the name of Meſſiah was often given to idolatrous, or infidel princes. God is ſaid to have ſent a prophet to anoint Jehu king of Iſrael; he ſignified the ſacred unction to Hazael king of Damaſcus and Syria, thoſe two princes being the Meſſiahs of the moſt high to puniſh the houſe of Ahab.

In the 45th of Iſaiah, the name of Meſſiah is expreſsly given to Cyrus. "Thus hath the Lord ſaid to his anointed (his Meſſiah) whoſe right hand I have holden to ſubdue nations before him."

Ezekiel, in the twenty-eighth chapter of his Revelations, gives the appellation of Meſſiah to the king of Tyrus, whom he alſo calls Cherubin. Son of man, ſays the eternal to the prophet, lift up thy voice and utter a lamentation concerning the king of Tyrus; and ſay unto him, thus ſaith the Lord, the eternal, thou waſt the ſeal of the likeneſs of God, full of wiſdom, and perfect in beauty: thou waſt the Lord's garden of Eden; or, according to other verſions, Thou waſt the Lord's whole delight. Thy garments were of ſardonix, topaz, jaſper, chryſolite, onyx, beryl, ſapphire, carbuncle, emerald, and gold. What thy tabrets and thy flutes could do was within thee; they were all ready on the day thou waſt created; thou haſt a cherubim, a Meſſiah.

This title of Meſſiah, or Chriſt, was given to the kings, prophets, and high-prieſts among the Hebrews. The Lord and his Meſſiah are witneſs, 1 Kings, chap. xii. ver. 3. that is, the Lord and the king whom he hath ſet up; and elſewhere, touch not mine anointed, and do my prophets no harm. David, who was divinely inſpired, in more than one place gives the title of Meſſiah to Saul his rejected father-in-law, who perſecuted him. God forbid, ſays he frequently, that I ſhould lay my hand on the Lord's anointed, the Meſſiah of God. The

As the name of Messiah, or anointed of the Eternal, has been given to idolatrous kings and reprobate persons, very often has it been used to indicate the true anointed of the Lord; the Messiah, by way of excellence, the Christ, the Son of God; lastly, God himself.

If all the oracles usually applied to the Messiah, were to be compared, it may give rise to some seeming difficulties, and which the Jews have made use of to justify their hardness of belief and obstinacy, did it admit of an apology? Several eminent divines allow, that the Jews, groaning under an oppressive slavery, and having so many repeated promises from the Eternal, might well long for the coming of a Messiah, who was to deliver them and subdue their enemies; and that they are in some measure, excusable for having not immediately perceived Jesus to be this deliverer and conqueror.

It was agreeable to the plan of eternal wisdom, that the spiritual ideas of the real Messiah should be unknown to the blind multitude; and so far were they unknown, that the Jewish doctors have denied that those passages which we produce, are to be understood of the Messiah. Many affirm that the Messiah is already come in the person of Hezekiah; and this was the famous Hillel's opinion. Others, and these are many, say, that the belief of the coming of a Messiah, so far from being a fundamental article of faith, was only a comfortable hope, no such thing being mentioned in the Decalogue, or in Leviticus.

Several Rabbins tell you, that they do not in the least question the Messiah's being come at the time decreed; that he is not however growing old, but remains in the world concealed, and waits till Israel shall have duly celebrated the Sabbath, to reveal himself. The

The famous Rabbi, Solomon Jarchy or Raſchy, who lived in the beginning of the twelfth century, ſays, in his Talmudics, that the antient Hebrews believed the Meſſiah to have been born on the very day of the final deſtruction of Jeruſalem by the Romans. This anſwers to the common ſaying, of ſending for the doctor when a man is dead.

The rabbi Kimchy, who alſo lived in the twelfth century, preached that the Meſſiah, whoſe coming he imagined to be at hand, would drive the Chriſtians out of Judea, which was then in their poſſeſſion. The Chriſtians, indeed, were diſpoſſeſſed of the Holy Land; but this was done by Saladin; and had that conqueror taken the Jews under his protection, it is very probable that, in their enthuſiaſm, they would have made him their Meſſiah.

The ſacred authors, and our Lord Jeſus himſelf, often compare the Meſſiah's reign, and the eternal beatitude, to a wedding and banquet; but theſe parables have been ſtrangely wreſted by the Talmudiſts. According to them, the Meſſiah will gather together all his people in the land of Canaan, and give them an entertainment, where the wine will be that which Adam himſelf made in the earthly Paradiſe, and which he keeps in vaſt cellars, dug by angels in the center of the earth.

The firſt courſe will be the famous fiſh called the great Leviathan, which at once ſwallows a fiſh, leſs than itſelf; yet it is three hundred leagues in length; and the whole maſs of waters is ſupported on this Leviathan. God at firſt created a male and a female; but, leſt they might overturn the earth, or crowd the univerſe with their offspring, he killed the female and ſalted it down for the Meſſiah's banquet.

The

The Rabbins add, that there will likewise be killed the bull called Behemoth, of such a monstrous size, that every day it eats the herbage of a thousand mountains. This bull's female was slain at the beginning of the world, to prevent the multiplication of such prodigious species, which must have been extremely detrimental to other creatures; but they say, that the Eternal did not salt it, cow's flesh not being so good salted as that of the female Leviathan. So firmly do the Jews believe all these rabbinical chimeras, that it is common among them to swear by their share of the Behemoth.

With such coarse ideas concerning the coming of the Messiah and his reign, is it to be wondered at, that the Jews, both ancient and modern, and several even of the first Christians, unhappily prepossessed with all these reveries, could not raise their conceptions to the idea of the divine nature of the Lord's anointed, or perceive God in the Messiah? See the sentiments of the Jews concerning this, in a work, intitled, Judæi Lusitani questiones ad Christianos, Quest. 1, 2, 4, 23. "To acknowledge a man God, say they, is imposing on one's self, it is forming a monster, a centaur, the strange compound of two natures incompatible with each other." Adding, that the prophets never taught the Messiah's being Man-God; that they expresly distinguish between God and David; that they plainly declare the former to be master, and the latter servant, &c.

It is sufficiently known that the Jews servilely adhered to the letter of the scriptures, never like us, penetrating into the spirit.

When the Saviour appeared, the prejudiced Jews declared against him. And Jesus Christ himself, that their blindness might not be too much irritated, seems extremely reserved in the article of his divinity, meaning, says St. Chrysostom, insensibly to accustom his hearers to believe a mystery so very much above bare reason: his assuming the divine prerogative of pardoning sins, shocked all the bye-standers; his most manifest miracles convinced not even those for whose relief they were operated, that he was God. When with a modest circumlocution, he owned himself the Son of God before the high priest's judgment seat; the high priest, filled with indignation, rent his cloaths, and cried out Blasphemy! Before the mission of the Holy Ghost, the apostles themselves had not the least apprehension of their master's divinity; he asks them what the people think of him? and their answer is, that some took him for Elias, others for Jeremiah, or some other prophet; and it was by a particular revelation that St. Peter knew Jesus to be the Christ, the Son of the living God.

The Jews being irreconcileably scandalized at the divinity of Jesus, have left no stone unturned to explode it; perverting the sense of their own oracles, or not applying them to the Messiah. They affirm that the name of God, Eloi, is not peculiar to the Deity; and that it is by sacred authors given to judges, to magistrates, and in general to all persons in authority: they do indeed quote a great number of passages, which countenance this observation, but without in the least invalidating those strong and clear terms of the antient oracles, which manifestly relate to the Messiah.

Lastly, say they, if the Saviour, and after him, the evangelists, the apostles, and primitive Christians did call Jesus, Son of God; this august term in the gospel-times imported no more than the contrary to the sons of Belial, i. e. a good man, a

servant

servant of God, in oppofition to a wicked man, or to one who does not fear God.

The Jews, befides denying Chrift his quality of Meffiah, and his divinity, have omitted nothing to render him contemptible, expofing his birth, life, and death, with all the ridicule, virulence, and contumely, which their guilty rancour could fuggeft.

Of all the works which Jewifh blindnefs has produced, none in extravagance and impiety exceed the antient book, intitled, Sepher Toldos Jefchut, which has been refcued from the worms by M. Vagenfeil, in vol. ii. of his work, called, Tela Ignea.

This Sepher Toldos Jefchut has a moft fhocking hiftory of the life of our Saviour, forged with the utmoft falfity and malice: for inftance, they have dared to write, that one Panther or Pandera, who dwelt at Bethlehem, feduced a young woman married to Jochaman; and the fruit of this foul commerce was a child, whom they named Jefus or Jefu. The father being obliged to fly the place, withdrew to Babylon. As for young Jefus, he was fent to fchool; but, adds the author, he had the infolence to raife his head and uncover himfelf before the priefts, contrary to the ufage, which was to appear in their prefence with the head hanging down and the face covered; a petulance for which he received a fmart check: this occafioning an enquiry into his birth, it was confequently found to be impure, and he became expofed to public ignominy.

That deteftable book, Sepher Toldos Jefchut, was known fo early as the fecond century; Celfus cites it with exultation, and Origen in his ninth chapter confutes it.

There

There is another book which likewise bears the title of Toledos Jesu, published in 1705 by M. Huldric, which is more consonant with the evangelical history of our Saviour's birth, but swarms with the grossest anachronisms and other errors. It makes Christ to have been born and have died under Herod the Great; and affirms, that the complaint of Panther's adultery with Mary the mother of Jesus, was brought before that prince.

The author, who calls himself Jonathan, and if his word may be taken, was cotemporary with Christ, and lived at Jerusalem, affirms that Herod, relatively to Jesus Christ, consulted the senators of a city in the land of Cesarea; but such an absurd author, with all his contradictions, we shall leave to himself.

These calumnies, however, serve to foment the implacable hatred of the Jews against the Christians and the gospel; so that they have stuck at nothing to falsify the chronology of the Old Testament, and to spread doubts and difficulties about the time of our Saviour's coming.

Ahmed-ben Cassum-al Anacousy, a Moor of Grenada, who lived towards the close of the sixteenth century, quotes an ancient Arabic manuscript, found in a cave near Grenada, together with sixteen sheets of lead, on which some tales in Arabic characters were engraved. Don Pedro y Quinones, archbishop of Grenada, has certified this fact. These famous Grenadian sheets have been since carried to Rome, where, after an examination of several years, they were at last condemned as apocryphal under the Pontificate of Alexander VII. Their contents are only some fabulous tales concerning Mary and her son.

The name of Messiah, joined to the epithet of false, is likewise given to those impostors, who, at several

several times, have made it their business to deceive the Jewish nation. Some of these false Messiahs set up even before the coming of the true anointed of God. The wise Gamaliel, Acts chap. v. ver. 34, &c. mentions one named Theudas, whose history is to be found in Josephus's Antiquities, b. 20. chap. 2. He boasted that he could pass the Jordan dry footed, and was joined by considerable numbers; but the Romans, coming to an action with his raw men, soon dispersed them; and taking the chief prisoner, set up his head in Jerusalem.

Gamaliel further speaks of Judas the Galilean, doubtless the same whom Josephus mentions in the twelfth chapter of the second book of his Jewish wars. He says that this false prophet had got together near 30,000 men; but the Jewish historian is noted for hyperboles.

So early as the apostolic times, Simon, surnamed the Magician, made his appearance; and to such a degree had he seduced the people of Samaria, that they accounted him the power of God; Acts chap. viii. ver. 9.

In the year 178 and 179 of the Christian æra, Adrian being then emperor, the false Messiah, Barchochebas, asserted his pretensions at the head of an army. Julius Severus, being sent against him, hemmed in the insurgents at the city of Bither, which after an obstinate siege he carried; and Barchochebas being taken, was put to death. Adrian, as the best expedient for preventing the continual revolts of the Jews, issued an edict against their going to Jerusalem; and even guards were posted at the city gates to keep them out.

Socrates, an ecclesiastic historian, book 2. ch. 38. relates, that in the year 434, a false Messiah started up in the island of Candia, under the name of Moses, and as the ancient deliverer of the Hebrews raised from the dead to effect a second deliverance for them.

The next century, in 530, saw in Palestine a false Messiah, named Julian; he recommended himself to the people as a great conqueror, who at the head of his nation should destroy all Christians whatever; and the Jews were so far seduced by his promises, that they ran to arms, and massacred great numbers of Christians. The emperor Justinian's forces engaging him, the false Christ was taken and executed.

In the beginning of the eighth century, Serenus, a Spanish Jew, stood for the Messiahship, preached and gained followers; but the upshot was, that both followers and leader came to a miserable end.

The twelfth century produced several false Messiahs, particularly one in France under Lewis the Younger; but both he and his adherents were hanged, without so much as the names of master or disciples being known.

The thirteenth century was still more fertile in false Messiahs; of these the more remarkable were seven or eight who appeared in Arabia, in Persia, in Spain, and Moravia: one of them who stiled himself David el Re, is reckoned to have been a very great magician; his artifices so far succeeded with the Jews, that he saw himself at the head of a considerable party; but this fair prospect terminated in his being murdered.

James Zieglerne, a Moravian, who lived in the middle of the 16th century, promulgated the approach of the Messiah's manifestation, assuring the people that this Messiah had been born fourteen years before, and that he himself had seen him at Strasbourgh; and he carefully kept a sword and a scepter, to put into his hands when he should be of age to teach.

In the year 1624 another Zieglerne confirmed the former prediction.

In the year 1666 Zabathei Sevi, a native of Aleppo, gave himself out to be the Messiah, foretold by the Zieglernes. He began by preaching in the highways and fields, and while his disciples admired him, the Turks laughed at him. It appears that at first his preaching had no very extraordinary success, for the chiefs of the Smyrna synagogue went so far as to pronounce sentence of death against him; but his punishment was mitigated to exile.

He contracted three marriages without consummating any, saying it was beneath him. He took a partner named Nathan Levi, who was to act the part of Elias, as the Messiah's harbinger. They repaired to Jerusalem, and Nathan there preached up Zabathei-Sevi as the deliverer of the nations. The Jewish populace declared for him, whilst they who had any thing to lose anathematized him.

Sevi, to shun the storm, withdrew to Constantinople, and from thence to Smyrna: Nathan Levi deputed to him four ambassadors, who, besides acknowledging his dignity, did him homage publicly as Messiah; this embassy dazzled the commonalty and even some doctors, who declared Zabathei-Sevi, Messiah, and king of the Hebrews; but the Smyrna synagogue condemned their king to be impaled.

Zabathei put himself under the cadi of Smyrna's protection, and soon had on his side the whole Jewish people; he even had two thrones set up, one for himself and the other for his favourite spouse, assuming the title of king of kings: his brother Sevi he created king of Judah; and to the

Jews themselves he gave the most positive assurances, that the Ottoman empire should soon be their own; in the height of his insolence, he had the emperor's name struck out of the Jewish Liturgy, and his own substituted in its stead.

He was confined in the castle of the Dardanelles, and the Jews gave out that his life was spared, only because the Turks very well knew him to be immortal. The governor of the Dardanelles made a great fortune by the presents which the Jews poured on him for leave to visit their king, their Messiah, who in his fetters maintained his dignity, and even the ceremony of kissing his feet.

The Sultan, however, who then kept his court at Adrianople, was for putting an end to this farce; and sending for Sevi told him, that if he was the Messiah, he must be invulnerable. This Sevi allowed; but on the grand seignior's ordering him to be placed as a mark for his icoglans or pages to discharge their arrows at, the Messiah owned that he was not invulnerable, and protested that God sent him only to bear testimony to the holy Mahometan religion. After undergoing a severe flagellation by the ministers of the law, he turned Mahometan, and lived and died despised both by Jews and Mussulmen. This adventure has brought the profession of a false Messiah into such disrepute, that since Sevi nobody has taken it up.

METAMORPHOSIS,

Metempsychosis.

IS it not very natural that all the various metamorphoses with which the earth may be said to be covered, should have led the orientals, whose imagination is so luxuriant, to imagine that our souls

souls passed from one body to another? An almost imperceptible point grows to be a worm, and this worm becomes a butter-fly; an acorn changes to an oak, an egg to a bird; water becomes clouds and thunder; wood is turned into fire and ashes: in a word, all nature is more or less a metamorphosis. Souls being accounted tenuous forms, were soon concluded to partake of that property, which was sensibly seen in more dense and heavy bodies. The metempsychosis is perhaps the most antient doctrine in the known world, and still prevails in a great part of India and China.

It is likewise very natural that those antient fables, collected and embellished by Ovid in his admirable work, took rise from the several metamorphoses with which our eyes are conversant. The very Jews have not been without their metamorphoses. If Niobe was changed into marble, Hedith, Lot's wife, was turned into salt. As Euridice was detained in hell for looking back, a like indiscretion cost Lot's wife her human nature. The country town in Phrygia where lived the hospitable Baucis and Philemon, is changed into a lake; the same submersion has befallen Sodom. Arius's daughters turned water into oil; the Scripture mentions a change something similar, but more sacred and real. Cadmus was turned into a serpent, and the like was seen in Aaron's rod.

The pagan deities very often assumed a human disguise; and when angels appeared to the Jews, it was always as men; with Abraham they partook of a repast. St. Paul, in his epistle to the Corinthians, says, that the messenger of Satan cuffed him: Αγγελος Σατανα με κολαφιζει.

MIRACLE.

MIRACLE (I).

A Miracle, in the energetic sense of the word, means something wonderful; and thus every thing is a miracle. The order of nature, the

---

(I) As our author does not absolutely deny the possibility of miracles, but acknowledges those which have been operated in favour of our holy religion by Christ and his apostles; he cannot be charged on that account with infidelity. But viewing the matter in a philosophic light, and abstracting from faith, he starts several doubts, which had he dealt with candour, he ought to have solved. He seems to have borrowed great part of this article from the Essay on Miracles, written by the learned historian Mr. Hume, whom he imitates in his cant language of resting our holy religion on faith, and not on reason; a test which he says it is by no means fitted to endure.

It has been the practice of modern deists to deny the possibility of miracles in general: observing that the frame and order of the world is preserved according to fixed laws or rules in an uniform manner, they weakly conclude, that there are in matter certain necessary laws or powers, the result of which they call the course of nature; this they think impossible to be changed, and consequently that there can be no miracle. But if they would consider things duly, they would find that lifeless matter is utterly incapable of obeying any laws, or of being endued with any powers; and therefore what they call the course of nature can be nothing more than the arbitrary will and pleasure of God, acting continually upon matter, according to certain rules of uniformity and proportion. Hence it follows, that it is altogether as easy to alter the course of nature, as to preserve it. Those effects which are produced in the world regularly and constantly, and which we call the works of nature, prove the constant providence of the Deity: those which upon any extraordinary occasion are produced in such a manner, as it is manifest they could neither have been done by any power or art of man, nor by what we call chance; these undeniably prove

the rotation of a hundred millions of globes round a million of suns, the activity of light, the life of animals, are perpetual miracles.

According to the received notion, however, a miracle is a violation of the divine and eternal laws. An eclipse of the sun and moon, a dead man walking two leagues with his head in his hands, are what we call a miracle.

Several naturalists affirm that, in this sense, there are no miracles; and their arguments are these:

A miracle is a breach of the mathematical, divine, immutable, eternal laws; now this definition alone makes a miracle a contradiction in terms. A law cannot be both immutable and broken; but it is answered, Cannot a law of God's making be suspended by its author? They boldly answer, no; and it cannot be that the infinitely wise Being should

---

prove to us the immediate interposition of the Deity, in order to signify his pleasure on that particular occasion. The true definition therefore of a miracle, as the learned Dr. Clarke observes, is " a work effected in a manner different from the " common method of Providence, by the interposition of " the Deity, for the proof of some particular doctrine, or in " attestation to the authority of some particular person." In this sense the miracles which the disciples of Christ saw him perform, were a compleat demonstration to them, that he had truly a divine commission, as it was certain that God would not himself interpose in the usual order of nature, to lead men into a necessary and invincible error. These miracles were worked to attest a doctrine, that tended in the highest degree to promote the honour of God, and the general reformation of mankind. This is an answer to all the queries of the philosophers in the following article, and is a sufficient reason for the miracles recorded in the Scriptures, in support of the true religion. With regard to such as are said to have been performed since the establishment of Christianity, that is another question, which we leave to the antagonists of the late Dr. Middleton to settle.

have

have made laws, and afterwards break them. If, say they, he made any alteration in his machine, it would be to make it go the better: now it is clear, that God has framed this immense machine as good as it possibly could be; if he saw that any imperfection would hereafter be occasioned by the nature of the materials, he at first provided against any such future defect, so that there would be no cause for any after-change.

Besides, God can do nothing without reason; now what reason should induce him to disfigure his own work for any time?

It is for man's sake, say their opponents. It is to be hoped then, answer they, that it is for the sake of all men, it being impossible to conceive that the divine nature should work for some particular men, and not for all mankind: and even all mankind is but a very little thing; less than an ant's nest in comparison of all the beings which fill the immensity of space. Now what can be more low and absurd, than to imagine that the infinite Being will, for the sake of three or four hundred ants on that little clod of mud, suspend or alter the eternal play of those immense springs on which depends the motion of the universe.

But supposing that God had been pleased to distinguish a small number of men by particular favours, must he therefore alter what he has settled for all times and all places? He certainly can favour his creatures without any such inconstancy and change; his favours are comprised in his very laws; every thing has been wisely contrived and arranged for their good; and they all irrevocably obey the force which he has originally implanted in nature.

Wherefore is God to work a miracle? to accomplish a design he has for some living beings!
that

that is making God to say, I have not been able, by the fabric of the universe, by my divine decrees, by my eternal laws, to compass such a design: I see I must make an alteration in my eternal ideas, my immutable laws, as what I intended cannot be executed by those means. This would be an acknowledgment of weakness, not a declaration of power; it would be the most inconceivable contradiction. So that to suppose God works any miracles is, if men can insult God, a downright insult to him; it is no less than saying to him, You are a weak and inconsistent Being. Therefore to believe miracles is an absurdity; it is, in some measure, scandalizing the Deity.

A farther reply to these philosophers is, Your crying up the immutability of the Supreme Being, the eternity of his laws, with the regularity of his infinite worlds, signifies nothing; our small heap of dirt has been covered with miracles; in history prodigies are as frequent as natural events. The daughters of the high-priest Anius changed whatever they would into wine or oil; Athalida, daughter to Mercury, rose from the dead several times; Esculapius restored Hypolitus; Hercules delivered Alcestes from death; heroes returned upon earth after staying a fortnight in the infernal regions; Romulus and Remus were the issue of a god and a vestal; the Palladium dropped from Heaven into the city of Troy; Berenice's tresses became a constellation; Baucis and Philemon's hut was changed to a stately temple; Orpheus's head uttered oracles after his death; the walls of Thebes were formed before numbers of Greeks, by stones moving of themselves to the sound of a flute; innumerable cures were performed in Esculapius's temple; and we have still monuments with the names of ocular witnesses to his miracles.

Name

Name me one nation where incredible prodigies have not been performed, especially in times when reading and writing were little known.

All the answer unbelieving philosophers give to these objections is a sneer and a shrug; but those who profess Christianity say, We make no doubt of the miracles wrought within our holy religion; yet it is by faith we believe them, and not by reason; as for the latter we turn the deaf ear to it; for we know, that when faith speaks, reason is to be mute: the miracles of Jesus Christ and his apostles we are fully and firmly persuaded of; but allow us to doubt a little of several others; indulge us, for instance, in suspending our judgment concerning what is related by a weak man (K), who yet has been surnamed the Great. He affirms that a little monk got such a custom of working miracles, that, at length, the prior forbad him to exercise his supernatural talent. The monk conformed to the order, but one day seeing a bricklayer falling from the roof of a house, he hesitated between monastical obedience and charity in saving the poor man's life, and only ordering him to remain in the air till he got orders, he ran to acquaint the prior with the case. The prior gave him absolution for the sin of beginning a miracle without leave, and allowed him to go through with it, but never to do the like again. It is granted to philosophers that this story may be a little mistrusted.

But it is again said to them, How will you dare to deny that St. Gervase and St. Protais appeared in a dream to St. Ambrose, and informed him of the place where their reliques lay; that St. Ambrose had them taken up; and that a blind man was

---

(K) Gregory the Great.

cured

cured by them? St. Auftin was then at Milan, and it is he who relates this miracle in Book XXII. of his City of God, and that it was performed "immenfo populo tefte." Here is a miracle with every circumftance of proof. Philofophers, however, fay, that they believe nothing at all of Gervafe and Protais appearing; that to know where the remains of their carcafes lie, is a thing of no concern to mankind; and that they give no more credit to that blind man than to Vefpafian's; that it is an ufelefs miracle; that God does nothing ufelefs; and in a word, they abide immoveable by their principles. My regard for St. Gervafe and St. Protais will not allow me to fide with thofe philofophers; I only give an account of their incredulity. They are vaftly fond of a paffage of Lucian in the death of Peregrinus, " a dexterous juggler turning Chriftian is fure of making his fortune;" but Lucian is a profane author, and, of courfe, fhould be of no weight among us.

Thefe philofophers cannot bring themfelves to believe the miracles of the fecond century, though eye-witneffes have in writing declared, that the bifhop of Smyrna, St. Policarpe, having, purfuant to the fentence paffed on him, been thrown into a blazing fire, they heard a voice from heaven calling out, " Chear up, Policarpe, be ftrong in the Lord, and fhew thy felf a man;" at which the flames of the pile drawing back from his body, formed a fiery canopy over his head, and out of the pile flew a dove; at laft they were obliged to cut off the good bifhop's head. To what purpofe was this miracle? fay unbelievers; how came it that the flames deviated from their nature, and the executioner's ax had the natural effect? how is it that fo many martyrs, after coming fafe and found out of boiling oil, have fallen under the edge of the fword?

The

The ufual anfwer is, that fuch was God's will; but philofophers will believe no fuch thing, unlefs they had feen it with their own eyes.

They who improve their reafonings by ftudy, will tell you that the fathers of the church have themfelves often owned that miracles were ceafed in their time. St. Chryfoftom fays exprefsly, "The extraordinary gifts of the fpirit were "given even to the unworthy, becaufe the church "then ftood in need of miracles; but at prefent "they are not fo much as given to the worthy, "the church no longer ftanding in need of them." Afterwards he acknowledges that there was nobody then who raifed the dead, or fo much as cured the fick.

St. Auftin himfelf, as if he had forgot the miracle of Gervafe and Protais, fays in his City of God, "Why are thofe miracles, which were per-"formed fome time ago, at prefent ceafed?" and he gives the fame reafon, "Cur, inquiunt, nunc illa miracula quæ prædicatis facta effe, non fiunt? Poffem quidem dicere, neceffaria prius fuiffe, quam crederet mundus, ad hoc ut crederet mundus."

It is objected to the philofophers, that St. Auftin, notwithftanding this avowal, fpeaks of an old cobler at Hippo, who having loft his cloak, went to pray for relief at the chapel of the Twenty Martyrs, and in his return home found a fifh, in the body of which was difcovered a gold ring; the cook who dreffed it giving it to the cobler, faid, There is a prefent for you from the Twenty Martyrs.

To this the philofophers anfwer, that in that ftory there is nothing contrary to the laws of nature; that a fifh may very naturally have fwallowed a gold a gold ring; and that there is no miracle in the cook's giving that ring to the cobler.

If the philosophers are put in mind that, according to St. Jerom, in his Life of the hermit Paul, this devout person had several conversations with satyrs and fauns; that a raven for thirty years together daily brought him half a loaf for his dinner; and a whole loaf the day St. Anthony paid him a visit; they may still reply that nothing of all this is absolutely contrary to nature; that satyrs and fauns may have existed; and that, after all, if this story be a puerility, that does not in the least affect the real miracles of our Saviour and his apostles. Several good Christians have rejected the story of St. Simeon Stilites, written by Theodoret: many miracles accounted authentic in the Greek church have been questioned by Latin writers; so in return, Latin miracles have been suspected by the Greeks; in process of time came the Protestants, who have made very free with the miracles of both churches.

A learned Jesuit (L) who preached a long time in the Indies, complains, that neither his brethren nor he could ever perform one single miracle. Xavier, in several letters, laments his not having the gift of tongues: he says that he is but as a dumb image among the Japonese; yet, according to the narrative of the Jesuits, he restored eight dead persons to life, and that is a great many; but it must withal be considered, that the scene of those restorations was six thousand leagues off. Some persons of later times make the suppression of the Jesuits in France a much greater miracle than all those of Xavier and Ignatius put together. Be

---

(L) Ospinian, p. 230.

that as it may, all Christians hold the miracles of Jesus Christ and his apostles to be indisputably true and real, but allow that some miracles of our modern times, and which are without any certain authenticity, may very well be doubted of.

It were to be wished, that for the legal verification of a miracle, it should be performed before the Academy of Sciences at Paris, or the Royal Society, and the College of Physicians at London, with a detachment of the guards to keep off the people, whose tumultuous indiscretion might hinder the performance of the miracle.

A philosopher was one day asked what he would say if the sun should stand still, that is, if the motion of the earth round that body ceased; if all the dead arose; and if all the mountains went and threw themselves into the sea; and all this to prove some important truth, we will suppose versatile grace. What I should say, answered the philosopher, I would turn Manichee, and say, that there is a principle which undoes what the other has done.

MOSES.

IT (M) has been the groundless opinion of many learned men that the Pentateuch cannot have been written by Moses. They say that, according to the

---

(M) So fond is our author of paradox, that in the following article he supposes Moses not to have been the author of the Pentateuch, or the five books commonly attributed to that legislator, viz. Genesis, Exodus, Leviticus, Numbers, and Deuteronomy. It is true, as he acknowledges those books to have been written by an inspired writer, it is not essential to religion, whether Moses was the author of them or not.

But

the scripture itself, the first known copy was found in the time of king Josias, and that this only copy

But for the sake of historical truth, we shall give a few remarks on this subject. The Pentateuch was called the law by way of excellence, because the principal part of it contained the law which Moses had received from God on Mount Sinai. Now it can hardly be questioned but this legislator was the author of the Pentateuch, if we attentively consider the 24th chapter of Exodus and the 31st of Deuteronomy. In the former, it is expressly said, " And Moses wrote all the " words of the Lord;" in the latter, " And Moses wrote this " law, and delivered it unto the priests, the sons of Levi:" Again, " And it came to pass when Moses had made an end " of writing the words of this law in a book until they were " finished." Besides, all antiquity, both sacred and profane, acknowledges Moses to have been the legislator of the Jews. That whole nation has always carefully preserved his books, and looked upon them as containing their law. When the tribes were divided into two kingdoms, both of them preserved the same respect for those books as being written by Moses. Prophane authors have spoken of those books, as penned by the same legislator. In short, it is as certain that the books which go by the name of Moses are his own, as that those ascribed to Thucydides and Livy, &c. appertain to those whose names they bear. It is possible there may have been some additions and alterations made in them; but the body of the history and the laws could not be altered. Thus the death of Moses is clearly mentioned in the last chapter of Deuteronomy; whence it is probable, that either Joshua or Esdras added the eight last verses of that book; though Josephus pretends that Moses, finding his dissolution approaching, wrote those lines himself, in order to certify his death at the end of his books, left the Jews, from too great a regard to his memory, should deny his death, and give out that he had been translated into Heaven. Notwithstanding this evidence of Moses's being the author of the Pentateuch, some late writers, as Pere Simon and Le Clerc, have espoused the contrary opinion of Hobbes and Spinosa, which seems also to be adopted by M. Voltaire. The difficulties started by those writers may appear plausible at first sight, but are fully refuted by M. du Pin, in his preliminary dissertation to the Bible, to which we refer the reader.

was brought to the king by Saphan the scribe. Now the interval from Moses to this circumstance of Saphan the scribe, according to the Hebrew computation, makes a space of 1167 years; for God appeared to Moses in the burning-bush in the year of the world 2213, and Saphan the scribe made public the book of the law in the year of the world 3380. This book, which had been found under Josias, was unknown till the return from the captivity of Babylon; and Esdras is said, by divine inspiration, to have brought to light all the sacred writings.

But whether Esdras or any other was the compiler of this book, is absolutely a matter of indifference, admitting its being inspired. The Pentateuch does not say that Moses was the author of it; so that it might, without profaneness, be attributed to any other sacred penman, if the church had not positively decided, that this book was written by Moses.

Some adversaries add, that no prophet has quoted any of the books of the Pentateuch; that not the least mention is made of it in the Psalms; in the books attributed to Solomon; nor in Jeremiah, nor in Isaiah; nor, in a word, in any canonical book of the Jews. Then the words answering to those of Genesis, Exodus, Numbers, Leviticus, Deuteronomy, are not to be found in any other book received as authentic by that nation.

Others more sanguine have put the following questions:

1. In what language could Moses have written in a wilderness? It could be only in the Egyptian, for, from this very book it is clear, that Moses and his whole people were born in Egypt, and very probably acquainted with no other language.

S

guage. The Egyptians were yet strangers to the use of the papyrus; they had their hieroglyphics cut in marble and wood; the very tables of the commandments are said to have been engraved on stone: so that here were five volumes to be engraved on polished stones; a work of prodigious time and labour!

2. Is it probable that in a wilderness, where the Jewish people had neither shoemaker nor taylor, and where the God of the universe was obliged to work a continual miracle to preserve their old cloaths and shoes, they should have among them persons of such skill as to engrave the five books of the Pentateuch on marble or wood? It will be said that workmen were found among them who could make a golden calf in one night, and afterwards reduce the gold to dust; (an operation beyond the skill of common chemistry, an art not yet invented) who could build the tabernacle, adorn it with thirty-four brass pillars, with silver chapiters; who wove and embroidered linen veils with hyacinth, purple, and scarlet: but this very thing strengthens the adversaries opinion, and they rejoin that it is not in nature that such curious works should have been made in a desert, and under the want of every thing; that shoes and coats would have been the things to have begun with; that people wanting necessaries scarce think of luxury; and that to say they had founders, engravers, carvers, dyers, embroiderers, when they had not so much as cloaths, sandals, nor bread, is gross and palpable contradiction.

3. If Moses had written the first chapter of Genesis, would the reading of that chapter have been forbidden to all young people? would the legislator be treated with such disregard? had it been Moses who said that God punishes the iniquities of the

the fathers to the fourth generation, would Ezekiel have presumed to say the contrary?

4. Had Moses written Leviticus, could he have contradicted himself in Deuteronomy? Leviticus forbids the marrying a brother's wife, Deuteronomy enjoins it.

5. Would Moses have spoken of towns which were not known in his time? Would he have said that towns which, relatively to him lay east of Jordan, were west of that river?

6. Would he have assigned to the Levites forty-eight towns in a country which never had ten; and in a wilderness where he had never so much as a house during all his wanderings?

7. Would he have laid down rules for the Jewish kings, whilst that people not only had no kings, but abhorred them, and there was no probability that they would ever have any? How! would Moses have given precepts for the conduct of kings, who did not come till about five hundred years after him, and say nothing concerning the judges and high priests, his immediate successors? Does not this reflection incline one to believe, that the Pentateuch was written in the time of the Kings; and that the ceremonies instituted by Moses were only traditional.

8. Is it possible that he should say to the Jews, ye were six hundred thousand men when I brought you out of the land of Egypt under the protection of your God? Would not the Jews have answered? Then you must have been a faint-hearted creature not have led us against Pharoah; he had not an army of two hundred thousand men to oppose us. Egypt never had so many men on foot; we should easily have defeated him, and made ourselves masters of his country. How! the God, who speaks to you, has, to please us, killed all the

first-born in Egypt; and if that country contained three hundred thousand families, there's three hundred thousand men carried off in one night to revenge us; and you have not seconded your God. You have not given us that fruitful country which was likewise defenceless. You made us come out of Egypt like thieves and poltroons, that we might perish in wildernesses among rocks and precipices: you might at least have led us by the direct way into that land of Canaan, to which we have no right (N), and which you promised us, but have not yet brought us thither.

It was natural that from the land of Goshen, we should have taken the way towards Tyre and Sidon along the Mediterranean; but you have made us traverse almost the isthmus of Suez, have brought us again into Egypt as far as beyond Memphis, and behold we are now at Bel-Sephon on the Red Sea, with the land of Canaan behind us, after a march of fourscore leagues in that very country which we were for shunning; and, after all, in imminent danger of perishing either by the sea or Pharoah's army.

Had your intention been to deliver us up to our enemies, what other measures could you have taken? God, you say, has saved us by a miracle, the sea opened to let us pass through; but, after such kindness, should you have brought us to die with hunger and weariness, in the horrible deserts of Ethan, Kadesh-Barnea, Mara, Elim, Oreb, and Sinai? All our fathers perished in those dreadful wildernesses, and after forty such calamitous years,

---

(N) Mr. Bachiene, gographer to the prince of Orange, has, in his Sacred Geography, proved the Israelites right to the land of Canaan.

you come and tell us, that God took particular care of our fathers.

This is what those murmuring Jews, those perverse children of vagabond fathers, who died in the deserts, might have said to Moses, had he read Exodus and Genesis to them: and what ought they not to have said, and even to have done, on account of the golden calf? How! you dare tell us that your brother made a golden calf for our fathers, whilst you was with God on the mount; you who sometimes say, that you spoke to God face to face, and sometimes that you could only see his hinder parts. Well, but you was with God, and your brother cast a golden calf in one day, and set it up for us to worship; but instead of punishing your worthless brother, you make him our high priest, and order your Levites to slay three-and-twenty thousand of your people. Would our fathers have tamely suffered this? Would they have let themselves been knocked down by sanguinary priests like so many victims. You farther tell us, as if this butchery was not sufficient, that another time you ordered twenty-four thousand of your poor followers to be massacred, because one of them had lain with a Midianite, and you yourself married a Midianite; and after this, you add, that you are the meekest of all men. A few more such meek procedures would have made an end of mankind.

No, had you been capable of such cruelty, had you been able to carry it into execution, you would have been the most barbarous of men; it would have been so enormous a guilt, that no punishment could have been equal to it.

These are pretty nearly the objections made by the learned to those who hold Moses to have been the author of the Pentateuch. But these rejoin, that the ways of God are not like those of men; that God, by a wisdom unknown to us, has tried and alternately protected and forsaken his people; that the Jews themselves, for above two thousand years, have universally believed Moses to be the author of those books; that the church, which has succeeded to the synagogue, and is endued with the like infallibility, has decided this point of controversy; and that the learned should keep silence, when the church speaks.

PETER

IN ITALIAN Piero, or Pietro; in SPANISH Pedro, in LATIN Petrus, in GREEK Petros, in HEBREW Cepha.

How comes it that Peter's successors have had so much power in the west and none in the east? This is asking why the bishop of Wurtzburg and Saltzburg have in troublesome times assumed royal prerogatives, whilst the Greek bishops have remained subjects. Time, opportunity, and the ambition of some, and the weakness of others, do every thing in this world, and ever will.

To these troubles was added opinion, and opinion rules men; not that they in reality have a very determinate opinion, but they are as tenacious of words.

It is related in the Gospel, that Jesus said to Peter, "I will give thee the keys of the kingdom of heaven." The sticklers for the bishop of Rome maintained, about the eleventh century, that he who gives the greater gives the less; that the heavens encompassed the earth; and that Peter, having the keys of the containing, had also the keys of the contents. If by the heavens we mean all the stars and all the planets, then the keys given to Simon Bar-jona, furnamed Peter, were a *paffe-par-tout*. If by the heavens are meant the clouds, the atmofphere, the ether, the fpace in which the planets roll, there are few lock-fmiths, fays Meurfius, who can make a key to fuch doors.

In Paleftine, keys were a wooden peg faftened with a leathern thong. Jefus fays to Bar-jona, "What thou fhalt bind on earth fhall be bound in heaven." From this the pope's theologians have inferred, that the popes are invefted with a power of binding and loofening fubjects from the oath of allegiance to their kings, and of difpofing of all kingdoms at their pleafure: a notable inference indeed! The commons at a general affembly of the ftates of France in 1302, in their petition to the king, fay, "that Boniface VIII. was a fcoundrel," believing that God bound and imprifoned in heaven all whom Boniface bound on earth. A famous German Lutheran (I think it was Melancthon) could hardly believe that Jefus fhould have faid to Simon Bar-jona, Cepha or Cephas, "Thou art Peter, and on this rock, will I build my church." He could not conceive that God had made ufe of fuch a play of words, fo very extraordinary a pun, and that the pope's power was founded on a quibble.

Peter has been thought the firft bifhop of Rome; but it is fufficiently known that then, and for a long time after, there was no particular fee. It was not till towards the end of the fecond century, that the Chriftians were moulded into a regular body.

It is poffible that St. Peter went to Rome; it is even poffible that he was crucified with his head downwards, though that was not cuftomary; but of all this we have no proof. A letter, bearing his name, is ftill extant, in which he fays that he is at Babylon. Judicious canonifts will have this Babylon to mean Rome; so that had he dated his letter from Rome, it might have been inferred that the letter had been written from Babylon: such inferences are of a long standing; and thus it is that the world has been governed.

A very pious man, who had been exorbitantly imposed on at Rome in relation to the purchase of a benefice, a practice, which is called simony, being asked whether he thought that Simon Peter had ever been in that country, answered, I see no marks of Peter's having been there, but I am very certain Simon was.

As to Peter's person, Paul is not the only one who has taken offence at his behaviour: both he and his successors have often been withstood to their face. St. Paul keenly reproached him for eating prohibited meats, as pork, puddings, hare, eels, &c. Peter, in justification of himself, alledged that, about the sixth hour, he had seen the heavens opened, and a large table-cloth full of eels, beasts, and birds descending from the four quarters of the heavens; and that the voice of an angel called out, "Kill and eat." Probably, says Wolaston, it was the same voice, which has called to so many popes, "Kill every body, and eat up the people's substance."

Casaubon could not approve Peter's beyaviour to Ananias and his wife (O), who were a good

---

(O) The punishment of Ananias and Sapphira might appear very severe for a fault, which does not seem at first sight to be considerable; but the offence was grievous, since they made so slight of lying to the Holy Ghost. For it is thought by some eminent writers, that they had taken an oath not to reserve any thing to themselves; but to devote their estates to the common use of the faithful. Their crime therefore was a kind of perjury and sacrilege: and it was severely punished, because it was requisite in the beginning to give sanction to the laws of Christianity.

sort

sort of people: What right, says he, had a Jew, a slave under the Romans, to order or allow all who believed in Jesus to sell their substance, and lay the produce at his feet. Were an Anabaptist preacher at London to order his brethren to bring him all their money, would he not be taken up as a mover of sedition, a robber, and as such sent to Tyburn? Was it not a horrid thing to strike Ananias dead, only because out of the money for which he had sold his estate, he secretly reserved a few pounds against a rainy day, bringing the far greater part to Peter. Scarce was the breath out of Ananias's body, when in comes his wife. Peter, instead of kindly informing her that he had just killed her husband for keeping a few pence, and telling her to take care of what she had, allures her into the snare. He asks her whether her husband had brought in all his money for the saints; the poor woman answers, yes, and instantly drops down dead. Something hard this!

Corringius asks why Peter, who thus demolishes those who brought him alms, did not rather go and kill all the doctors who had a hand in putting Jesus to death, and had caused himself to be scourged several times. Fie, Peter, to kill two Christians who had brought you a good purse of money; and they who crucified your God, you allow to live!

It is to be supposed that Corringius, when he put forth these bold questions, was not in a country subject to the inquisition. Erasmus has concerning Peter a pretty singular remark, that the head of the Christian religion began his apostleship by denying Jesus Christ; and the high priest of Judaism began his ministry by making a golden calf, and worshipping it.

However it be, Peter is transmitted to us as poor, and humbly instructing the poor; he is like
those

those founders of orders who lived in indigence, but whose successors are become great men.

The pope, St. Peter's successor, has both won and lost: however, he has still remaining, in the several parts of the world, besides his immediate subjects, about fifty millions of people, who in many articles acknowledge his laws.

To have a master three or four hundred leagues from one's home; to forbear thinking till that man shall have seemed to think; not to dare to try definitively a process between our fellow-citizens, but by commissioners of this foreigner's nomination; to transgress the laws of one's country, by which a person is restrained from marrying his niece, and yet to render this a legitimate marriage, by giving a still more considerable sum to that foreign master; not to dare take possession of any fields or vineyards conferred by one's own sovereign, without paying a large sum to this foreign master; not to dare plough one's grounds on a day appointed by a foreigner for commemorating an unknown person, whom he has placed in heaven by his own private authority; these are the advantages of acknowledging a pope; these are the liberties of the Gallican church.

Other nations there are who carry submission still farther. We have in our times seen a sovereign ask the pope leave to bring to a trial, in his royal court of justice, some monks accused of regicide, fail in his follicitations for leave, and not dare to try those wretches.

It is well known that, formerly, the popes power was still of greater extent. They were much superior to the gods of antiquity; for those deities were only imagined to dispose of empires, but the popes disposed of them in reality.

Sturbinus says, that they who doubt of the pope's divinity and infallibility are excusable, when it is considered that St. Peter's see has been profaned by forty schisms, and twenty-seven of them have been attended with murders, massacres, and wars.

That Stephen VII. a priest's son, had his predecessor, Formosus, dug up, and the corpse's head cut off.

That Sergius III. was convicted of assassinations, and had a son by Marozia, who inherited the papacy.

That John X. Theodoras's gallant, was strangled in his bed.

That John XI. son of Sergius III. was known only for his scandalous intemperance.

That John XII. was murdered at his strumpet's house.

That Benedict IX. bought the pontificate, and sold it again.

That Gregory VII. was the author of civil wars, which were continually prosecuted by his successors for the space of five hundred years.

That lastly, among so many debauched, ambitious, and sanguinary popes, there has been an Alexander VI. whose name always excites no less horror and detestation than those of Nero and Caligula.

This, it is said, proves the divinity of their character, that it should have subsisted amidst so many crimes; but had the behaviour of the califs been still more flagitious and execrable, they would then have been still more divine. This is Dermius's argument; but the Jesuits have answered him.

PREJUDICES.

PRejudice is an opinion void of judgment: thus every where many opinions are instilled into children before they are able to judge.

There are universal and necessary prejudices, and such are essential to virtue. In every country, children are taught to believe in a God, who punishes and rewards; to respect and to love their father and mother; to hold theft a crime; a selfish lye a vice, before they can so much as guess what vice or virtue is.

Thus there are very good prejudices, and these are such as on being brought to the test, judgment ratifies.

Sentiment is not mere prejudice; it is much stronger. It is not because the mother has been told that she must love her son, that she loves him; she, happily, cannot help her fondness for him. It is not from prejudice that a man runs to assist an unknown child, whom a beast is near devouring, or who is in any other danger.

But it is from mere prejudice that you respect a man dressed in a particular manner, and grave in his carriage and discourse. Your parents have told you to bow to such a man; thus you come to respect him, before you know whether he deserves your respect. Being grown up, and your knowledge enlarged, you begin to see that this man is a hypocrite, eaten up with pride, selfishness, and craft; hereupon you despise what you venerated, and prejudice is superseded by judgment. You have, from prejudice, believed the fables with which you was amused in your childhood; you were told that the Titans waged war against the Gods; and that Venus was in love with Adonis. These fables at twelve years of age go down with you as realities; but, at twenty, you perceive them to be only ingenious allegories.

Let us briefly, for order sake, examine the different sorts of prejudices; we may perhaps find ourselves like those who perceived that at the time of the Mississippi, they had been calculating in aginary riches.

Prejudices of the Senses.

Is it not very odd that our eyes always deceive us, even when we see very well; whereas we are never deceived by our ears? If a sound ear hears these words, You are handsome, I love you; it is very certain that the person speaking did not say, I hate you, you are ugly: but the apparent smoothness of a looking-glass is a deception; a microscope shews the surface to be in reality very rugged. The sun seems to be about two feet in diameter; whereas it is demonstrated to be a million of times larger than the earth.

God apparently has put truth in your ears, and error in your eyes: but study optics, and you will find that God has not imposed on you; and that it is impossible, in the present state of things, objects should appear otherwise than you see them.

Physical Prejudices.

That the sun rises and sets, and the earth is immoveable, are prejudices naturally imbibed: but that lobsters are good for the blood, because in boiling they turn red; that eels cure the palsy, because of their frisking; that the moon has an influence on diseases, because a stronger symptom of a fever was observed in a patient in the wane of the moon: these notions, with a thousand others, were entertained by the empyrics of old, who judged without reasoning, and led others into their mistakes.

Historical Prejudices.

Most stories have been credited without examination, and such belief is a prejudice. Fabius Pictor

Pictor relates, that several ages before him, a vestal virgin of the city of Alba, going with her pitcher to draw water, was ravished and brought into the world Romulus and Remus; and that these twins were suckled by a she-wolf, &c. This fable the Roman people greedily swallowed, without examining whether, at that time, vestal virgins were known in Latium; whether it was likely that a king's daughter should go out of her convent with a pitcher in her hand; and whether it was agreeable to nature, that a she-wolf, so far from eating two infants, should suckle them. The prejudice took root.

A monk wrote that Clovis, being in great danger at the battle of Tolbiac, made a vow, if he escaped safe, to turn Christian; but is it natural in such an exigency to apply to a foreign deity? Is it not in extremities, that our native religion acts with the greatest force? What Christian in a battle against the Turks would not call on the Blessed Virgin, rather than on Mahomet? It is added, that a dove brought a phial in its bill for anointing Clovis; and that an angel brought the oriflamme or banner to be carried before him. All such little tales, prejudice readily credited; but they who are acquainted with human nature very well know, that both the usurper Clovis and the usurper Rollo, or Rolf, turned Christians, that they might more safely rule over Christians, as the Turks, on their becoming masters of the empire of Constantinople, turned Mussulmen, to ingratiate themselves with the Mussulmen.

RELIGIOUS PREJUDICES.

If your nurse has told you that Ceres presides over grain; or that Visnou and Xaca have several times

times become men; or that Sanmoncodom came upon earth, and cut down a forest; or that Odin expects you in his hall towards Jutland; or that Mahomet, or some other, has made a journey into heaven; lastly, if your governor afterwards inculcates into your brain the traces made in it by your nurse, you will never get rid of them during your life. Should your judgment attempt to efface these prejudices, your acquaintance, and especially your female acquaintance, will charge you with impiety, and terrify you; then your dervise, lest his income may suffer some curtailment, will accuse you to the cadi; the cadi will do his best to have you impaled, for he would have all under him blockheads, thinking that blockheads make tamer subjects than others; and thus things will go on till your acquaintance, the dervise, and the cadi shall begin to perceive that folly does no good, and that persecution is abominable.

RELIGION.

QUESTION I.

DR. Warburton, bishop of Gloucester, author of one of the most learned pieces that ever appeared, in vol. i. p. 8. expresses himself to this purpose: " A religion, or society, not founded on " the belief of a future state, ought to be supported " by an extraordinary providence: the Jewish reli- " gion was not founded on the belief of a future " state; therefore it must have been supported by " an extraordinary providence."

Several divines have declared against him, and, disputant like, have retorted his argument on himself.

" A re-

"A religion not founded on the doctrine of the
"soul's immortality, and eternal rewards, must be
"false. Now Judaism had no such tenets; there-
"fore Judaism, so far from being supported by
"providence, was, according to your principles,
"a false and savage religion, which denied any
"such thing as providence."

Others of the bishop's adversaries maintained that the immortality of the soul was known among the Jews, even in Moses's time; but he very evidently proved against them, that neither in the Decalogue, nor Leviticus, nor Deuteronomy, is one single word said of this belief; and that it is ridiculous to go about wresting and corrupting a few passages of the other books, in support of a truth about which their book of laws is silent.

The bishop, though he composed four volumes to demonstrate that the Jewish law proposed neither punishments nor rewards after death, has not been able to give his adversaries any very satisfactory answer. They urged, "either Moses was
"acquainted with this doctrine, and then he de-
"ceived the Jews in not making it public: or he
"was ignorant of it; and if so, he was incapable
"of founding a good religion. Indeed, had the
"religion been good, why was it abolished? A
"true religion should suit all times and places; it
"should be like the light of the sun, which shines
"in all lands and throughout all generations."

This prelate, with all his erudition and sagacity, has been hard put to it in making his way through all these difficulties; but what system is without difficulties?

QUESTION II.

Another learned person, a much greater philosopher, and one of the most profound metaphysicians

cians of the times, produces strong reasons to prove, that the first religion was Polytheism; and that, before improved reason came to see there could be only one Supreme Being, men began with believing several gods.

I, on the contrary, presume to believe that they began with worshipping only one God, and that, afterwards, human weakness adopted several others; and I conceive the thing to be thus.

It is not to be doubted but villages and country towns were prior to large cities; and that men were divided into small republics before they were united in large empires. It is very natural, that a town, terrified at the thunder; distressed by the ruin of its harvest; insulted by a neighbouring town; daily feeling its weakness, and every where perceiving an invisible power, soon came to say, There is some being above us, which does us good and hurt.

It seems to me impossible that they should have said: there are two powers; for wherefore several? In every thing we begin with the simple, then proceed to the compound, and often an improvement of knowledge brings us back again to the simple: this is the process of the human mind.

Which being was first worshipped? was it the sun, was it the moon? I can hardly believe it. Only let us take a view of children; they are pretty nearly on a footing with ignorant men. The beauty and benefit of that luminous body which animates nature, make no impression on them; as insensible are they of the conveniences we derive from the moon, or of the regular variations of its course; they do not so much as think of these things; they are accustomed to them. What men do not fear, they never worship. Children look up to the sky with as much indifference as on the ground; but, at a tempeſt, the poor creatures tremble and run and hide themſelves. I am inclined to think it was ſo with primitive men. They who fiiſt obſerved the courſe of the heavenly bodies, and brought them to be objects of admiration and worſhip, muſt neceſſarily have had a tincture of philoſophy; the error was too exalted for rude illiterate huſbandmen.

Thus the cry of a village would have been no more than this: There is a power which thunders, which ſends down hail on us, which cauſes our children to die, let us, by all means, appeaſe it; but which way? Why, we ſee, that little preſents will ſooth angry people, let us try what little preſents will do with this power. He muſt alſo to be ſure have a name or title; and that, which naturally preſents itſelf firſt, is chief, maſter, lord: thus is this power called my Lord. Hence it probably was, that the fiſt Ægyptians called their god Knef; the Syrians, Adoni; the neighbouring nations Baal or Bel, or Melch or Moloc; the Scythians Pape, all words ſignifying Lord, Maſter.

In like manner almoſt all America was found to be divided into multitudes of little colonies, all with their patron deity. The Mexicans and Peruvians themſelves, who were large nations, had but one only God; the former worſhipping Mango Kapack, the other the God of war, whom they called Vilipuſti, as the Hebrews had ſtiled their lord, Sabaoth.

It is not from any ſuperiority or exerciſe of reaſon, that all nations began with worſhipping only one Deity; for had they been philoſophers, they would have the univerſal God of nature and not the god of a village; they would have examined the infinite teſtimonies acknowledged of a creating and preſerving being; but they examined

mined nothing; they only perceived, and such is the progress of our weak understanding. Every town perceived its weakness and want of a powerful protector. This tutelary and terrible being they fancied to reside in a neighbouring forest, or mountain, or in a cloud. They fancied only one such power, because in war the town had but one chief; this being they imagined to be corporeal, it being impossible they could have any other idea. They could not but believe that the neighbouring town had also its god. Accordingly Jephtha says to the inhabitants of Moab: "You lawfully possess "what your god Chamos has made you conquer; "and you ought to let us quietly enjoy what our "god has given us by his victories (P)."

This speech from one foreigner to another is very remarkable. The Jews and Moabites had outed the natives, with no other right than force; and one says to the other, Thy god has supported thee in thy usurpation, allow my god likewise to support me in mine.

Jeremiah and Amos both ask, "Wherefore has "the god Moloch seized on the country of Gad "(Q)?" These passages shew that antiquity attributed a guardian god to every country, and traces of this theology are likewise to be met with in Homer.

It is very natural that, from the heat of fancy and a vague increase of knowledge, men soon multiplied their gods, and assigned guardians to the elements, seas, forests, springs, and fields. The more they surveyed the heavenly bodies, the greater

---

— (P) The sense in our version is very different. Judges xi. 24.
— (Q) Here the difference is still greater. Jer. xi. 1. Amos says nothing like it.

must their astonishment have been. Well might they who worshipped the deity of a brook, pay their adorations to the sun: and, the first step being taken, the earth was soon covered with deities; so that at length cats and onions came to be worshipped.

However, time must necessarily improve reason: accordingly it produced some philosophers, who saw that neither onions nor cats, nor even the heavenly bodies, had any share in the disposition of nature. All those philosophers, Babylonians, Persians, Egyptians, Scythians, Greeks, and Romans, acknowledged only one Supreme God, rewarding and punishing.

This they did not immediately make known to the people, for a word against onions and cats spoken before old women and priests, would have cost a man his life; those good people would have stoned him. He who should have ridiculed some Egyptians for eating their gods, would have been eaten himself, since Juvenal relates as fact, that in a controversial dispute, an Egyptian was killed and eaten quite raw.

Well! what was to be done? Orpheus and others institute mysteries, which the initiated swear by execrable oaths never to reveal; and of these mysteries the principal is, the worship of one only God. This great truth spreads over half the earth; the number of the initiated swells immensely; the antient religion indeed still subsists, but not being contrary to the tenet of God's unity, it is connived at. The Romans had their Deus Optimus Maximus; the Greeks their Zeus, their Supreme God. All the other deities are only intermediate beings; heroes and emperors were classed among the gods, which meant no more than the blessed, for it is not to be supposed, that Claudius, Octavius, Tiberius, and Caligula, were accounted the creators of heaven and earth.

In a word, it seems demonstrated that, in Augustus's time, all who had any religion acknowledged one supreme eternal God, with several classes of secondary deities; the worshipping of whom has since been called idolatry.

The Jewish laws never countenanced idolatry; for though they admitted Malachim, Angels, and inferior orders of cœlestial beings; their law appointed no manner of worship for these secondary deities. Indeed they adored angels, that is, when they saw any, they prostrated themselves before them; but as this was a very uncommon case, no ceremonial, or legal worship, had been instituted for them; neither was any homage paid even to the cherubim of the ark. It is manifest that the Jews worshipped openly one single God, even as the innumerable crowds of the initiated worshipped him privately in their mysteries,

Question III.

At this time, when the worship of one Supreme God universally prevailed in Asia, in Europe, and Africa, among all who made a due use of their reason, it was that the christian religion received its birth.

Platonism greatly promoted the understanding of its dogmas. The Logos, which in Plato signifies the wisdom, the reason of the Supreme Being, with us was made the word, and the second person of the Deity. Thus religion was wrapped up in metaphysics, to human reason unfathomable.

How Mary was afterwards declared mother of God; how the consubstantiality of the Father and the word were established, together with the procession of the Pneuma, the divine organ of the divine Logos; two natures and two wills resulting from the Hypostasis; and lastly, the superior manducation, in which both soul and body are fed with the members of the incarnate God, worshipped and eaten in the form of bread, present to the sight, felt by the taste, and yet annihilated: these things we shall not repeat here. All mysteries have ever been sublime.

So early as the second century, the expulsion of devils was performed, by pronouncing the name of Jesus; whereas before, the name of Jehovah, or Yhaho, was made use of in such miracles: for St. Matthew relates that Jesus's enemies having spread abroad, that it was by the name of the prince of the devils that he cast out the devils, he made them this answer: "If I cast out devils by Beelze-"bub, by whom do your children cast them out?"

At what time the Jews acknowledged Beelzebub, a foreign deity, to be prince of the devils is not known; but we know, and learn it from Josephus, that at Jerusalem there were exorcists, whose immediate province it was to dislodge the devils from the bodies of the possessed, that is men labouring under uncommon distempers; which, in those times, a great part of the world attributed to malignant genii.

Thus the demoniacs were relieved by the true pronunciation of the word Jehovah; now lost, together with other ceremonies at present buried in oblivion.

Exorcisms by Jehovah, or other of God's names, continued to be practised even in the early ages of the church. Origen against Celsus, N°. 262, says, "If when invoking God or swearing by him, he "is termed the God of Abraham, Isaac, and Ja- "cob,

"cob, certain things will be done by thofe names,
"fuch being their nature and force, that devils
"are fubject to thofe who utter them; whereas if
"called by any other appellation, as god of the
"tumultuous fea, or the deftroyer, no effect fol-
"lows. The word Ifrael tranflated into Greek will
"do nothing; but on pronouncing it in Hebrew,
"along with the other requifite words, the magi-
"cal operation will take place."

The fame Origen, N°. 19, has thefe remarkable words: "There are names of a natural vir-
"tue, as thofe ufed by the wife men in Egypt,
"the Magi in Perfia, and the Brachmans in In-
"dia. Magic, as it is called, is no vain and chi-
"merical art, as the Stoics and Epicureans pretend;
"neither were the names of Sabaoth or Adonai
"made for created beings, but appertain to a myf-
"terious theology concerning the Creator; hence
"comes the virtue of thefe names, when placed
"in order, and pronounced according to the
"rules, &c."

Origen, in fpeaking thus, only relates what was univerfally held, and does not deliver his own private opinion. All the religions then known admitted a kind of magic, and with two diftinctions, the celeftial and infernal magic, necromancy and theurgy; every nation had its prodigies, divinations, and oracles. The Perfians did not deny the Egyptian miracles, nor the Egyptians offer to difcredit the Perfian. God was pleafed to wink at the firft Chriftians efpoufing the Sybilline oracles, and fome other unconfequential errors, as not corrupting the effentials of religion.

Another very remarkable circumftance is, that the chriftians of the two firft centuries abhorred temples, altars, and images. This Origen owns, N°. 374, but on the church's being modelled into

a fet-a settled form, its discipline and every thing else became altered.

QUESTION IV.

When once a religion comes to be established by law, the magistrates are very vigilant in suppressing most of the things; which used to be done by the professors of that religion before it was publicly received. The founders held their private meetings, though forbidden under penalties; now none but public assemblies held under the eye of the law are permitted, and all clandestine associations made punishable. The old maxim was, It is better to obey God than man; now the opposite maxim comes into vogue, To obey God is to conform to the laws of the land. All places rung with obsessions and possessions, the devil was let loose upon earth; now the devil does not stir out of his den. Prodigies and predictions were necessary then; now a stop is put to them, and they are exploded: he who should openly take upon him to foretel any public calamity, would soon be shewn the way to Bedlam. The founders took money underhand from the believers; whereas a man collecting money to dispose of it as he pleases, without any legal warrant, would be taken to task. Thus the whole of the scaffolding used in the construction of the building, is taken away.

QUESTION V.

Next to our holy religion, to be sure the only good religion, which would be the least bad? Would it not be the most simple? Would it not be that which taught a great deal of morality and few doctrines? that which tended to make men
virtuous

virtuous without making them fools? that which did not impose the belief of things impossible, contradictory, injurious to the Deity, and pernicious to mankind; and which did not take on itself to threaten with eternal punishments all who had common sense? Would it not be that which did not support its articles by executioners, and deluge the earth with blood for unintelligible sophisms? that in which a quibble, a pun, and two or three supposititious maps, would not suffice to make a priest a sovereign and a God, though noted for the most profligate morals and execrable practices? that which did not make kings subject to this priest? Would it not be that which taught only the adoration of one God, justice, forbearance, and humanity?

Question VI.

The religion of the Gentiles is said to be absurd in several points, contradictory, and pernicious. But have not its evils and follies been greatly exaggerated? Jupiter's carrying on his amours in the shape of a swan, a bull, with other such doings of the Pagan deities, is certainly the height of ridicule; but let any one, throughout all antiquity, shew me a temple dedicated to Leda lying with a swan or a bull. Did Athens or Rome ever hear a sermon to encourage girls to copulate with the swans in their court-yards? Did the collection of fables so beautifully embellished by Ovid, constitute their religion? Are they not like our Golden Legend, or Flower of the Saints? Should some Bramin or Dervise object to us the story of St. Mary the Egyptian, who not having wherewith to pay the sailors who had brought her into Egypt, voluntarily granted to each of them, in lieu of money, what

what is called favours, we fhould immediately fay to the Bramin, You are miftaken, father, the Golden Legend is not our religion.

We taunt the antients with their prodigies and oracles; but could they return on earth, and were the miracles of our lady of Loretto, and thofe of our lady of Ephefus, to be numbered, in whofe favour would the ballance of the account be?

Human facrifices have been introduced almoft among all nations, but very rarely were they practifed. Jephtha's daughter and king Agag are the only two we meet with among the Jews, for Ifaac and Jonathan were not facrificed. The Grecian ftory of Iphigenia is not thoroughly verified: human facrifices are very rarely heard of among the antient Romans; in a word, very little blood has the Pagan religion fhed, and ours has made the earth an aceldama. Ours, to be fure, is the only good, the only true religion; but by our abufe of it, we have done fo much mifchief, that when we fpeak of other religions, it fhould be with temper and modefty.

Question VII.

If a man would recommend his religion to ftrangers or his countrymen, fhould he not go about it with the moft winning compofure, the moft infinuating mildnefs? If he fets out with faying that what he declares is demonftrably true, he will meet with ftrong oppofition; and if he takes upon him to tell them that they reject his doctrine, only becaufe it condemns their paffions; that their heart has corrupted their mind; that they have only a falfe and prefumptuous reafon, he excites their contempt and refentment, and overthrows what he was for building up.

If the religion which he preaches be true, will passion and insolence add to its truth? Do you storm and rage when you say that men should be mild, patient, benevolent, just, exact in the discharge of all the duties of society? No; here every body is of your mind; why then such virulent language to your brother when you are preaching to him metaphysical mysteries? It is because his good sense irritates your self-love. You proudly require that your brother should submit his understanding to yours; and pride disappointed blazes into rage; from hence, and hence only, arises your passion. A man who receives ever so many musket-shot in a battle, is never seen to express any anger; but a doctor, at the denial of assent, kindles into implacable fury.

RESURRECTION (R).

THE Egyptians are said to have built their superb pyramids only for tombs, where their bodies being embalmed outwardly and inwardly, lay till, at the expiration of a thousand years, their souls returned into them. But if their bodies were

---

(R) The doctrine of the resurrection is one of the fundamental points of our holy religion. M. Voltaire does not attempt to weaken our belief of it, but to shew his learning by enumerating the opinions of the Heathens, as well as of the primitive Christians relative to that article. We shall only observe that his explication of the famous passage of Job, ch. xix. ver. 25, is taken from the very learned bishop of Gloucester, who in his Divine Legation, book vi. sect. 2. p. 543, has given us a beautiful account of this whole book, and cleared up all the difficulties in it; but particularly makes it appear, that the words in question can relate only to a temporal deliverance.

to come to life again, and it was their first operation, why did the embalmers pierce the scull with a hook, and draw the brain out? To think of a man's coming to life again without brains, inclines one to apprehend that the Egyptians had little or none when living; but it must be considered, that most of the antients believed the soul to reside in the breast. And why in the breast sooner than any other part? because it is well known that under all our sensations, if any thing violent, we feel a dilatation or contraction about the region of the heart; and this produced the opinion, that there was the soul's residence. This soul was something aerial, a light figure roving about where it could, till it had joined its body again.

The belief of the resurrection is much more antient than the historical times. Athaladas, Mercury's son, could die and come to life again at pleasure; Esculapius restored Hyppolitus to life; Hercules conferred the like kindness on Alcestes; and Pelops, who had been cut into pieces by his father, the gods made whole again: Plato relates that Heres returned to life only for a fortnight.

It was not till a very long time after Plato, that the Pharisees among the Jews adopted the tenet of the resurrection.

The Acts of the Apostles mention a very singular transaction, and well worthy of notice. St. James and several of his companions advised St. Paul, though so thorough a Christian, to go into the temple of Jerusalem, and observe all the ceremonies of the antient law, to the end all may know, say they, that every thing which is said of you is false, and that you still continue to observe Moses's law.

St. Paul accordingly went into the temple for seven days; but being known on the seventh, he was

was accufed of having brought ftrangers into it, with a view of prophaning it.

Now Paul perceiving that fome of the crowd were Sadducees and others Pharifees, he cried out in the council, "Brethren I am a Pharifee, the fon "of a Pharifee; it is for the hope of another life, "and the refurrection of the dead, that I am in "danger of being condemned," Acts xxiii. ver. 6. In all this affair not a word had been faid about the refurrection of the dead; but Paul's drift in mentioning it was to raife a quarrel between the Pharifees and Sadducees.

Ver. 7. "And Paul having faid, there arofe a "diffenfion between the Pharifees and Sadducees, "and the multitude was divided."

Ver. 8. "For the Sadducees fay, there is no re- "furrection, neither angel nor fpirit; but the Pha- "rifees confefs both, &c."

It has been affirmed that Job, who doubtlefs is of great antiquity, was acquainted with the doctrine of the refurrection; and, in proof of it, the following words are quoted: "I know that my re- "deemer liveth, and that one day his redemption "will rife on me, or that I fhall rife again from the "duft; that my fkin will return; and that I fhall "again fee God in my flefh."

But feveral commentators underftand no more by thefe words, than that Job hopes he fhall foon get over his diftemper, and fhall not always be lying in the ground as he then was: the fequel fufficiently proves the truth of this explanation; for the moment he cries out to his falfe and harfh friends, "Why then fay you, let us perfecute him, or be- "caufe you fhall fay, Becaufe we have perfecuted "him (S). Does not this evidently mean, you will

---

(S) See our tranflation, chap. xix. ver. 25 and 28.

repent of having infulted me, when you fhall fee me again in my former ftate of health and opulence? A fick perfon fays, I fhall recover, not I fhall rife from the dead: to give forced meanings to clear paffages, is the fure way never to underftand one another.

According to St. Jerome, the fect of the Pharifees began but a very little time before Jefus Chrift. Rabbi Hillel is accounted its founder, and he was cotemporary with Gamaliel, St. Paul's mafter.

Many of thefe Pharifees believed that it was only the Jews who were to rife again; and that as to the reft of mankind, they were not worth while. Others affirmed that the refurrection would be only in Paleftine, and that bodies buried in other parts would be fecretly conveyed to the neighbourhood of Jerufalem, there to be united to their foul. St. Paul tells the inhabitants of Theffalonica, " That the fecond coming of Jefus Chrift " is for them and for him; and that they fhall be " witneffes of it."

Ver. 16. " For on the fignal being given by the " archangel and the trumpet of God, the Lord " himfelf fhall defcend from heaven, and they who " fhall have died in Jefus Chrift fhall rife firft."

Ver. 17. " Then we who are alive, and who fhall " have remained till then, fhall be caught up with " them in the clouds, to go and meet the Lord in the " air; and thus we fhall live for ever with the Lord." 1 Theffalonians, chap. iv.

Does not this important paffage evidently prove, that the firft Chriftians made themfelves fure that they fhould fee the end of the world; and St. Luke actually foretels it, as what fhould happen in his life-time?

St.

St. Austin thinks that children, and even still-born infants, shall rise at the age of maturity. Origen, Jerome, Athanasius, Basil, did not believe that women were to rise again with the distinctions of sex.

In a word, there have ever been disputes about what we were, what we are, and what we shall be.

SOLOMON (T).

SURELY Solomon could not be so rich as he is said?

The book of Chronicles tells us that Melk David his father left him one hundred thousand talents

---

(T) This whole article is liable to great exceptions, and betrays a spirit of licentiousness in the author. He takes upon himself to strike what books he pleases out of the canon of the scriptures, because they do not suit his fancy, or because he meets with a few difficulties, which are easily solved. We are sorry to own that he shews himself in this article to have joined that class of Deists, whom Dr. Clarke mentions as not capable of being argued with. These are they who endeavour to turn the most sacred things into ridicule; and shew as great a disregard to common decency as to religion. They pretend to expose the abuses and corruption of religion: but the profane and lewd images with which they affect to dress up their discourse, demonstrate that they do not intend to deride any vice or folly, but rather to foment the vicious inclinations of others. By turning every thing alike into ridicule, they plainly declare that they have no regard for virtue or religion. Such men are not to be argued with, till they learn to use arguments instead of drollery. For banter is not capable of being answered by reason, not because it has any strength in it; but because it runs out of all the bounds of reason and good sense, by extravagantly joining together such images as have not in them-

talents of gold * and one thousand talents of silver; so enormous a sum, that it is quite incredible. There themselves any manner of similitude or connection; thus all things are alike easy to be rendered ridiculous, by being represented only in an absurd dress.

This is what our author has unhappily done in regard to the Song of Solomon. Whether this book, as well as those of Proverbs and Ecclesiastes, were written by that prince, is not at all material to our religion; but it is certain that they belong to the canonical books, and their authority is the same as that of the other parts of the scripture, of which there never was any doubt in the church.

The Song of Songs is generally believed to have been written by king Solomon. It contains an epithalamium, in which the lover and his spouse are represented speaking their parts. King Solomon is named several times in the body of the work; so that there can be no doubt of its being written in his time. In regard to the impropriety which some imagine of inserting a book of this kind among those of holy writ, it must be observed, that there is a double meaning to be understood; the historical and the mystical. In the historical sense, it is a song for the nuptials of Solomon, and the daughter of the king of Egypt, who is called Shulamite. According to the mystical sense, of which the historical is only the foundation, it denotes the union between Christ and his church, which in the scripture is compared to that between man and wife. Such is the mystery represented by the nuptials of Solomon. But we are afraid our author is too carnally minded, to attend to the mystical sense of this or any other part of scripture.

Our author's objections against the books of Proverbs and Ecclesiastes are puerile, and scarce deserving of notice. But it is very droll to see him displaying his erudition on the French translation of the 31st verse in the 23d chapter of Proverbs: " Ne regardez point le vin quand il paroit clair, et " que sa couleur brille dans le verre:" because verre signifies glass, which is a recent invention. But it is highly probable the French translators meant no more than a cup, as the original implies, and as it is rendered in the English version; when

* A talent of gold is generally estimated about 5075 l. sterling.

There is not so much cash in all the nations of the whole

"when it giveth his colour in the cup." The book of Ecclesiastes was certainly written by Solomon, since it is mentioned to be the work of the son of David, king of Jerusalem, who excelled in wisdom and magnificence. It is a discourse made to a congregation, upon the vanity and emptiness of all worldly things. That the passages which our author finds fault with, are to be considered as objections which Solomon makes to himself, appears from the whole tenour of the book, and cannot bear any other construction. But does not Solomon clearly explain his meaning in other passages? as in this, "Rejoice, oh! young man, in thy youth, and let "thy heart cheer thee in the days of thy youth, and walk in "the ways of thy heart, and in the sight of thine eyes; but "know, that for all these things God will bring thee into "judgment." Does this breathe the air of libertinism? We sincerely wish our author had never been more licentious than Solomon shews himself in this book; the public then would never had so much reason to complain of some of his writings.

In regard to the objections our author starts at the entrance of this article against the opulence of Solomon, they only discover his ignorance of the Jewish history. The scripture says, (1 Chron. xxix. 4.) "That David left behind him "for the building of the temple, three thousand talents of "gold, of the gold of Ophir, and seven thousand talents of "refined silver." Now Dean Prideaux observes (Connect. book I.) two things concerning this immense quantity of gold; first, that it was the gold of Ophir; from whence he concludes that David must have established a navigation to that place in his time, by the assistance of Hiram's expert sailors, without which it cannot be conceived how he could have amassed so vast a treasure. Thus Solomon did but improve what his father had begun in regard to the encouragement of commerce. Secondly, this sum, as he says, is so prodigious, as gives reason to think, that the talents were another sort of talents, of a far less value than the Mosaic talents. For what is said to be given by David, and contributed by his princes, towards the building of the temple at Jerusalem, if valued by the Mosaic talents, exceeded the value of eight hundred millions of our money, which was enough to have built all that temple of solid silver.

whole world; and it is not easy to conceive that David

Solomon was a far more powerful prince than many people imagine: his dominions were not confined to the little country of Palestine, as M. Voltaire is pleased to call it; they reached from the river Euphrates, or even beyond it, to the Nile, or borders of Egypt; and all the kings of those countries were tributaries to him (1 Kings iv. 24.) What standing army he kept, the scripture does not mention; yet, besides his fourteen hundred chariots and horses, the text says he had twelve thousand horsemen, which some take to have been rather saddle horses; and others, his life-guards. In regard to the forty thousand stalls of horses for his chariots, mentioned in the first book of Kings, chap. iv. this passage we must own has created some difficulty, especially as in the second book of Chron. chap. ix. it is said, he had only four thousand stalls. But we must observe that M. Voltaire very unfairly magnifies the number of horses in the first passage, by making use of the word *ecurie*, *stable*; whereas in the original it signifies only *præsepe*, a *crib*, that is a division of the stable, so many cribs to each stable. Hence Buxtorff supposes that the book of Kings means the horses, that of Chronicles the stables, viz. that there were forty thousand horses in four thousand stables. Recourse must be therefore had to an hypallage; he had *forty thousand stables*, viz. *forty thousand horses in his stalls*; and the latter were four thousand according to the book of Chronicles. Some interpreters think that the number in the book of Chronicles has been corrupted; but this is said without any authority; therefore the plain and easiest way of solving the whole difficulty is, that in the book of Kings the word *præsepium*, or *stable*, is taken in its proper sense for a crib, or division of the stable; in the book of Chronicles, it is a synecdoche, and signifies a stable containing ten divisions, or cribs for ten horses: that is, there were four thousand *equiha majora*, *quæ* forty thousand *minora conficiebant*. And this difference of signification is pointed out by the very words in the original, as may be seen in Pool's *Synopsis Criticorum*.

Be that as it may, Solomon was the first who introduced the use of chariots and horses in Israel, at least to any degree of magnificence. For it is certain that the multiplying of chariots and horses, was expressly forbidden by the Mosaic law. These

he

David amassed such treasures in so small a country as Palestine (U).

Solomon,
he sent for out of Egypt, not only for his own use, but for that of several neighbouring kings, whom he obliged to pay him six hundred shekels for every chariot and four horses, and one hundred and fifty for every single horse. He had likewise abundance of yarn, linen, and other commodities, brought to him out of Egypt, which he sold to his subjects and merchants at a certain price (1 Kings x.); all this produced an immense revenue. He did not keep all his horses and chariots at Jerusalem, but disposed them in several of his strong cities, reserving only a convenient number about his person, either for guards or grandeur (ibid.) but not quite so many as four hundred and twelve thousand, as our facetious author pretends, to escort his concubines in taking the fresh air along the lake of Genesareth, or that of Sodom.

In order to supply his vast expences, Solomon built a navy at Ezion-geber, a sea-port near Eloth, in the land of Edom upon the Red Sea, and put it under the care of some Syrian mariners, to whom many of his own people were joined. The fleet sailed to Ophir, and in about three years brought him back an immense weight of gold and silver, besides several kinds of precious stones, spices, ebony, and other curious woods, ivory, peacocks, monkeys, and other rarities (1 Kings ix.) The gold itself amounted to four hundred and fifty talents yearly, besides the profit he made of all the other commodities. Ophir not only afforded the greatest quantity of gold, but exceeded all other gold in fineness and value (1 Kings x.) Various are the opinions of the learned in regard to the situation of Ophir; but the most probable conjecture places it in some of those remote rich countries of India beyond the Ganges, and perhaps as far as China or Japan. The latter still abounds with the finest gold, and with several other commodities imported by Solomon's fleet; and by its distance best answers to the length of the voyage. Thus by encouraging navigation and commerce, Solomon became the richest prince of his time, and his kingdom the most flourishing in the world.

(U) See Gentleman's Magazine for November or December, 1764.

Solomon, according to the first book of Chronicles, had forty thousand stables for his chariot-horses. Each stable containing ten horses, makes four hundred thousand, which, with his twelve thousand saddle horses, amount to four hundred and twelve thousand good war horses; a great many for a Jewish melk who never was engaged in a war. Never was the like magnificence seen in a country breeding only asses, and at present without any other beast for the saddle. But probably times are altered; indeed so wise a prince having a thousand concubines, might very well have four hundred and twelve thousand horses, were it only to give his seraglio an airing along Genesareth lake, or that of Sodom, or toward Cedron brook, one of the most delicious spots on earth, except that this brook is dry nine months of the year, and the ground a little stoney.

But is this same wise Solomon really author of the works fathered on him? is it likely, for instance, that the Jewish eclogue called the Song of Songs is of his writing?

A monarch who had a thousand mistresses, may have said to one of these charmers, Kiss me with the kisses of thy mouth, for thy breasts are better than wine. A king and a shepherd amidst such amorous indearments may very naturally talk alike: but it is something odd, that it is the girl who is made to talk thus wantonly about kisses and her sweetheart's breasts.

I likewise will not deny but a courtly prince may make his mistress say, My husband is like a cluster of myrrh, he shall lye all night betwixt my breasts. A cluster of myrrh is to me something obscure; but I very well understand the charmer's meaning, when she bids her beloved lay his left hand over her neck, and embrace her with his right.

There are some expressions in which the author's

thor's elucidation is wanted, as when he says, Your navel is like a goblet in which there is always something to drink; your belly is like a bushel of wheat; your breasts are like two young roes; your nose is as the tower of Lebanon.

This I own is not the stile of Virgil's Eclogues; but all have not a like stile, and a Jew is not obliged to write like Virgil.

I suppose it may likewise be another beautiful strain of eastern eloquence to say, Our sister is yet little; she has no breasts; what shall we do for our sister? If she be a wall, let us build on her; if a door, let us shut her.

We will allow that such words might have escaped Solomon, though the wisest of men, in a merry mood: This composition is said to be an epithalamium on his marriage with Pharaoh's daughter: but is it natural that Pharaoh's son-in-law should leave his beloved in the night, to go and saunter in his walnut-yard; and that the queen should run after him bare-footed? that the city watch should beat her, and take her gown from her?

Could a king's daughter have said, I am brown, yet am I beautiful like Solomon's furrs (W). Such expressions might be overlooked in a home-spun swain; though, after, all there can be little affinity between furrs and a girl's beauty. Well, but Solomon's furrs might be exceedingly admired in their time; and for a low-lived Jew in a lay to his sweetheart, to tell her in his Jewish gibberish, that never any Jewish king had such fine furred gowns as her dear self, was not at all out of character; but Solomon must have been strangely infatuated with

―――― . (W.) The Geneva and Dutch translations say, Curtains: Beza has it, Similis sum inhabitantibus aulæa Schelomonis. The author seems disingenuous in most of his quotations.

his furrs to compare them to his miſtreſs. Were a king in our times to write ſuch an epithalamium on his marriage with a neighbouring monarch's daughter, he would forfeit all title to the laurel.

Several Rabbis have advanced that this luſcious eclogue not only is not Solomon's, but is not ſo much as authentic. Theodore de Mopſueſte was of the ſame opinion; and the celebrated Grotius calls the Song of Songs a libidinous work, *flagitioſus*; yet is it received as canonical, and reputed to be throughout an allegory of Chriſt's and his church's eſpouſals. The allegory muſt be owned a little forced; and what the church could mean by its little ſiſter having no bubbies, and that if a wall, ſhe muſt be built on, is impenetrably obſcure (X).

Eccleſiaſtes is of a more ſerious turn, but no more Solomon's than the Song of Songs. The author is commonly thought to be Jeſus the ſon of Sirach, whilſt others attribute it to Philo of Biblos; but whoever he was, the Pentateuch ſeems not to have been known in his time, elſe he would not have ſaid that, at the time of the deluge Abraham was going to ſacrifice Iſaac, or have ſpoken of Joſeph the patriarch as a king of Egypt.

The Proverbs have been attributed to Iſaiah, Elziah, Sobna, Eliakim, Joake, and many others; but to whomſoever we owe this collection of eaſtern ſentences, we may be ſure it does not come from a royal hand. Would a king have ſaid, The wrath of a king is as the roaring of a lion? This is the language of a ſubject or ſlave, who trembles at a frown from his maſter. Would So-

---

―― (X) The Rabbis I think compare the book of Proverbs to the outward court of the temple, Eccleſiaſtes to the inward court, and the Song of Songs to the ſanctuary.

lomon

lomon have harped so much on a whorish woman? would he have said, Look not on wine when it appears bright in the glass, and its colour shines?

I very much question whether drinking-glasses were made in Solomon's time; the invention is but modern: the antients drank out of wooden or metal cups; and this single passage betrays that book to be the work of some Alexandrine Jew, and written long since Alexander.

We now come to Ecclesiastes, which Grotius affirms to have been written in the time of Zorobabel. This author's freedom is known to every body; he says, "That men are in nothing bet-
"ter than beasts; that it is better never to have
"been born than to exist; that there is no other
"life; that the only good is to eat and drink, and
"be merry with the woman one loves."

Solomon perhaps might have talked in this manner to some of his women, and some construe these sayings as objections which he makes to himself; but, besides the libertinism of which they strongly favour, they have nothing of the appearance of objections; and to make an author mean the contrary of what he says, is an insult on the world.

However, several of the fathers tell us, that Solomon repented, and imposed on himself a severe penance: now this should silence all animadversions on his conduct.

But though these books were written by a Jew, what is that to us? The Christian religion is indeed founded on Judaism, but not on all the Jewish books. Why should the Song of Songs be held more sacred among us than the fables of the Talmud? The answer is, because we have included it in the Hebrew canon. And what is this same canon? It is a collection of authentic works. Well, and must a work of course be divine, for being au-
U 4 thentic?

thentic? For instance, a history of the kings of Juda and of Sichem, what is it but a history? A strange prepossession, indeed! We despise and abhor the Jews; and yet we insist, that all such of their writings which we have collected, bear the sacred stamp of divinity. Never was such a contradiction heard of!

SENSATION.

Oysters, we are told, have two senses, moles four, and other animals, like men, have five. Some are for admitting a sixth, but it is evident that the voluptuous sensation, which is what they mean, comes within the touch; and that five senses make up our whole portion. We cannot conceive or desire any thing beyond.

The inhabitants of other globes may have senses which we know nothing of: the number of the senses may gradually increase from globe to globe; and the being endued with innumerable senses and all perfect, may be the apex or period of all beings.

But we with our five organs, what power have we over them? It is always involuntarily that we feel, and never from our own inclination; in the presence of the object it is impossible not to have the sensation appointed by our nature. The sensation, though in us, does not at all depend on us; we receive it, and in what manner? Is there any affinity between the vibrations of the air, the words of a song, and the impression which these words make on my brain?

Thought seems to us something strange; but sensation is no less wonderful: a divine power equally shews itself in the sensation of the meanest insect, as in a Newton's brain. Yet at seeing thousands of little animals destroyed, you are not in the least concerned what becomes of their sensitive faculty, though this faculty be the work of the Being of beings. You look on them as machines in nature, born to perish and make room for others.

Wherefore and how should their sensations subsist, when they no longer exist? What need is there for the author of every thing that has being, to preserve properties of which the subject is extinct? It may as well be said, that the power of the Sensitive Plant, to draw in its leaves towards its twigs, subsists when the plant is withered. Here undoubtedly it will be asked, how it is that the sensation of animals perishing with them, man's faculty survives him? That is a question beyond the verge of my knowledge; all I can say to it is, the eternal Author both of sensation and thought, alone knows how he imparts it, and how he preserves it.

It was the current opinion of all antiquity, that nothing is in our understanding, which was not before in our senses. Descartes, in his Philosophical Romances, advanced that we had metaphysical ideas before we so much as knew our nurse's breasts. A college of divines condemned this dogma, not because it was an error, but a novelty: afterwards it adopted this very error, because it had been overthrown by Locke, an English philosopher; and an Englishman, to be sure, must be in the wrong. After such shifts of opinion, it has again proscribed that antient truth, that the senses are the inlets to the understanding. It seems to have acted like governments loaded with debts, sometimes giving a currency to certain notes, and afterwards suppressing them. But this college's notes have quite lost their currency for some time past.

In spight of all the colleges of the world, philosophers will still see that our first knowledge we
receive

receive from our sensations; and that our memory is no more than a continued sensation: a man born without any of his five senses would, could he live, be totally void of any ideas. It is owing to the senses that we even have our metaphysical notions: for how should a circle or a triangle be measured, without having seen or felt a triangle? How can we form an idea, imperfect as it is, of infinitude, but by enlarging boundaries? and how can we throw down boundaries, without having seen or felt them?

An eminent philosopher (Traité des Sensations, tom. ii. p. 128) says, Sensation includes all our faculties.

What must be inferred from all this? That I leave to reflective readers (X).

SOUL (Y).

IT would be a fine thing to see one's soul. Know thyself, is an excellent precept, which God alone can practise. Who but he can know his essence?

We call soul, that which animates; and so contracted is our understanding, that we know little
more

———, (X) Mr. Voltaire does not tell us what inferences we are to draw from the foregoing doctrine of sensations; but we must confess, the whole article contains the substance of the Lucretian arguments against the immateriality of human souls, which is this; that, since the five senses are the only means we have of perception, and these depend upon the corporeal organs, the soul without the body is incapable of perception, and therefore is nothing. In answer to which we must observe, first, that though the senses or perceptions depend on the corporeal organs, as to their present exercise, yet in their nature they are really distinct powers, and cannot arise from any of the known properties or qualities of matter, as the
learned

more of it. Three-fourths of our species do not
go

learned Dr. Clarke hath fully demonstrated. Secondly, our five senses cannot be said to be the only possible ways of perception, by an absolute necessity in the nature of the thing: these are purely arbitrary; and the same power that gave us these, may have given others to other beings: if they be purely arbitrary, the want of them does not imply a total want of perception; but the same soul which in the present state has the powers of reflection, reason, and judgment, which are faculties intirely different from sense, may as easily in another state have different ways of perception. To say that the senses are necessarily the only ways of perception, is a mere prejudice arising from custom; for supposing men had never known the use of sight, would not they have the same reason to conclude, there were but four possible ways of perception, and that sight is an impossible, imaginary power, as they now presume the faculties of immaterial beings to be so? Men from their own mere negative ignorance, should never dispute against the possibility of things. See Dr. Clarke on the Being and Attributes of God.

(Y) This article abounds with metaphysical questions concerning the immortality of the soul, which our author says can be only made known to us by faith. We apprehend he is much mistaken, and shall therefore give the reader the proofs of the immortality of the soul, or of a future state of rewards and punishments. This we have attempted the rather, as throughout his whole work he seems inclined to discredit this doctrine, the basis of all natural as well as of revealed religion. With regard to the notions of schoolmen, mentioned by M. Voltaire, they are a matter of no consequence, as they do not affect the doctrine itself, but are only designed to amuse an idle curiosity.

I. In this present world the natural order of things is so perverted, that vice often flourishes in great prosperity, and virtue falls under the heaviest calamities; whence we conclude, there must be a future state of rewards and punishments. For if there be a God, he is infinitely just and good; and it must needs be his will, that all rational creatures shall imitate his moral perfections; he cannot therefore but be pleased with such as obey his will, and displeased with those who dis-
obey

go that length, and little concern themselves about the

---

obey it; thence it follows, that in vindication of the honour of his government, he must signify his approbation or displeasure some time or other, by making finally a suitable difference between those who obey him, and those who act otherwise; consequently there must be a state of rewards and punishments after this life, wherein all the present difficulties of providence shall be cleared up by an exact administration of justice. To say, that virtue is sufficient to its own happiness, is talking idly with the Stoics; since in the present state of things, virtue is not itself the chief good, but only the means to obtain it; and he who dies for the sake of virtue, is not really more happy, abstracted from a regard to futurity, than he who dies for any fond opinion or humour.

II. Considering the nature and operations of the soul itself, none of the known qualities of matter can in any possible variation, division, or composition, produce sense and thought. The powers of the soul are the most remote from the known properties of matter. It is absurd to suppose the soul made up of innumerable consciousnesses, as matter of innumerable parts; therefore the seat of thought must be a simple substance, such as cannot be divided into pieces like matter; consequently, the soul is not liable to be dissolved along with the body; therefore it will naturally be immortal.

III. A third argument in favour of a future state, is drawn from men's natural desire of immortality. For it is not at all probable, that God should have given men appetites, which were never to be satisfied; desires, that had no objects to answer them; and unavoidable apprehensions of what was never to happen.

IV. A fourth argument is drawn from men's conscience, or judgment of their own conduct. Virtuous actions are attended with self-applause and expectation of rewards; crimes, on the other hand, are followed by remorse, and dread of punishment. Hence it is not therefore at all likely, that the Deity should have so framed the mind of man, as necessarily to pass upon itself a judgment, which shall never be verified; and stand perpetually convicted by a sentence, which shall never be confirmed.

V. A

the thinking being; the other fourth is seeking, but nobody has found, nor ever will find.

Thou poor pedant feest a vegetating plant, and thou fayeft Vegetation, or even Vegetative foul. Thou obferveft bodies have and give motion, and this with thee is ftrength. Thy hound's aptnefs in learning to hunt, under thy inftruction, thou calleft inftinct, fenfitive foul; and as thou haft combined ideas, thou termeft fpirit.

But pray what do you mean by thefe words, This flower vegetates? But is there a real being named Vegetation? One body impels another, but is there in it a diftinct being called Strength? This hound brings thee a partridge; but is there a being called Inftinct? Wouldft thou not laugh at a philofopher, had he even been Alexander's preceptor, who fhould tell thee: All animals live; therefore there is in them a being, a fubftantial form, which is life?

Could a tulip fpeak, and fhould it fay to thee, We are evidently two beings united, wouldft thou not contemptuoufly turn thy back on the tulip?

Let us firft fee what thou knoweft, and of what

V. A fifth and laft argument is drawn from man's being by nature an accountable creature, and capable of being judged. Every moral action a perfon performs proceeds either from fome good, or bad motive; is either conformable or contrary to right reafon, and worthy of praife, or difpraife. Therefore it is highly reafonable to fuppofe, that fince all the moral difference of our actions confifts in the right ufe or abufe of thofe faculties, which we have received from a fuperior being, there will at fome time or other be an inquiry made into the grounds of our feveral actions, whether they have been agreeable or difagreeable to the rule that was given us, and a fuitable judgment be paffed upon them. See further concerning this fubject, Dr. Clarke on the Being and Attributes of God, and Woolafton's Religion of Nature delineated.

thou

thou art certain: that thou walkest with thy feet; that thou digestest by thy stomach; that thou feelest all over thy body; and that thou thinkest by thy head. Let us see if thy reason alone could give thee so much insight, as to conclude, without any supernatural help, that thou hast a soul?

The first philosophers, both Chaldeans and Egyptians, said: There must be something in us that produces our thoughts. This something must be very subtile; it is a breath; it is fire; it is æther; it is a quintessence; it is a light form; it is an entelechia; it is a number; it is a harmony. According to the divine Plato, it is a compound of the same and of the other; and Epicurus from Democritus has said, that it is thinking atoms in us: but, friend, how does an atom think? Own your ignorance here.

The opinion which, unquestionably we should embrace, is that the soul is an immaterial being; but as certainly you do not conceive what this immaterial being is. No, answer the learned; but we know that its nature is to think. And how come you to know that? We know it, because it does think. O doctors! O schoolmen! I am very much afraid that you are as ignorant as Epicurus. The nature of a stone is to fall, because it falls; but I ask you what makes it fall?

We know, continue they, that a stone has no soul. Granted, I believe it as well as you. We know that a negative and an affirmative are not divisible, are not parts of matter: I am of your opinion. But matter, otherwise unknown to us, has qualities that are not divisible, as gravitation towards a center given it by God. Now this gravitation has no parts, is not divisible. The motory force of bodies is not a being composed of parts; neither can it be said that the vegetation of all organized bodies,

their

their life, their inſtinct, are diſtinct, or diviſible beings. You can no more cut in two the vegetation of a roſe, the life of a horſe, the inſtinct of a dog, than you can cut in two a ſenſation, a negation, or an affirmation. Thus your fine argument, taken from the indiviſibility of thought, proves nothing at all.

What then do you call your ſoul? what idea have you of it? All you can of yourſelf, without a revelation, allow to be in yourſelf, is a power unknown to you of feeling and thinking.

Now, honeſtly tell me, is this power of feeling and thinking, the ſame as that by which you digeſt and walk? You tell me it is not: for it would be in vain for your underſtanding to ſay to your ſtomach, digeſt; it will do no ſuch thing if it be out of order; and to as little effect would your immaterial being command your feet to walk; they will not budge, if the gout be in them.

The Greeks were well aware that thought often had no concern with the play of our organs; inſtead of thoſe organs, they ſubſtituted a ſenſitive ſoul, and for the thoughts, a more fine and more ſubtile ſoul, a *nous*.

But let us come to this ſoul of thought, which on a thouſand occaſions has the ſuperintendency over the ſenſitive ſoul. The thinking ſoul orders its hands to take, and they take; but it never tells its heart to beat, its blood to flow, or its chyle to form itſelf; all this is done without it. Thus are two ſouls full of buſineſs, and very little miſtreſſes in their own home.

Now certainly that firſt ſenſitive ſoul does not exiſt; it is nothing but the motion of your organs. Obſerve this, O man! that thy weak reaſon affords thee no more proof that the other ſoul exiſts. It is only by faith that thou canſt know it. Thou art born; thou liveſt; thou acteſt; thou thinkeſt; thou

hou sleepest and wakest without knowing how. God has given thee the faculty of thinking, as he has given thee all thy other appurtenances; and had he not come at the time appointed by his providence to inform thee, that thou hast an immaterial and immortal soul, thou wouldst have been without any proof of it.

Let us now take a view of the fine systems which philosophy has struck out concerning the souls.

One says that the soul of man is part of the substance of God himself; another, that it is part of the great all; a third, that it has been created from all eternity; a fourth, that it is made and not created; others affirm, that God makes them as they are wanted; and that they come at the instant of copulation: one cries they are lodged in the seminal animalcules: not at all, says another, they take up their residence in the Falopian tubes. One coming in at the heat of the dispute, bawls, You are all out, the soul stays six weeks till the fœtus be formed, and then possesses itself of the pineal gland; but if germ prove addle, it goes away to whence it came, till a better opportunity. The last opinion makes its abode to be in the callous body. This is the situation assigned to it by La Peironie. Indeed none under the king of France's first surgeon could provide such an apartment for the soul. However, the surgeon has got into better vogue than his callous body.

St. Thomas, in his 75th question, &c. says, that the soul is a form *Subsistens per se*; that it is all in all; that it's essence differs from it's power; that there are three vegetative souls, the nutritive, the augmentative, and the generative; that the memory of spiritual things is spiritual, and the memory of corporeal things is corporeal; that the rational soul is an immaterial form as to the operations;

and

and material in essence. St. Thomas has written two thousand pages all of this force and perspicuity. No wonder that schools stile him the angelic doctor!

As many systems have been invented on the manner of this soul's perceptions, when it shall have quitted this body by which it perceived, how it will hear without ears, smell without a nose, and feel without hands; what body it will afterwards re-assume, whether that which it had at the age of two years, or of fourscore? how the Me, the identity of the same person, will subsist? how the soul of a man, who was seized with ideotism at the age of fifteen, and died in that state at seventy, will recover the train of ideas which it had at its age of puberty? by what dexterity, a soul, one of whose legs was cut off in Europe, and which lost an arm in America, will find this leg and arm again, after their several mutations into esculent herbs, and the blood of some other animal? There would be no end of enumerating all the extravagancies which this poor human soul has broached concerning it's self.

We live upon this earth in the same manner as the man with the iron mask spent his days in prison, without knowing his original, or the reason of his being confined, which excited a general curiosity.

If any man has discovered a ray of light in this region of darkness, perhaps it is Mallebranche, notwithstanding the general prejudices against his system. It does not differ greatly from that of the Stoics; and who knows but these two opinions, properly rectified, come nearest the truth? There is, I think, something very sublime in that antient notion: "We exist in God; our thought, our "sentiments, are derived from the Supreme Being."

A most

A most remarkable circumstance is, that in the laws of God's people, not a word is said of the soul's spirituality and immortality, nothing in the Decalogue, nothing in Leviticus, nor in Deuteronomy.

It is very certain, it is manifest, that Moses no where proposes to the Jews rewards and punishments in another state; that he never mentions to them the immortality of their souls; that he never encourages them with the hopes of heaven, nor does he threaten them with hell; his promises and menaces are all temporal.

Before his death, he tells them in Deuteronomy:

"If, after having children and grand children, you deal falsely, you shall be cut off from the land, and be made little among the nations.

"I am a jealous God, punishing the iniquity of the fathers to the third and fourth generation.

"Honour thy father and mother, that thy life may be long.

"You shall never want food.

"If you follow after strange gods, you shall be destroyed——

"If you obey the Lord, you shall have rain in spring and autumn; corn, oil, wine, and fodder for your beasts, that you may eat and be satisfied.

"Put these words into your hearts, about your hands, between your eyes; write them on your doors, that your days may be multiplied.

"Do as I order you, without adding or taking away any thing.

"If a prophet arise among you, foretelling strange things, and his prophecy is true, and what he says comes to pass; should he say to you, Come, let us follow strange gods, ye shall immediately kill him; and all the people smite him after you.

"When

" When the Lord shall have delivered the na-
" tions into your hands, put them all to the sword,
" without sparing one single man; thou shalt not
" pity any one.

" Eat no unclean birds, as the eagle, and the
" ossifrage, and the ospray, &c.

" Eat no creatures which chew the cud and are
" not cloven footed, as the camel, the hare, and
" the cony.

" Whilst you observe all those ordinances you
" shall be blessed in your houses and in your
" fields; the fruits of your body, of your land,
" of your cattle shall be blessed.

" If you fail to observe all these ordinances and
" ceremonies, cursed shall ye be in your houses
" and in your fields.——

" Famine and poverty shall come on you; you
" shall die, distressed by cold, want, and sick-
" ness; you shall have the itch, the scab; you shall
" have ulcers in your knees, and in your legs.

" The strangers shall lend to you on usury----
" because ye have not served the Lord.

And ye shall eat the fruit of your bodies, and
" the flesh of your sons and of your daughters."

Do not all these promises and threatnings relate
intirely to things of time and this world? is there
a single word in them concerning the soul's immortality, and a future life?

Several celebrated commentators have thought,
that those two capital doctrines were very well
known to Moses, and in proof of it produce Jacob's words, who apprehending that his son had
been devoured by wild beasts, says in his grief, I
shall go down with my son to the grave, *in infer-
num*, into hell; that is to say, as my son is dead,
let me die.

They farther prove it by passages from Isaiah

and Ezekiel; but the Hebrews, to whom Moses was speaking, knew nothing of those two prophets, as not living till some ages after.

To dispute about Moses's private sentiments is wasting words to no purpose. The certain fact is, that in his public laws he had never so much as once made mention of a life to come, limiting all punishments and all rewards to the present state. If he was acquainted with a future life, why did he not expresly set forth such an important tenet? and if he was a stranger to it, what was the scope of his mission?

This is a question advanced by several great men: and in answer to it they say, that Moses's Lord, who is the lord of all men, reserved to himself the prerogative of explaining to the Jews in his own time, a doctrine which they were not in a condition to understand, when in the wilderness.

Had Moses taught the doctrine of the immortality of the soul, a great school among the Jews would not always have opposed it. Nay, that great school, the Sadducees, would not have been allowed of in the state, much less would they have held the chief employments; and still much less would high-priests have been taken from such a body.

It appears that the Jews were not divided into three sects, the Pharisees, the Sadducees, and the Essenes, till after the foundation of Alexandria. Josephus the historian, who was a Pharisee, says in book XIII. of his antiquities, that the Pharisees believed the metempsichosis. The Sadducees held that the soul perished with the body. The opinion of the Essenes was, that souls were immortal and came down into bodies from the upper regions of the air in an aerial form; that their return thither is by a rapid attraction; and, after death, those which belong-

belonged to good persons have mansions assigned them beyond the ocean, in a country where there is neither heat nor cold, wind nor rain, whilst the souls of the wicked go to a quite contrary climate; such was the theology of the Jews.

He who alone was to set mankind right came and overthrew these three sects; but without him we never should have been able to know any thing of the soul: for philosophers never had any determinate idea of it; and Moses, the only true legiflator of the world before our divine teacher; Moses, who spoke to God face to face, and who saw only his hinder parts, has left mankind in their natural ignorance of this momentous article: so that it is but seventeen hundred years since there has been any certainty of the existence and immortality of the soul.

Cicero had only surmises; his grand-son and grand-daughter might have learned farther from the first Galileans who came to Rome.

But before, and since that time, in all the parts of the earth, where the apostles had not preached the gospel, every one might say to his soul, Who art thou? whence comest thou? what art thou doing? whither art thou going? Thou art, I know not what; thou thinkest and perceivest; and wert thou to perceive and think a hundred thousand millions of years, never wouldst thou, by thine own faculties, without the assistance of God, know a jot more than thou knowest now.

Know man, that God has given thee understanding to guide thy behaviour, and not to penetrate into the essence of the things which he has created.

SUPERSTITION (Y).

WHatever goes beyond the adoration of one Supreme Being, and a submission of the heart to his eternal orders, is generally superstition; and a most dangerous superstition is the annexing of the pardon of crimes to certain ceremonies.

> " Et nigras mactant pecudes et manibus divis
> " Inferias mittunt.
> " O faciles nimium qui tristia crimina cædis
> " Fluminea tolli posse putatis aqua."

You imagine that God will forget your having killed a man, only for your washing yourself in a river, sacrificing a black sheep, and some words being said over you. Of course then a second murder will be forgiven you at the same easy rate, and so a third; and a hundred murders will only cost you a hundred black sheep, and a hundred ablutions! Poor mortals! away with such con-

---

(Y) The doctrine contained in this article may come very well from the mouth of Cicero, Seneca, or Plutarch; but if it intends to suppress all external ceremonies of religion, it is not suitable to a believer of Christianity. We are taught that every particular or national church hath authority to decree and appoint ceremonies or religious rites, without being charged with superstition. And we believe that Baptism and the Lord's-Prayer, which constitute a part of our external worship, were ordained by Christ, and consequently a divine institution. Superstition properly consists in the practice of such ceremonies as are repugnant to reason, or the word of God.

ceits;

ceits; the best way is, commit no murder, and so save your black sheep.

How scandalous is it to imagine that a priest of Isis and Cybele can reconcile you to the deity, by playing on cymbals and castanets! And what is this priest of Cybele, this vagrant gelding, who lives by your weakness, that he shall set up to be as a mediator between heaven and you? Has he any commission from God? He takes money from you only for muttering some strange words; and you can think that the Being of Beings ratifies what this hypocrite says.

Some superstitions are innocent; you dance on Diana or Pomona's festivals, or those of any of the secondary gods in your calendar: be it so; dancing is pleasant, healthy, and exhilarating; it hurts no body; but do not take it into your head that Pomona and Vertumnus are mightily pleased at your having frolicked in honour of them; and that should you fail to do so, they would make you smart for it. The gardener's spade and hoe are the only Pomona and Vertumnus. Don't be so weak as to think that your garden will be destroyed by a tempest, if you omit dancing the pyrrhic or the cordax.

There is another superstition which perhaps is excusable, and even an incentive to virtue; I mean deifying great men who have been signal benefactors to their own species. To be sure it would be better only to look on them as venerable personages, and especially to endeavour to imitate them: therefore revere, without worshipping, a Solon, a Thales, a Pythagoras; but by no means do not pay thy adorations to Hercules for having cleansed Augeas's stables, and lying with fifty girls in one night.

Especially forbear setting up a worship for wretches without any other merit than ignorance, enthusiasm, and nastiness; who made a vow of idleness and beggary, and gloried in such infamy: fit subjects indeed for deification after their death; who were never known to do the least good when living!

Observe that the most superstitious times have ever been noted for the greatest enormities.

TOLERATION.

WHAT is toleration? It is a privilege to which human nature is entitled: we are all made up of weakness and errors; it therefore behoves us mutually to forgive another's follies. This is the very first law of nature.

Though the Gueber, the Banian, the Jew, the Mahometan, the lettered Chinese, the Greek, the Roman Catholic, the Quaker, traffic together on the 'Change of Amsterdam, London, Surat, or Bassora; they will never offer to lift up a poniard against each other, to gain proselytes: wherefore then, since the first council of Nice, have we been almost continually cutting each other's throats?

Constantine began with issuing an edict, allowing the exercise of all religions; and some time after turned persecutor. Before him, all the severe treatment of the Christians proceeded purely from their beginning to make a party in the state. The Romans permitted every kind of worship, even of the Jews and Egyptians, both which they so very much despised. How then came Rome to tolerate these forms? It was because neither the Egyptians nor the Jews themselves went about to exterminate the antient religion of the empire; they did not
cross

cross seas and lands to make proselytes; the getting of money was all they minded; whereas it is indisputable, that the Christians could not be easy, unless their religion bore the sway. The Jews were disgusted at the statue of Jupiter being set up in Jerusalem; but the Christians would not so much as allow it to be in the capitol of Rome. St. Thomas candidly owns, that it was only for want of power that the Christians did not dethrone the emperors: they held that all the world ought to embrace their religion; this of course made them enemies to all the world, till its happy conversion.

Their controversial points likewise set them at enmity one against another concerning the divinity of Christ: they who denied it, were anathematized as Ebionites; and these anathematized the worshippers of Jesus.

If some would have all goods to be in common, as they alledged was the custom in the Apostles time; their adversaries call them Nicolaitans, and accuse them of the most horrid crimes. If others set up for a mystical devotion, they are branded with the appellation of Gnostics, and opposed with extreme vehemence and severity. Marcion, for disputing on the Trinity, got the name of an idolater.

Tertullian, Praxeas, Origen, Novatus, Novatianus, Sabellus, and Donatus, were all persecuted by their brethren before Constantine's time: and no sooner had Constantine established the Christian religion, than the Athanasians and Eusebians fell foul of one another; and ever since, down to our own times, the Christian church has been deluged with blood.

The Jewish people were, I own, extremely barbarous and merciless; massacring all the inhabitants of a little wretched country, to which it had

no

no more right *(Z)* than their vile descendants have to Paris or London. However, when Naaman is cured of his leprosy by dipping seven times in the river Jordan, and by way of expressing his gratitude to Elijah, from whom he had the secret of that easy cure, he tells him that he will worship the God of the Jews; he yet reserves to himself the liberty to worship his sovereign's God likewise; and asks Elisha's leave, which the prophet readily grants *(A)*. The Jews worshipped their God, but never were offended at, or so much as thought it strange, that every nation had its own Deity. They acquiesced in Chamoth's giving a tract of land to the Moabites, provided they would let them quietly enjoy what they held from their God. Jacob made no difficulty of marrying an idolater's daughter; for Laban had another kind of god than he whom Jacob worshipped. These are instances of toleration among the most haughty, most obstinate, and most cruel people of all antiquity; and we, overlooking what little indulgence was among them, have have imitated only their sanguinary rancour.

Every individual persecuting another for not being of his opinion, is a monster; this is evident beyond all dispute: but the government! men in power,

---

(Z) This is a mistake of M. Voltaire. The Israelies treated the Cananites with great severity by the express command of God, who would have these nations extirpated because of their horrid impiety, which soon made them unworthy of the lands they possessed, and was the cause of their being given away to the Israelites.

(A) This story of Naaman is not fairly represented. Naaman does not ask Elisha's permission to worship his master's God, but to bow himself down along with his master, who leaned upon his hand; so that it was not a religious, but a civil ceremony, in the discharge of his office. Thus Abraham, Gen. xxiii. 7. bowed himself to the people of the land.

princes!

princes! how are they to deal with those of a different worship from theirs? If foreigners and powerful, it is certain a prince will not disdain entering into an alliance with them. Francis I. though his most Christian majesty, unites with the Mussulmen against Charles V. likewise a most Christian monarch. Francis supplies the German Lutherans with money to support their revolt against the emperor; but, according to custom, burns them in his own country: thus, from policy, he pays them in Saxony; and, from policy, makes bonfires of them at Paris. But what was the consequence? Persecution ever makes proselytes. France came to swarm with new Protestants, who at first quietly submitted to be hanged, and afterwards hung others; civil wars came on; and St. Bartholomew's day, or the massacre of Paris, crowned all. Thus this corner of the world became worse than all that ever the antients or moderns have said of hell.

Ye fools, never to pay a proper worship to the God who made you! wretches, on whom the example of the Noachidæ, the lettered Chinese, the Persees, and all wise men have had no influence! monsters, to whom superstitions are necessary as carrion to crows! You have been already told it, and I have nothing else to tell you; whilst you have but two religions among you, they will be ever at daggers drawing; if you have thirty they will live quietly. Turn your eyes to the grand signior, he has among his subjects Guebers, Banians, Greeks, Latins, Christians, and Nestorians. Whoever goes about to raise any disturbance is surely impaled; and thus all live in peace and quietness.

TYRAN-

TYRANNY.

BY a tyrant is meant a sovereign who makes his humour the law, who seizes on his subjects substance, and afterwards inlists them to go and give his neighbours the like treatment. These tyrants are not known in Europe.

Tyranny is distinguished into that of one person and of many; a body invading the rights of other bodies, and corrupting the laws that it may exercise a despotism apparently legal, is the latter tyranny; but Europe likewise has none of these tyrants.

Under which tyranny would you chuse to live? Under none; but had I the option, the tyranny of one person appears to me less odious and dreadful than that of many. A despot has always some intervals of good humour; which is never known in an assembly of despots. If a tyrant has done me an injury, there is his mistress, his confessor, or his page, by means of whom I may appease him, and obtain redress; but a set of supercilious tyrants is inaccessible to all applications. If they are not unjust, still they are austere and harsh; and no favours are ever known to come from them.

Under one despot, I need only stand up against a wall when I see him coming by, or prostrate myself, or knock my forehead against the ground, according to the custom of the country; but under a body of perhaps a hundred despots, I may be obliged to repeat this ceremony a hundred times a day, which is not a little troublesome to those who are not very nimble. Another disagreeable circumstance is, if my farm happens to be in the neighbourhood of one of our great lords, it is unknown what damages I am obliged to put up with; and if I have a law-suit with a relation to a relation of one of their high-mightinesses, it will infallibly go against me. I am very much afraid that in this world things will come to such a pass, as to have no other option than being either hammer or anvil. Happy he! who gets clear of this alternative.

V I R T U E (B).

WHAT is virtue? Doing good to others. How can I give the name of virtue to any one but to him who does me good? I am in want, you relieve me; I am in danger, you come to my assistance; I have been deceived, you tell me the truth. I am ill used, you comfort me; I am ignorant, you instruct me: I must say then you are virtuous. But what will become of the cardinal and theological virtues? Let some e'en remain in the schools.

(B) Our author may give some offence to minute critics in the following article, but upon consideration the reader will find the whole to be a logomachia. By virtue he means charity and beneficence. The cardinal and theological virtues he calls excellent qualities, but does not allow them to be virtues in regard to our neighbour. No body pretends they are; but they are virtues in regard to ourselves, and to the Deity; or they are excellent qualities, for we shall not dispute about the word. We do not perceive, nevertheless, how M. Voltaire can be said to give indirect encouragement in this article to private vices, for he acknowledges that gluttony, drunkenness, &c. are blemishes or defects in a hermit, tho' not pernicious to society, because he does not live in a social state.

What

What is your temperance to me? It is no more than an observance of a rule of health; you will be the better for it; and much good may it do you. If you have faith and hope, better still; they will procure you eternal life. Your theological virtues are heavenly gifts, and those you call cardinal are excellent qualities for your guidance in life; but, relatively to your neighbour, they are no virtues. The prudent man does good to himself; the virtuous to men in general. Very well was it said by St. Paul, that charity is better than faith and hope.

But how! are no virtues to be admitted but those by which others are benefited? No indeed. We live in a society; consequently there is nothing truly good to us, but what is for the good of such society. If a hermit is sober and devout, and among other mortifications wears a sackcloth shirt; such a one I let down as a saint; but before I shall style him virtuous, let him do some act of virtue which will promote the well being of his fellow creatures. Whilst he lives by himself, to us he is neither good nor bad; he is nothing. If St. Bruno reconciled families, and relieved the indigent, he was virtuous; if he prayed and fasted in the desert, he was a saint. Among men virtue is a mutual exchange of kindnesses, and whoever declines such exchanges, ought not to be reckoned a member of society. Were that saint to live in the world, probably he would do good in it; but whilst he keeps out of it, the world will only do his saintship justice, in not allowing him to be virtuous. He may be good to himself, but not to us.

But, say you, if a hermit be given to drunkenness, sensuality, and private debauchery, he is a vicious man; consequently with the opposite qualities, he is virtuous. That is what I cannot come into: if he has those faults he is a very filthy man; but

but, with regard to society, as it is not hurt by his infamies, he is not vicious, wicked, or deserving of punishment. It is to be presumed, that were he to return into society, he would do much harm, and prove a very bad man. Of this there is a greater probability, than that the temperate and chaste hermit will be a good man; for in public life, faults increase, and good qualities diminish.

A much stronger objection is, that Nero, pope Alexander VI. and other such monsters did some good things. I take upon me to answer, that when they did, they were virtuous.

Some divines, so far from allowing that excellent emperor Antoninus to have been a good man, represent him as a conceited Stoic, who, besides ruling over men, coveted their esteem; that in all the good he did to mankind, his own reputation was the end; that his justice, application, and benevolence, proceeded purely from vanity; and that his virtues were a downright imposition on the world. At this, I cannot forbear crying out, O! my God, be pleased in thy goodness, often to give us such hypocrites.

W A R.

FAmine, the plague, and war, are the three most famous ingredients in this lower world. Under famine may be classed all the noxious foods, which want obliges us to have recourse to; thus shortening our life, whilst we hope to support it.

In the plague are included all contagious distempers; and these are not less than two or three thousand. These two gifts we hold from providence; but war, in which all those gifts are concentered,

centered, we owe to the fancy of three or four hundred persons scattered over the surface of this globe, under the name of princes and ministers; and on this account it may be, that in several dedications, they are called the living images of the Deity.

The most hardened flatterer will allow, that war is ever attended with plague and famine, especially if he has seen the military-hospitals in Germany; or passed through any villages where some notable feat of arms has been performed.

It is unquestionably a very noble art to ravage countries, destroy dwellings, and *communibus annis*, out of a hundred thousand men to cut off forty thousand. This invention was originally cultivated by nations, assembled for their common good; for instance, the diet of the Greeks sent word to the diet of Phrygia and its neighbours, that they were putting to sea in a thousand fishing-boats, in order to do their best to cut them off root and branch.

The Roman people, in a general assembly, resolved that it was their interest to go and fight the Vejentes or the Volscians before harvest; and some years after, all the Romans being angry with all the Carthaginians, fought a long time both by sea and land. It is otherwise in our time.

A genealogist sets forth to a prince that he is descended in a direct line from a count, whose kindred, three or four hundred years ago, had made a family-compact with a house, the very memory of which is extinguished. That house had some distant claim to a province, the last proprietor of which died of an apoplexy. The prince and his council instantly resolve, that this province belongs to him by divine right. The province, which is some hundred leagues from him, protests that it is does not so much as know him; that it is not disposed

posed to be governed by him; that before prescribing laws to them, their consent, at least, was necessary: these allegations do not so much as reach the prince's ears; it is insisted on that his right is incontestable. He instantly picks up a multitude of men, who have nothing to do, nor nothing to lose; cloaths them with coarse blue cloth, one sou to the ell; puts them on hats bound with coarse white worsted; makes them turn to the right and left; and thus marches away with them to glory.

Other princes, on this armament, take part in it to the best of their ability, and soon cover a small extent of country, with more hireling murderers than Gengis-Kan, Tamerlane, and Bajazet had at their heels.

People, at no small distance, on hearing that fighting is going forward, and that if they would make one, there are five or six sous a day for them, immediately divide into two bands, like reapers, and go and sell their services to the first bidder.

These multitudes furiously butcher one another, not only without having any concern in the quarrel, but without so much as knowing what it is about.

Sometimes five or six powers are engaged, three against three, two against four, sometimes even one against five, all equally detesting one another; and friends and foes, by turns, agreeing only in one thing, to do all the mischief possible.

An odd circumstance in this infernal enterprize is, that every chief of these ruffians has his colours consecrated; and solemnly prays to God before he goes to destroy his neighbour. If the slain in a battle do not exceed two or three thousand, the fortunate commander does not think it worth thanking God for; but if, besides killing ten or twelve thousand men, he has been so far favoured by heaven, as totally to destroy some remarkable place, then a verbose hymn is sung in four parts, composed in a language unknown to all the combatants, and besides stuffed with barbarisms. The same song does for marriages and births, as for massacres; which is scarce pardonable, especially in a nation of all others the most noted for new songs.

All countries pay a certain number of orators to celebrate these sanguinary actions; some in a long black coat, and over it a short docked cloak; others in a gown, with a kind of shirt over it; some again over their shirts have two pieces of a motley-coloured stuff hanging down. They are all very long-winded in their harangues, and to illustrate a battle fought in Weteravia, bring up what passed thousands of years ago in Palestine.

At other times these gentry declaim against vice; they prove by syllogisms and antitheses, that ladies, for slightly heightening the hue of their cheeks with a little carmine, will assuredly be the eternal objects of eternal vengeance; that Polyeucte and Athalia (C) are the devil's works; that he, whose table on a day of abstinence, is loaded with fish to the amount of two hundred crowns, is infallibly saved; and that a poor man, for eating two penny-worth of mutton, goes to the devil for ever and ever.

Among five or six thousand such declamations, there may be, and that is the most, three or four, written by a Gaul named Massillon, which a gentleman may bear to read; but in not one of all those discourses has the orator the spirit to animadvert on war, that scourge and crime which includes

---

(C) Two French Tragedies.

all

all others. These groveling speakers are continually prating against love, mankind's only solace, and the only way of repairing it: not a word do they say of the detestable endeavours of the mighty for its destruction.

Bourdaloue, a very bad sermon have you made against impurity, but not one either bad or good on those various kinds of murders, on those robberies, on those violences, that universal rage, by which the world is laid waste! Put together all the vices of all ages and places, and never will they come up to the mischiefs and enormities of only one campaign.

Ye bungling soul-physicians, to bellow for an hour and more against a few flea-bites, and not say a word about that horrid distemper, which tears us to pieces. Burn your books, ye moralizing philosophers! Whilst the humour of a few shall make it an act of loyalty to butcher thousands of our fellow-creatures, the part of mankind dedicated to heroism will be the most execrable and destructive monsters in all nature. Of what avail is humanity, benevolence, modesty, temperance, mildness, discretion, and piety; when half a pound of lead discharged at the distance of six hundred paces shatters my body; when I expire at the age of twenty under pains unspeakable, and amidst thousands in the same miserable condition; when my eyes at their last opening see my native town all in a blaze; and the last sounds I hear are the shrieks and groans of women and children expiring among the ruins, and all for the pretended interest of a man who is a stranger to us!

The worst is, that war appears to be an unavoidable scourge; for if we observe it, the god Mars was worshipped in all nations; and among the Jews, Sabaoth signifies the god of armies: but in

Homer, Minerva calls Mars a furious hare-brained infernal deity.

WHATEVER IS IS RIGHT.

WHAT a clamour was raised in the schools, and even among sober thinkers, when Leibnitz, paraphrasing on Plato, built his structure of the best of possible worlds, affirming that all things went in the best manner, and that God could make but one world. Now, Plato had allowed that God could make five, there being five regular solid bodies; the tetraedron or three-faced pyramid, with the base equal, the cube, the exaedron, the dodecaedron, and hicoaedron. But our world is not of the form of any of Plato's bodies, so that he should have allowed God a sixth manner.

So much for the divine Plato. Leibnitz, who certainly was his superior both in metaphysics and geometry, in the tenderness of philanthropy shewed mankind, that we ought to be very well satisfied, and that God had done all he could for us; that he had necessarily, among all possibilites, made choice of what was indisputably the best.

What becomes of original sin? was the cry of many. Let what will come of it, said Leibnitz and his friends; but in his public writings he makes original sin necessarily a part of the best world.

How! our first parents to be driven out of a delightful abode, where they were to have lived for ever, had they not eaten an apple! How! in wretchedness to beget children loaded with a variety of wretchedness, and making others as wretched as themselves! How! to undergo such diseases; to feel such vexations; to expire in pain; and by way of refreshment to be burned through all the ages of eternity; was this the best portion? That is not over good for us; and in what can it be good for God?

Leibnitz was sensible this admitted of no answer; accordingly he falls to making of large books unintelligible to his very self.

To deny that there is any evil, may be said as a banter by a Lucullus full of health, and feasting in his saloon with his mistress and jocund cronies; but only let him look out at the window, and he will see some unhappy people; and a fever will make the great man himself so.

I am not fond of quoting; it is usually a critical task; it is neglecting both what precedes and follows the passage quoted, and bringing on one's self complaints and quarrels: yet I must quote Lactantius, a father of the church, who, in his thirteenth chapter on the Divine Anger, puts the following words into Epicurus's mouth; "Either God
" would remove evil out of this world, and cannot;
" or he can or will not; or he has neither the
" power nor will; or lastly, he has both the power
" and will. If he has the will and not the power,
" this shews weakness, which is contrary to the
" nature of God; if he has the power, and not
" the will, it is malignity; and this is no less con-
" trary to his nature. If he is neither able nor
" willing, it is both weakness and malignity; if
" he be both willing and able (which alone is
" consonant to the nature of God) how came it
" that there is evil in the world?"

This is a home argument; and accordingly Lactantius gives but a sorry answer to it, in saying that God wills evil, but that he has given us wisdom for acquiring good. This answer must be allowed to fall very short of the objection; as sup-

posing

posing that God, without producing evil, could not have given us wisdom; if so, our wisdom is a dear bargain.

The origin of evil (D) has ever been an abyss, the bottom of which lies beyond the reach of human eye; and many philosophers and legislators, in their perplexity, had recourse to two principles, one good and the other evil; Tiphon was the evil principle among the Egyptians, and Arimane among the Persians. This divinity is well known to have been espoused by the Manichees; but these wise folks, having never conversed with either the good

---

(D) How difficult soever this great question of the cause and original of evil may appear to our author, it has been admirably well solved by the learned Dr. Clarke, in the inference he draws from the proofs of the possibility and real existence of liberty. For liberty implying a natural power of doing evil as well as good, and the imperfect nature of finite beings making it possible for them to abuse their liberty to an actual commission of evil, and it being necessary to the order and beauty of the whole, there should be different degrees of creatures, some less perfect than others; hence there necessarily ariseth a possibility of evil, though the Creator is infinitely good. Evil is either natural or moral. *Moral evil* arises wholly from the abuse of liberty, which God gave to his creatures for other purposes, and which it was reasonable and fit to give them for the perfection and order of the whole creation: but they, contrary to the divine intention and command, have abused what was necessary for the perfection of the whole, to the corruption and depravation of themselves. *Natural evil* is either counterpoised in the whole, with as great or greater good; such are the afflictions and sufferings of good men, and then it is not properly an evil: or it is a punishment, and then it is a necessary consequence of moral evil. As for death, it is not a natural evil, though generally counted such; since it is only the want of immortality, a perfection which does not belong to our nature, and such a want is not properly an evil. See Dr. Clarke on the Being and Attributes of God.

or the evil principle, I think they are not to be believed on their bare word.

Amidst the absurdities which swarm in the world, and may be classed among its evils, it is no slight error to have supposed two Almighty Beings struggling which should bear the greater sway in the world, and making an agreement together, like Moliere's two physicians, Allow me the puke, and I will allow you the bleeding.

Basilides, from the Platonics, affirmed, so early as the first century of the church, that God gave our world to be made by his lowest angels; and that by their aukwardness and ignorance things are as they are. This theological fable falls to pieces before the terrible objection, that it is not in the nature of an infinitely wise and powerful God to cause a world to be constructed by ignorant architects, who know not how to conduct such a task.

Simon, aware of this objection, obviates it by saying, that the angel who acted as surveyor is damned for his bungling; but this bungling of the angel does not mend our case.

Neither does the Grecian story of Pandora solve the objection any better. The box with all evils in it, and hope remaining at the bottom, is indeed a charming allegory; but this Pandora Vulcan made purely to be revenged of Prometheus, who had formed a man of mud.

The Indians are not a whit nearer the mark: God on creating man gave him a drug, by which he was to enjoy perpetual health; the man put his drug on his ass; the ass being thirsty, the serpent shewed it the way to a spring, and whilst the ass was drinking, the serpent made off with the drug.

The Syrians had a conceit, that the man and the woman having been created in the fourth heaven, they took a fancy to eat a bit of cake instead of ambrosia,

ambrosia, their natural regale. Ambrosia perspired through the pores; but after eating the cake they had a motion to go to stool, and asked an angel the way to the privy. Do you see, said the angel, yon little planet, scarce visible, about sixty millions of leagues off? that is the privy of the universe; make the best of your way thither. They marched, and there they were left to continue; and ever since this our world has been what it is.

But the Syrians are gravelled when asked, why God permitted man to eat of the cake, and why it should be productive of such dreadful evils to us?

To shorten my journey, I shoot away from the fourth heaven to lord Bolingbroke. This personage, who it must be allowed had a great genius, gave the famous Pope his plan of WHATEVER IS IS RIGHT, which accordingly occurs word for word in lord Bolingbroke's posthumous works; and the same sentiment occurs before in lord Shaftesbury's Characteristics. In his treatise entitled the Moralist, are these words:

" Much is alledged in answer, to shew why
" nature errs, and how she came thus impotent
" and erring from an unerring hand. But I deny
" she errs ——'Tis, on the contrary, from this or-
" der of inferior and superior things, that we ad-
" mire the world's beauty, founded thus on con-
" trarieties; whilst from such various and disagree-
" ing principles, an universal concord is established.

" Thus in the several orders of terrestrial forms,
" a resignation is required, a sacrifice and yielding
" of natures one to another. The vegetables by
" their death sustain the animals; and animal
" bodies dissolved, enrich the earth, and raise again
" the vegetable world. Numerous insects are re-
" duced again by the superior kinds of birds and
" beasts; and these again are checked by man,
" who

"who in his turn submits to other natures, and
"resigns his form a sacrifice in common to the rest
"of things. And if in natures so little exalted,
"and pre-eminent above each other, the sacrifice
"of interest can appear so just; how much more
"reasonably may all inferior natures be subjected
"to the superior nature of the world! — The
"central powers, which hold the lasting orbs in
"their just poise and movement, must not be
"controuled to save a fleeting form, and rescue
"from the precipice a puny animal, whose brittle
"frame, howe'er protected, must of itself so soon
"dissolve. The ambient air, the inward vapours,
"the impending meteors, or whatever else is nu-
"trimental or preservative of this earth, must ope-
"rate in a natural course; and other constitutions
"must submit to the good habit and constitution
"of the all-sustaining globe."

Bolingbroke, Shaftesbury, and Pope their artist, are not more satisfactory than the others; their WHATEVER IS IS RIGHT, imports no more, than that all is directed by immutable laws; and who knows not that? You tell us nothing in observing with every little child, that flies are born to be devoured by spiders; spiders by swallows; swallows by magpies; magpies by eagles; and eagles to be shot at by men, and men to kill one another, and to be eaten by worms; and afterwards by devils, at least a thousand to one.

Thus we see a clear and stated order throughout every species of creatures: in short, there is order in all things. The formation of a stone in my bladder is a wonderful mechanism: stony particles insensibly get into my blood; are filtrated in my kidnies; pass through the urethra; settle in my bladder; and there, by an admirable Newtonian attraction, concrete. The stone forms and grows
bigger,

bigger, and by the finest dispositions in the world, I undergo tortures worse than death: a surgeon, having improved Tubal Cain's invention, comes and stabs a sharp and edged steel instrument into my ———, lays hold of my stone with his forceps; but by a necessary mechanism it breaks as he is trying to extract it, and by the same mechanism I expire as on the rack. As what ever is is right, all this must be likewise right; it is evidently a consequence of the unalterable physical principles granted; and I know it as well as yourself.

Had we no feeling, no objection would lye against such a system: but that is not the point; what we ask is, whether there are no sensible evils, and whence they are originated? Pope, in his fourth epistle on WHATEVER IS IS RIGHT, says, " There " is no evil, or all partial evil is universal good."

An odd general good, truly; composed of the gout, the stone, pains, afflictions, crimes, sufferings, death, and damnation!

The fall of man is the plaister we lay on all these partial diseases of soul and body, which you term general health; but with Shaftesbury and Bolingbroke, original sin is a mere jest, and Pope is silent about it; their system manifestly undermines Christianity, and explains nothing at all.

This system, however, has lately been countenanced by several divines, who make no difficulty of contrarieties: well, let no body be grudged the comfort of reasoning in his way on the deluge of evil, with which the world is overwhelmed; incurable patients should be allowed to gratify their appetites in eating what they like; some have even cried up this system as consolatory.

A strange comfort I own! And do not you find great relief in Shaftesbury's prescription, who says, that God will not change his eternal laws for so

paltry

paltry a creature as man? It muſt however be owned, that this paltry animal has a right humbly to lament, and, amidſt his lamentations, to endeavour at comprehending why thoſe eternal laws are not adapted to the well-being of every individual.

This ſyſtem of WHATEVER IS IS RIGHT, repreſents the Author of nature merely as a powerful cruel king, who, if he does but compaſs his deſigns, is very eaſy about the death, diſtreſſes, and afflictions of his ſubjects.

So very far, then, is the opinion of the beſt world poſſible from being conſolatory, that it puzzles thoſe philoſophers who embrace it. The queſtion of good and evil remains an inexplicable chaos to candid enquirers; cavillers may trifle with it; they are galley-ſlaves playing with their chains. As to the thoughtleſs commonalty, they are not unlike fiſhes taken out of a river and put into a reſervoir, little thinking they are to undergo a ſecond removal in Lent; ſo we of ourſelves are totally ignorant of the cauſes of our deſtiny.

At the end of almoſt every chapter of metaphyſics, we ſhould put the two letters uſed by the Roman judges when a cauſe was obſcure, N. L. *non liquet*, I don't underſtand it.

WICKED, WICKEDNESS (E).

WE are perpetually told that human nature is eſſentially perverſe, that man is born a child of the devil. Now nothing can be more imprudent,

---

(E) Our author talks very favourably of humanity under this article, which is inconſiſtent with the horrid picture he gives

prudent; for, my friend, in preaching to me that all the world is born in wickedness, thou informest me that thou art born so, and that behoves me to beware of thee, as I would of a fox or crocodile. O! not at all, sayest thou, I am regenerated, I am no unbeliever or heretic, I may be trusted: so then, the remainder of mankind being either heretics, or what thou callest infidels, will be a mere herd of monsters; and whenever thou art speaking to a Lutheran or a Turk, thou shouldest conclude that they are for robbing and murdering thee, for they are the devil's spawn; one is not regenerated, and the other is degenerated. Much more rational and much more handsome would it be to say to men, " You are all born good; consider how dreadful it " would be to defile the purity of your being." Mankind should be dealt with as individuals. If a prebendary leads a scandalous life, a friend says to him, Is it possible that you can thus disgrace the dignity of a prebendary? A counsellor or judge is reminded that he has the honour of being counsellor to the king; and that it is his duty to be an example of virtue. The encouragement to a soldier is, Remember you belong to the regiment of Champagne; and every individual should be told, Remember your dignity as a man.

Say or do what you will, this must at length be the case: for what can mean this saying, so

---

gives of it in his Universal History. As he would insinuate, however, that human nature is exempt from original sin, he is guilty of a very great error; for it is an essential dogma of Christianity, evidently laid down in scripture, that we have all sinned in Adam, " as by one man sin entered into the " world, and death by sin; so death passed upon all men, " for that all have sinned." From this, and in consequence of original sin, it may be said, that man is of his own nature inclined to evil.

common among all nations, Reflect within thyself. Now, were you born a child of the devil; were your origin criminal; were your blood formed of an infernal liquor: to bid you reflect within yourself would import, Consult your diabolical nature, and follow its *suggestions*; cheat, **rob**, murder, it is your father's law.

Man is not born wicked; he becomes so, as he falls sick. Should some physicians come and tell him you are born sick, it is certain that these physicians, whatever they might say or do, will not cure him if his disease be inherent in his nature; and these reasoners are themselves very sick.

Bring together all the children of the universe, you will see nothing in them but innocence, gentleness, and fear; were they born wicked, spightful, and cruel, some signs of it would come from them, as little snakes strive to bite, and little tygers to tear. But nature having been as sparing of offensive weapons to man as to pigeons and rabbits, it cannot have given them an instinct to mischief and destruction.

So man is not born wicked: how comes it then that so many are infected with the pestilence of wickedness? It is because they who bear rule over them, having caught the distemper, communicate it to others; as a woman, having the distemper which Christopher Columbus brought from America, has spread the venom all over Europe. By the first ambitious man was the world corrupted.

You will say that this first monster only fecundated that germ of pride, rapine, fraud, and cruelty, which is in all men. I own, that in general, the greater part of our brethren easily contract these qualities: but has every body the putrid fever, the stone, and gravel, because every body is liable to those distempers?

There

There are whole nations which are not wicked; the Philadelphians, the Banyans have never shed human blood. The Chinese, the people of Tonquin, Lao, Siam, and even of Japan, have lived in the most profound tranquility for these hundred years past. In the space of ten years scarce any of those enormities at which human nature stands astonished, is heard of in the cities of Rome, Venice, Paris, London, and Amsterdam; cities, where yet cupidity, the mother of all crimes, is flagrant.

If men were essentially wicked, and all born under the sway of a being as malignant as wretched, who, in revenge for his punishment, inspired them with all his rage, we should every morning hear of husbands being murdered by their wives, and fathers by their children, just as fowls are found killed by a polecat, who came in the night and sucked their blood.

If we suppose there are ten hundred millions of men upon the earth, it is a great many; and this makes about five hundred millions of women, who sew and spin, feed their little ones, keep the house or hut clean, and backbite their neighbours a little. I do not see any great harm these poor simpletons do on earth. Of this number of inhabitants on the globe, there are at least two hundred millions of children, who certainly neither kill nor plunder, and about as many who, through age and sickness, are not capable of those crimes. Thus there remains, at most, but a hundred millions whom youth and vigor qualify for the commission of crimes. Of these hundred millions we may say, that ninety are continually taken up with prodigious labour, inforcing the earth to furnish them with food and raiment: now these have scarce time to perpetrate outrages.

In

In the remaining ten millions will be included idlers and jocund companions, who love peace and feſtivity; the men of talents, who are taken up with their ſeveral profeſſions; magiſtrates and prieſts, whom it manifeſtly behoves to lead an irreproachable life, at leaſt in appearance. So that the real wicked men are reduced to ſome few politicians, either ſecular or regular, who will always be for diſturbing the world; and ſome thouſands of vagrants, who hire their ſervices to thoſe politicians. Now never is a million of theſe wild beaſts employed at once, and among theſe I reckon highwaymen; ſo that at moſt, and in the moſt tempeſtuous times, there is but one man of a thouſand who may be called wicked, and he is not ſo always.

Thus is wickedneſs on earth infinitely leſs than is talked of and believed. To be ſure, there is ſtill too much misfortune, diſtreſs, and horrible crimes; but the pleaſure of complaining and magnifying is ſuch, that at the leaſt ſcratch you cry out: the earth is deluged with blood. If you have been cheated, then the world is full of perjury. An atrabilarious mind, on having been wronged, ſees the univerſe covered with damned ſouls; as a young rake, ſeated at ſupper with his doxy after the opera, does not dream that there are any diſtreſſed objects.

F I N I S.

www.ingramcontent.com/pod-product-compliance
Lightning Source LLC
Chambersburg PA
CBHW030008240426
43672CB00007B/871